Reading *Stargate SG-1*

To the younger Dr Beeler and my daughter, Amelia
S.B.

To The Geeks
L.D.

READING
STARGÅTE
SG • 1

EDITED BY
STAN BEELER
AND **LISA DICKSON**

I.B. TAURIS

Published in 2006 by I.B.Tauris & Co. Ltd
6 Salem Road, London W2 4BU
175 Fifth Avenue, New York NY 10010
www.ibtauris.com

In the United States and Canada distributed by Palgrave Macmillan, a
division of St Martin's Press, 175 Fifth Avenue, New York NY 10010

ISBN 10: 1 84511 183 4
ISBN 13: 978 1 84511 183 0

A full CIP record for this book is available from the British Library
A full CIP record for this book is available from the Library of Congress
Library of Congress catalog card: available

Typeset in Ehrhardt by Dexter Haven Associates Ltd, London
Printed and bound in India by Replika Press Pvt. Ltd

CONTENTS

ACKNOWLEDGEMENTS

There are many people who deserve thanks: Philippa Brewster at I.B.Tauris for having faith in the book, and for guiding us through the publication process; our publishers, I.B.Tauris, for producing this edition and promoting the advancement of cultural studies; Dr Max Blouw and the Office of Research at the University of Northern British Columbia for guidance and support, and the university in general for being a good place to be; the fans who allowed Lisa to take their pictures in their fannish regalia and natural habitats; huge thanks to The Geeks, who were a wonderful resource for all manner of things, popping up with immediate answers to the most esoteric of our questions, who let us exploit them and recruit them and whine to them, and whose enthusiasm for this project was absolutely indispensable when we were book-wrangling – Geek Power!; and finally to our spouses, Dr Karin Beeler and Dr Kevin Hutchings, who have to love us even when we're crazy, and little Amelia Beeler, whose tendency to stay up all night meant that Stan could watch the entire *Stargate SG-1* and *Stargate: Atlantis oeuvre* in the wee hours of the morning when brains are suggestible. (Note: Amelia learned to recognise the *Stargate SG-1* theme song at an extremely early stage of her development. The long-term effects of this are yet to be seen.)

NOTES ON CONTRIBUTORS

Stan Beeler is Chair of English at the University of Northern British Columbia, Canada. His areas of interest include Film and Television Studies, Popular Culture, Comparative Literature and Renaissance Literature. He has published a book on the literary history of the Rosicrucian movement, *The Invisible College: A Study of the Three Original Rosicrucian Texts* (AMS Press), and articles on contemporary television.

Lisa Dickson is an assistant professor of English at the University of Northern British Columbia, where she specialises in Renaissance literature, Shakespeare in performance and Cultural Studies. Her current research includes an investigation of the representation of violence in film and staged drama. She has published on Shakespeare's early histories and on the intersection of beauty and violence in Tarsem Singh's science fiction thriller *The Cell*.

Dave Hipple holds a first degree in English from the University of St Andrews, an MA in Education from the Open University and an MA in Science Fiction from the University of Reading. Following a career in university administration he has now returned to Reading, to pursue a Ph.D. on the cultural impact of visual science fiction and its reception by various constituencies. Topics of recent papers include *Star Trek*, the novel and film *Starship Troopers*, the TV series *Firefly*, the numerous versions of *The Hitchhiker's Guide to the Galaxy* and the characteristics of science fiction in general.

Lisa Kincaid has been a freelance writer, web designer and horse trainer, but still has not found a way to make a living through *Stargate* trivia. She is currently a full-time student in Oregon, where she is studying equine science.

Jeffrey A. Kyer is a long-time gamer who has authored a number of articles on RPGs (role-playing games), in addition to several RPG books, including *Stargate SG-1: Friends and Foes, Season 2*, an episode-by-episode guide for gamers.

Christine Mains is a Ph.D. candidate at University of Calgary, currently writing a dissertation on the representation of the wizard/ scientist as teacher and the transmission of knowledge-power in popular culture. Her MA thesis focused on the quest of the female hero in the work of American fantasist Patricia A. McKillip, and she has published several articles on McKillip as well as on the figure of the wizard, the work of Canadian fantasist Charles de Lint, and the television series *Stargate SG-1*. She is the editor of the *SFRA Review* and serves on the executive board of the International Association for the Fantastic in the Arts.

Melanie Manzer Kyer is an Assistant Professor of German at the College of Charleston. She holds a Ph.D. from Pennsylvania State University.

Rachel McGrath-Kerr is a postgraduate student in Communication and Cultural Studies at the University of Canberra, Australia, where she is examining the transformation of female identity with respect to violence in cult television series.

Gaile McGregor is Director of Social Research for Terraconnaissance Inc. and an Adjunct Professor in the Department of Sociology at the University of Western Ontario. She is best known for her series of semio-ethnographic studies of post-frontier societies, beginning with *The Wacousta Syndrome: Explorations in the Canadian Langscape* [sic] (1986). In explaining the impetus for her chapter in this book, she describes herself as both a Canadian nationalist and an avid consumer of American-style pop culture.

Sabine Schmidt (Mannheim, Germany) has a Dr Phil. in German studies, Romance languages and literature studies, and Modern History, at the Universities of Mannheim and Lyon (France). She is co-editor of 'Geschlecht, Literatur, Geschichte I' (1999) and 'Korrespondenzen. Festschrift für Joachim W. Storck' (1999, 2nd edn 2001), and author of 'Das domestizierte Subjekt: Subjektkonstitution und Genderdiskurs in ausgewählten Werken Adalbert Stifters' (2004), in addition to numerous articles and essays. Her ongoing projects include 'Kathinka Zitz-Halein', 'Adalbert Stifter', 'Women Warriors in Literature and History' and 'Relationship Triangles in Early German Science Fiction (Kurt Laßwitz)'.

Jo Storm is a writer and academic who lives in Toronto, Ontario. She is also the author of a compendium on the *SG-1* series entitled 'Approaching the Possible: The World of *Stargate SG-1*'.

Judith Tabron, Ph.D., is the author of *Postcolonial Literature from Three Continents: Tutuola, H.D., Ellison, and White* as well as 'Girl on Girl Politics: Willow/Tara and new approaches to media fandom' in volume 4.1–2 of *Slayage: The Online Journal of Buffy Studies*. She has taught at Brandeis University and Slippery Rock University. She is the Director of Faculty Computing Services at Hofstra University in the Long Island area of New York. Her current research is about pop culture empires, across media, as a major American export throughout the twentieth century.

Martha Taylor holds a Master's Degree in English from UCLA. Her interest in genre television dates back to the 1960s, when she watched the original *Star Trek* through the bars of her crib. These days she lives and works in Chattanooga, Tennessee.

Stephanie Tuszynski is a Ph.D. candidate at Bowling Green State University. In addition to researching online groups and social interaction, her other areas of interest include film and television and the intersection between these 'old' media and new media. She produced and directed 'IRL (In Real Life)' – a documentary about an online community that looked at what separation (if any) existed between virtual and 'real' life for the community's members.

Michael W. Young teaches in the English Department at La Roche College and has a Ph.D. in Creative Writing and Literature from the University of Cincinnati. His published works include poetry, short fiction and scholarly articles on Writing, Literature and Teaching.

STARGÅTE SG-1
CAST LIST

Primary Cast

Lt. Col. Samantha Carter	Amanda Tapping
Gen. George Hammond	Don S. Davis
Dr Daniel Jackson	Michael Shanks
Gen. Hank Landry	Beau Bridges
Gen. Jonathan 'Jack' O'Neill	Richard Dean Anderson
Lt. Col. Cameron Mitchell	Ben Browder
Jonas Quinn	Corin Nemec
Teal'c	Christopher Judge

Secondary Cast

SGC/USAF Personnel

Maj. Paul Davis	Colin Cunningham
Dr Janet Fraiser	Teryl Rothery
Chief Master Sgt. Walter Harriman	Gary Jones
Maj. Charles Kawalsky	Jay Acovone
Catherine Langford	Elizabeth Hoffman
Dr Carolyn Lam	Lexa Doig
Dr Bill Lee	Bill Dow
Maj. Lorne	Kavan Smith
Col. Makepeace	Steve Makaj
Col. Harry Maybourne	Tom McBeath
Dr Rodney McKay	David Hewlett
Maj. Bert Samuels	Robert Wisden
Sgt. Siler	Dan Shea
Col. Frank Simmons	John de Lancie

| Gen. Vidrine | Steven Williams |

Other Earthlings, Friends and Foes

Cassandra (off-world refugee)	Katie Stuart
Jacob Carter/Selmak (Tok'ra)	Carmen Argenziano
Dr Sarah Gardner/Osiris (Goa'uld)	Anna-Louise Plowman
Senator Robert Kinsey	Ronny Cox
Martin Lloyd	Willie Garson
Pete Shanahan	David DeLuise
Agent Richard Woolsey	Robert Picardo

Jaffa

Master Bra'tac	Tony Amendola
Drey'auc	Salli Richardson/Brook Susan Parker
Gerak	Lou Gossett Jr.
Ishta	Jolene Blalock
Rya'c	Neil Denis

Abydonians

Kasuf	Erik Avari
Sha're/Amonet (Goa'uld)	Viatiare Bandera
Skaara/Klorel (Goa'uld)	Alexis Cruz

Tok'ra

Jacob Carter/Selmak	Carmen Argenziano
Malek	Peter Stebbings
Martouf/Lantesh	J. R. Bourne
Rosha/Jolinar of Malkshur	Tanya Reid

Goa'uld System Lords

Anubis	David Palffy
Apophis	Peter Williams
Baal	Cliff Simon

Nirrti	Jacqueline Samuda
Osiris/Dr Sarah Gardner	Anna-Louise Plowman
Yu the Great	Vince Crestejo

Other Aliens, Friends and Foes

Chaka (Unas)	Dion Johnstone
Doci (Ori)	Julian Sands
Fifth (Human-form Replicator)	G. Patrick Currie
Lya (Nox)	Frida Betrani
Vala Maldoran (space pirate?)	Claudia Black
Narim (Tollan)	Garwin Sanford
Oma Desala (Ancient)	Carla Boudreau

STARGÅTE: ATLANTIS
CAST LIST

Primary Cast

Dr Carson Beckett
Ronon Dex
Teyla Emmagan
Lt. Aiden Ford
Dr Rodney McKay
Maj./Lt. Col. John Sheppard
Dr Elizabeth Weir

Paul McGillion
Jason Momoa
Rachel Luttrell
Rainbow Sun Francks
David Hewlett
Joe Flanigan
Tori Higginson

Secondary Cast

Atlantis Expedition Members: Civilian

Dr Peter Grodin
Dr Kate Heightmeyer
Dr Kavanagh
Dr Simon Wallis
(declined the expedition)
Dr Radek Zelenka

Craig Veroni
Claire Rankin
Ben Cotton
Garwin Sanford

David Nykl

Atlantis Expedition: Military

Sgt. Bates
Col. Steven Caldwell
Col. Dillon Everett
Maj. Lorne
Sgt. Markham
Sgt. Stackhouse

Dean Marshall
Mitch Pileggi
Clayton Landey
Kavan Smith
Joseph May
Boyan Vukelic

Col. Marshall Sumner | Robert Patrick

Athosians

Halling | Christopher Heyerdahl
Wex | Casey Dubois

Genii

Cowan | Colm Meaney
Commander Acastus Kolya | Robert Davi
~~Sora~~ | ~~Erin Chambers~~

Aliens

Chaya Sar (Ancient) | Lenor Varela
The Keeper (Wraith) | Andee Frizzell
Male Wraith | James Lafazanos

INTRODUCTION

STAN BEELER
AND LISA DICKSON

In 1997 the series *Stargate SG-1* first aired on American cable television, initially on Showtime and then in later seasons on the Sci Fi channel. Through syndication, it has since ventured into Canadian and European markets. Although the series plot was originally based on the moderately successful 1994 feature film directed by Roland Emmerich, starring Kurt Russell and James Spader, over the course of nine seasons of production the show has evolved away from many of the basic premises of the film and developed its own unique mythological superstructure. Unlike its counterpart in the film, which opened a portal to a single planet, Abydos, the Stargate of the series differs in that it 'goes other places', taking the ensemble cast each week to a range of new planets where ancient human civilisations have been seeded as slave populations by the show's arch-villains, the parasitic, body-snatching Goa'uld. Thus, the series' premise effects a concatenation of ancient cultures, present-day political and social concerns, and award-winning special effects, aliens and advanced technologies, all anchored by the central icon of the Stargate, and the focus on the dynamic relationships among the show's main characters, the four-person first-contact team: SG-1. Series executive producer Richard Dean Anderson has referred to the Stargate itself as the 'best free-standing prop' in the industry.

Stargate SG-1 has blossomed into a series with a stable market share driven by fierce fan loyalty, as evidenced by media tie-ins such as novelisations and role-playing games, lively internet discussion groups, the proliferation of 'textual poaching' (to use Henry Jenkins' influential term) in fan fiction and art, and the popular annual conventions, both 'official', such as the *Wolf Cons* in Europe and *Gatecon* in Vancouver, and 'unofficial', such as the fan-run *MediaWest Con* and *Vividcon*, where *Stargate SG-1* holds its own in the kaleidoscope of media fandoms. Through syndication and DVD sales, the series has also developed a healthy viewership outside North America, especially in Great Britain, France and Germany. Moreover, the series has aired nine seasons so far and – what may be considered the Holy Grail of any television series – a spin-off. *Stargate: Atlantis* is in its second season of airing on the US Sci Fi cable channel and shows signs of the same popularity with its audience as its parent series. When we compare *Stargate SG-1* with other, often more critically acclaimed, science fiction and fantasy series, it is clear that there is something remarkable about its staying power. The only other American series that has approached *Stargate SG-1*'s longevity is Chris Carter's *The X-Files*, which also lasted nine seasons. Its spin-off, *The Lone Gunmen*, however, lasted less than one full season. None of Joss Whedon's three important fantasy series, *Buffy the Vampire Slayer*, *Angel* and *Firefly*, although popular among academics as well as the general fan base, has lasted as long. *Buffy* lasted seven seasons, *Angel* five, and *Firefly* was cancelled before the end of its first. Other series with strong fan groups and healthy DVD sales lost network support much earlier in their respective careers and have been relegated to the diminished status of reruns on speciality channels. *Babylon Five* lasted only five seasons, *Farscape* four, and James Cameron's stylish *Dark Angel* was cancelled after only two. Given the 'short and brutish' lifespan of the average fantasy/science fiction series it would seem appropriate to take a critical look at *Stargate SG-1* as it completes its ninth season and to attempt to discover the source of its staying power.

Reading Stargate SG-1 is a collection that will be of interest to both academic and popular audiences. We have divided this volume into two parts; *Part 1: The Host* offers textual studies of the series itself, and the chapters in *Part 2: The Symbiote* explore *Stargate SG-1*'s cultural role as both artefact and capital. However, all the chapters in this collection examine aspects of the series that contribute to its status as one of the longest-running science fiction series currently on television. Only the UK's apparently immortal *Doctor Who* and Gene Roddenberry's constantly reincarnated *Star Trek* franchise have exceeded the staying power of *Stargate SG-1* and its offspring, and the scholars contributing to this volume clearly answer the question of why this series holds such fascination for its audience.

The first chapter in *Part 1: The Host*, 'Seeing, knowing, dying in "Heroes, Parts 1 and 2"' by Lisa Dickson, is a detailed study of the combination of literary and cinematographic techniques in two episodes of *Stargate SG-1*. It is the best possible starting point for a collection devoted to revealing the underlying reasons for *Stargate SG-1*'s long-standing success, as it provides a detailed study of the qualities of writing, production and acting that are the driving force behind audience appreciation of the series. Since we would be remiss if we did not attempt to situate *Stargate SG-1* as a representative of its genre, Dave Hipple's engaging '*Stargate SG-1*: Self-possessed science fiction' positions *Stargate SG-1* in the traditions of science fiction television and film, incorporating a close examination of two episodes from season one and reflecting upon the show's use (and abuse) of science fiction strategies to reinforce its storytelling. Although series such as *Buffy the Vampire Slayer* and *Xena Warrior Princess* have done a lot to promote the cause of feminism in genre fiction, there is still some discussion as to the true effect of science fiction upon feminist goals. Stephanie Tuszynski's '"Way smarter than you are": Sam Carter, human being' uses *Stargate SG-1*'s Sam Carter as a paradigm to assess the overall quality of female representation in fantasy and science fiction television. Continuing with the exploration of the socio-ethical dimension of the series, in 'You know that "meaning of life" stuff?': Possessed of/by knowledge in *Stargate SG-1*', Christine Mains discusses the relationship between the use of knowledge in *Stargate SG-1* and the ethical concerns 'surrounding the subordination of the pursuit of knowledge to military needs'. Taking this enquiry into the domain of mythology, one of the grounding elements of the series' overall story arc and a key aspect of its appeal, Jo Storm's 'Sam, Jarred: The Isis myth in operation' covers a specific example of the use of traditional Egyptian mythology, while Michael W. Young's '*Stargate SG-1* and *Atlantis*: The gods of technology versus the wizards of justice' presents the series in the context of several modern myths. The popularity of *Stargate SG-1* even outside an English speaking environment is undeniable and Sabine Schmidt's chapter, entitled 'Gender roles, sexual identities and the concept of the Other in *Stargate: SG-1*', presents a uniquely German-speaking perspective on the series, and focuses on the ways that the series categorises 'self' and 'Other', friend and foe, in terms of the logic of sexual difference.

Turning from the details of the series' aesthetic and ideological content to its broader social, economic and consumer contexts, *Part 2: The Symbiote* opens with two essays which look at the role of *Stargate SG-1* and *Stargate: Atlantis* as Canadian cultural products. Gaile McGregor's '*Stargate* as cancult? Ideological coding as a function of location' and Stan Beeler's '"It's a Zed PM": *Stargate SG-1*, *Stargate:*

Atlantis and Canadian production of American television' consider different aspects of the *Stargate* franchise's Canadian identity. Nationalism is never as important as money in the continued success of a television series, and Judith Tabron's chapter, 'Selling the Stargate: The economics of a pop culture phenomenon', deals with this truism in detail. Sometimes aiding and abetting the financial machinery of popular television and sometimes working to subvert it, audience consumption and appreciation of science fiction and fantasy have been transformed by a contemporary desire to become actively involved in what have been traditionally passive pastimes of reading and watching television. The fictional worlds created by the writers of *Stargate SG-1* and *Stargate: Atlantis* have been significantly affected through feedback from role-playing games, while online fan fiction is only one of the many forms of 'unofficial' extrapolation from the series that enables active and invested participation on the part of fans. Melanie Manzer Kyer and Jeffrey A. Kyer consider the popularity of *Stargate* role-playing games in 'Reading *Stargate*/playing *Stargate*: Role-playing games and the *Stargate* franchise'. In the final chapter of *Reading Stargate SG-1*, 'Sam I am: Female fans' interaction with Samantha Carter through fan fiction and online discussion', Rachel McGrath-Kerr surveys fan writers in order to explore the influences of feminism and 'post-feminism' on their participation in and assessment of the series and its presentation of modern female role models.

As *Reading Stargate SG-1* is designed to be a comprehensive study of the popularity of the *Stargate* franchise and to be accessible to both diehard fans and those with a broader, perhaps more general, academic interest in television studies, we have included episode guides to *Stargate SG-1* seasons one to eight (by Martha Taylor) and *Stargate: Atlantis* (by Lisa Kincaid), a comprehensive glossary of series-related terms (by Lisa Kincaid), as well as a list of useful internet sources and a selected bibliography.

The contributions to this collection demonstrate that *Stargate SG-1* and *Atlantis* can repay the effort of serious academic exploration. In both aesthetic and economic terms, as examples of both intriguing world-building and savvy audience-building, the series and its spin-off prove to be fruitful ground for investigation. The new seasons – just beginning as we go to press – promise to continue the trend. The introduction of new characters to the SG-1 team (Ben Browder as Lt. Col. Cameron 'Cam Shaft' Mitchell, and Claudia Black as the piratical

Vala Maldoran) has revitalised the series, as has the invention of a new and more powerful enemy, the Ori, who, while better dressed than the Goa'uld, are also seemingly more insidious. On *Atlantis*, too, the flagship team has been augmented by Ronon Dex (Jason Momoa), who replaces Lt. Aiden Ford (Rainbow Sun Francks), now that he's gone 'darkside', while the base's ability to connect to Earth via both the Stargate and the starship *Daedaelus* offers up new and complex relationships and tensions to explore.

Where the shows go from here remains to be seen. What is certain is that many, many people will be watching.

PART 1:
THE HOST

PART 1

THEORIES

1

SEEING, KNOWING, DYING IN 'HEROES, PARTS 1 AND 2'

LISA DICKSON

In the seventh season episode 'Heroes, Part 2' (episode 718),[1] the popular recurring character Chief Medical Officer Janet Fraiser (Teryl Rothery) is killed in action. Much of this episode is designed as a sort of bait-and-switch in which the audience is led to believe that it is Jack O'Neill (Richard Dean Anderson) who is the casualty of the ill-fated rescue mission to the planet tellingly designated P3X 666. The revelation of the truth comes in the form of footage of Janet's death, accidentally captured on tape by Daniel Jackson (Michael Shanks), who is trying to record an injured airman's last message to his pregnant wife. We see the footage only in the latter part of the episode, when a film crew sent to document the operations of Stargate Command finally wrests the tape from Daniel's fiercely protective control. When this revelation is made, we might feel – as many fans did when the episode aired after much promotional advertising featuring the fallen O'Neill – that our perceptions and their affective power have been manipulated. The bait-and-switch, and its withholding of information, its use of misdirection and well-timed, carefully framed exposure, reflects a deeper thematic, structural and technical concern in the episode with the nature of 'truth', 'objectivity' and representation.

The episode's 'prequel', 'Heroes, Part 1' (717), sets the stage for this interrogation by showing us the SGC from an outsider's point of view, that of Emmett Bregman (Saul Rubinek) and his film crew as they try, and fail, to get the inside story. Staging a clash of perspectives represented by a number of on-screen cameras, the two episodes turn on the telling moment of revelation – Janet's on-camera death – and, through the struggle over Janet's recorded image, reveal the series' core values. 'Heroes, Part 1' posits a gap between the 'real' (as ostensibly represented by the 'objective' third-person camera) and its construction and interpretation (as represented by the limited scope of Bregman's documentary lens). 'Heroes, Part 2' is about the conflation of these points of view in a specifically ideological way, one which, like the bait-and-switch, challenges the notion of objective truth and substitutes a discourse of responsible interpretation. The two episodes stage a movement from antagonism to identification, distance to proximity, a progression made visible in the blocking of key scenes, and which parallels the discursive shift from an emphasis on the political to the idealisation of the personal. This progression places *Stargate SG-1* in a long lineage of war representations, from World War II aerial photography to the post-Vietnam war film, which tend to elide the 'Establishment' and create instead an alternative 'American' that is both individualised and personal on the one hand and at the same time iconic and representative of the American 'type' on the other. In this context, 'America' becomes its soldiers and *not* its foreign (or interplanetary) policy, and the thorny ethical questions that are the focus of 'Heroes, Part 1' are, in 'Part 2', subsumed in the suffering and triumphs of the 'mythic I', the episodes' eponymous 'heroes'.

Self-reflexively interested in the ways that 'truth' is constructed and communicated, the episodes demand that we look not only at their content but also at their mode of address and elements of style. As John Corner puts it, 'The question is then not only "how do we *know* what we are *seeing*?" ... but also what we might call "how do we *see* what we are *knowing*?"'[2] Corner goes on to observe, in his discussion of documentary film, that the camera will 'construct a viewing position, a stance of *looking*',[3] that we might call, after Graeme Burton, a 'mode of address', which 'positions the viewer in relation to the program and its potential meanings'.[4] For instance, conventionally realist television such as *Stargate SG-1* presents the action through the 'eye' of an 'objective' third-person camera, which takes on a role analogous to the third-person narrator of fiction, positing itself as a silent observer of the action, having special access to all the space that we can see, but still standing separate from the events that it records. The 'objective' camera can move anywhere, through space and across time, and while it may occasionally stand in for the perspective of a particular character – as in, for instance, the shot-reverse-shot structure of a staged conversation between two people – its ability seamlessly to take *anyone's* perspective invests it with omniscience, which in turn associates it more or less firmly with the 'objective' and the 'real'.

In this sense, this camera is 'invisible'; it doesn't appear onscreen at all, any more than our own eye is visible to us as we are looking through it. The conventions of realism embed us in this point of view and ask us to accept what we see as a mere rendering of 'what's there'. But this camera is not really 'objective' and it does not really simply 'record what's there' but rather shapes our responses in a variety of ways: a close-up can tell us that we must pay attention, that we are receiving important information about a character's inner life, that the events preceding the close-up are important enough to merit our 'close-up' attention to a character's response to them, and so on. For Burton, the 'objective' point of view 'helps naturalize ideological meanings in the program',[5] making them invisible by ensuring that the camera does not call attention to itself as a particular and particularly invested point of view.

This combination of suggestive power and invisibility is key to what Richard Maltby calls 'the consensus style'. Not associated with a specific ideological or political platform, the consensus style reflects an attitude towards narrative: 'The narrative operates as a closed unit, endorsing particular characters, attitudes and actions from within the restricted framework which it alone defines.'[6] In other words, a system of values and concerns is posited as neutral and objective, an effect enabled by the omniscience of the camera's point of view and by the seamlessness and continuity of the editing. 'Heroes, Parts 1 and 2' are particularly interesting in this context, because they do call attention to the issue of point of view by staging a complex relationship between four cameras: the 'objective' camera, which is our 'regular' way of seeing the programme; Bregman's documentary video camera; Woolsey's video camera in the interrogation room; and Daniel's handi-cam footage of the events on P3X 666. Each of these cameras is invested with its own conventions, and the interplay between them challenges any claim to absolute authority or even to a single 'truth', seeming, therefore, to challenge the consensus style. However, on closer examination, we see that what the two episodes demonstrate is the process by which the consensus style is constructed: the 'objective' point of view is first threatened by another perspective, and then assimilates that threat by restructuring that perspective in its own image.

For Maltby, the key to the consensus style is the invisibility of the 'means of production', so to speak. Continuity cutting is one of these methods of invisibility, which 'mold[s] the series of discontinuous events in time and space from which the film is constructed, into a perceptually continuous whole'.[7] Likewise, the camera will use conventional juxtaposition of shots, such as the 'shot-reverse-shot' that, in conjunction with 'conventional perspective relations', allows the viewer to see the diagetic space as seamless, orderly and comprehensible.[8] These methods produce the illusion that we are standing in a recognisable three-dimensional space, while careful attention is paid to the positioning of the camera so that we do not get disoriented in the scene.[9] Thus, in a shot-reverse-shot structure, there is a clear sense of where each character is in relation to each other and to us as the unseen viewers. 'Heroes I', however, disrupts the standard 'objective' point of view by playing with its invisible conventions.

First, the opening shot of the episode is an image of the Stargate as seen from the briefing room, familiar as an 'establishing shot' from any number of *Stargate SG-1* episodes. However, in this case, we hear Bregman's voice coaching the cameraman, Tech. Sgt. James (Tobias Slezak), and the image has the sharp-edged brightness of video, not the regular patina of film we associate with the 'objective' point of view. The shot 'quotes' the 'objective' camera perspective and, in doing so, reveals its conventionality, and that it does, in fact, arise from a *particular* point of view and from a *particular* deployment of cinematic skill aimed at eliciting a specific effect. It is not just recording 'what's there'. In a second telling scene, Senator Kinsey (Ronny Cox) confronts Jack in the mess hall, and their exchange is filmed by the 'objective' camera on one side and by Bregman's camera on the other. Thus, when we switch from one point of view to the other, it appears that Kinsey and Jack have switched places in the room, thus violating conventional perspective relations by disrupting our sense of relative position.[10] It is a clever visual pun on Kinsey's attempt to appropriate the SGC's position as his own, and the visual disorientation in the scene mirrors the moral and political disorientation produced by Kinsey's self-serving corruption of the system. Both instances use Bregman's camera to highlight the clash of perspectives by revealing or breaking with the cinematic conventions of the shots, thereby challenging the 'objective' camera's authority, omniscience and invisibility.

In this way, Bregman and his camera perform the function of 'defamiliarisation', or *ostranenie*, a Russian Formalist concept that describes how art, by framing the familiar in unusual ways, breaks us from our habitual perception of the world and allows us to see the mundane in new, invigorating, and revitalising ways.[11] On a thematic level, Bregman represents the 'real world' point of view whose presence in the SGC defamiliarises what has become mundane to us. All the things that we, the long-time viewers of the show, see as 'normal', or at least normal for the SGC, are thrown into a new light. For instance, we see Bregman strolling down the corridor with Daniel while Bregman reads from the report of Daniel's Ascension. Daniel corrects the bare-bones report by noting that he actually had to die first, and rather painfully, too, but his low-key delivery, in contrast to Bregman's obvious difficulty in getting his head around the idea, reflects the naturalisation of the fantastic, extraordinary nature of the experience within the 'objective' structure of the show.[12] The overexposed lighting of the scene in the corridor and the high-colour clarity of video clearly distinguish the interview scene from that of the 'objective' point of view, where Daniel's experience is normalised as simply part of the SGC's wacky past that everyone there, including the long-time viewer, now takes in their stride.

And the defamiliarisation works in two directions. Even as it allows us to reconnect with the sense of wonder in the face of the fantastic, it functions to elevate the prosaic to the level of the extraordinary. Murray Smith notes that key to the Formalist notion of defamiliarisation is its absence of judgement; it does not ask you to see the world in a specific way, only that you see it in a new way as the work of art 'renews our consciousness of and sensitivity towards a particular percept or concept'.[13] That said, he goes on, an artwork can nevertheless communicate a 'message' within the defamiliarising process: '[A]n artwork might address us *as if*, with a question[,] "it's like this isn't it?"'[14] Coming to visit Simon Wells (Julius Chapple) in the infirmary ('Part 2', 718), Daniel challenges Wells' feeling of responsibility for Janet's death. Daniel asserts that a Jaffa killed her, not Wells, and while she was doing her job, just as Wells was doing his. The everyday prosaic act of 'putting in the hours' is in this exchange imbued with heroic status. It was just Janet's job to lay down her life for a comrade, and just doing her job makes her, and Wells, heroic. The defamiliarising that takes place in the earlier scene sets the stage for this reciprocal movement, elevating the very prosaic nature of the individual, and addressing us *as if* to say, 'Here, at the SGC, old ways of defining what is "normal" or "insignificant" and what is "fantastic" or "extraordinary" don't work. New definitions are needed.'

So, the question remains, then, as to whose definition of these terms, particularly the term 'hero', is going to prevail. Initially, Bregman is figured as invasive and his perspective limited. In one of the most intense scenes of the two episodes ('Part 2', 718), Bregman comes to Daniel's lab after the ill-fated mission and realises that Daniel has captured 'something' on film. The blocking of the scene is telling. For much of the scene, Daniel is in the extreme foreground of the frame, pressed up so close, in fact, that he is often out of focus. He is forced into a corner by his grief, positioned as far away from Bregman as he can get, and this brings him closer to us, but uncomfortably so. He is isolated but crowded against the fourth wall with Bregman 'out there'. Mostly out of focus at the far end of the room, Bregman represents a force from the outside against whom we are aligned because Daniel is so close to us, and their incommensurate points of view are emphasised by the use of the zoom lens, which, with its shallow depth of field, cannot keep them both in focus at the same time. The 'objective' point of view, then, is shown to be not so much 'objective' as strongly partisan. And after Daniel gets up to order Bregman out of the room and to take the handi-cam back to his desk, his posture and the angle of the shot highlight his vulnerability to Bregman's invading perspective. In the reverse shot wherein we see from Bregman's position, Daniel is turned three-quarters away and, in the dim lighting of the room, he is almost lost in the gloom except for the bare, exposed line of his neck, his ear, his head angled defensively away. This shot and the vulnerability it communicates will be repeated in the footage of Janet's death. Attempting to convince Daniel to give him the film, Bregman tells the story of a war photographer, Martin Kristovsky, who accidentally snapped a picture of a lieutenant at the moment of his death, when the lieutenant is shot in the head while saving Kristovsky's life. As he tells his story, Bregman comes closer and closer to Daniel until he and Daniel are almost – but not quite – both in focus. He tells Daniel that revealing what is on the tape will not change what happened on 666, but what *will* change 'is how *you* feel about it'. The scene ends with Bregman exiting and Daniel once again crowded against the screen, only now he has been changed by Bregman's story, and the close-up in which he looks out of frame signals this shift.

The scene's blocking maps out nicely the progression from distance to proximity that characterises the realignment of points of view in the two episodes, and I will return to this, but first I want to note how

Bregman's defamiliarising perspective brings a new interpretive paradigm to the familiar. In the interviews that comprise most of 'Part 1', Bregman asks about the *ethics* of what the SGC does – its secrecy, its lack of public oversight, its cost and potential for catastrophic consequences for the people of Earth who have no say in its direction or even existence. His questions force the viewer to contemplate what is generally elided or naturalised in the space of the 'objective' view, where the SGC's viability and importance are a given,[15] and in so doing reveals the partiality of that perspective. Maltby asserts that the invisibility of the means of production, what he calls 'cosmetic disguise', 'limit[s] the spectator's self-awareness during the film, and stress[es] his or her direct relation, as receiver, of the film as an organic entity and of the message that was the film's story'.[16] Bregman's interviews seem to work against this consensus style by making the audience visible to itself. Let us consider the scene in the editing room during the second scroll credits ('Part 2', 718) where Bregman and James are cutting together Bregman's interviews with Sam and Daniel. Viewing the rough footage of Daniel's interview, we see Daniel occasionally looking directly, and suspiciously, into Bregman's camera. This is unusual in the show as a whole (characters never look directly into the camera unless the camera is standing in for another character in a conversation). So, Daniel's gaze flickering to the camera that is filming him is one of the techniques of self-reflexivity: the moment reminds us that we are looking through a camera, that is, from a particular perspective. Finally backed up against the wall by Bregman's pointed questions about whether the world should know about the Stargate programme, Daniel looks away from both Bregman and the camera and says: 'I think it's a relative question; *it depends on your point of view*' ('Part 2', 718). Up until this moment, we have been watching the interview full-screen. While the image is clearly video from Bregman's camera, however, the full-screen aligns this interview with the 'real' because of its size, which duplicates that of the 'objective' view. Thus, the boundaries between these points of view are blurred, and it takes a certain kind of vigilance to resist that conflation. The conflation is not complete, however; on this last line of Daniel's, we watch him, still full-screen, but now the image is obviously on the monitor (the tracking lines and shifted colours signal this). We are being reminded that we have been removed one additional step from the 'real'. The momentary confusion between the two points of view seems to align Bregman's perspective with the 'real' or the 'objective' but

15

Daniel's disruptive gaze and his words perform the reciprocal action of revealing the 'objective' point of view to be likewise mediated. 'The question is relative,' the camera insists. 'It depends on your point of view.' The last frames show us that we are not seeing the 'real' but just one point of view. Is it Daniel's? Bregman's? Bregman's version of Daniel's version? Once again, objectivity is foreclosed.

In the absence of an objective stance, we are left to contemplate the implications of point of view, who controls it, how they use it, and to what effect. These implications are given pointed emphasis by Daniel's struggle with Bregman over the handi-cam footage. By echoing the earlier scene between Bregman and Daniel in Daniel's lab, the footage of Janet's death asks us to compare these two moments and communicates the dangers of the 'wounding shot'. As in the lab scene where Daniel is crowded into the foreground, his head angled defensively away, Janet is similarly positioned so close to us that we can almost touch her, and, like Daniel, she is turned largely away from us, exposing that same stretch of unprotected face and ear and neck. Again, there is a subtle visual pun at work here, as the scenes compare 'shots' – from a staff weapon and from Bregman's invasive, interrogating camera/gaze – and assess their similarly deadly potential. The obvious difference is that Janet's exposed face is viewed from Daniel's clearly sympathetic and benevolent point of view, while Bregman's similar position in the earlier scene is coded as invasive. Nevertheless, the echoing of perspectives in the shots implicates Daniel in the struggle for ownership and interpretive control of this image, regardless of the fact that his motivation is distinguished by its protectiveness. And, as Woolsey's witch-hunt in the second episode demonstrates, Janet is particularly vulnerable to the vagaries of inter-pretation, for Woolsey uses the occasion of her death to challenge the SGC's policies and core values. Janet's vulnerability is related to her textualisation: we see her death only on Bregman's monitor; even the 'objective' footage we get of her in the field is framed by Daniel's flashback; and the 'fact' of her death is confirmed when Col. Rundell (Mitchell Kosterman) enters and reads the official report to the gathered film crew. Janet has become someone's 'story'.[17]

The point of the scene in which the film crew views Daniel's footage, and, indeed, of the entire dramatised struggle between Bregman and Daniel, is Daniel's *desire* or the need to protect Janet and her memory from the grosser effects of interpretation, regardless of the fact that they are always already infected by it. In a telling gesture in the screening room, when Bregman realises what he has on this tape, he throws down his pencil; his interpretive power is superseded by the greater power of the image, even as his capitulation is itself an act of interpretation that valorises the 'raw' power of the spectacle of pain. At issue here, these scenes suggest, is not the idea of interpretation itself, or how it can be escaped, but the social consequences of the fact that interpretation is inescapable.

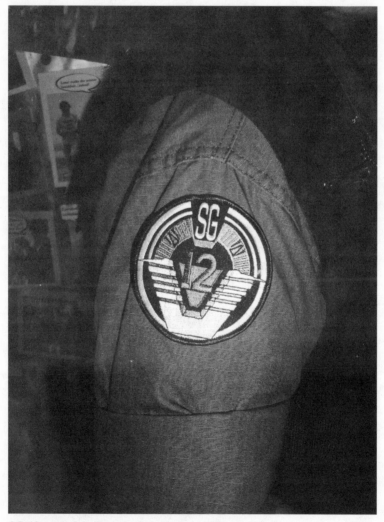

SG-12 arm patch. Photo by Lisa Dickson, 2005.

How, then, does this struggle for interpretation resolve itself within the visual and thematic language of the episodes? Thus far, we've seen how the presence of Bregman's documentary camera destabilises the 'objective' perspective, revealing that, indeed, there is no 'objective' position from which to address the questions the episode raises. The B-plot, that is, the wounding and rescue of Airman Wells, begins to put a point on those questions, as the consequences of the 'secret alien war' are graphically played out onscreen in individual, human terms. But remarkably, in the second episode, Bregman's antagonistic stance does not persist. This function is, rather, displaced onto Kinsey's political bagman, Woolsey (Robert Picardo), and the whole visual–ideological geography of the first episode is reversed as Bregman becomes increasingly *identified* with the SGC and the 'objective' (but clearly not impartial) perspective. This reversal is integral to the dramatisation of the episode's core value system, one that privileges the subjective, the emotive and the embodied, and which posits a particular representation of the 'American' soldier. At this juncture, however, the conflation is an uncomfortable one, and before it can represent a reconciliation, Bregman's antagonistic perspective must be broken down in order to be reconstituted. According to Burton, '[t]he visual narrative [of documentary film] is part of a drive to make things clear'.[18] However, Bregman's narrative *does not* initially make things clear. Bregman spends most of his time in the SGC's hallways, waiting to catch the action, his marginal position signalling the displacement of his perspective from the 'real story'. He is not allowed to film ongoing missions or to be in the Gateroom or control room when teams are departing or returning. The footage he does get is clearly at odds with what we know about the SGC and its personnel. Sam is twitchy, nervous and inarticulate, an image that clashes with our understanding of her competence and skill in extraordinary circumstances (she *does* blow up stars before breakfast and race spaceships for fun, after all). And when she is finally in her element, describing the function of the Stargate, Bregman, hungry for spectacle, responds, 'Can we get a shot of the Gate opening?' and Sam's pained 'Sure. It's really cool. Steam comes out if it and everything' ('Part 1', 717) reduces her to the equivalent of an amusement park ride operator. Likewise, the footage Bregman takes of Dr Lee describing the new lightweight ceramic shield inserts for the infantry flak vests seems like insignificant 'filler' that does little to capture the real excitement of the SGC. The two scenes are important because they demonstrate that Bregman, an outsider, is not equipped to determine what is or is not 'important' or 'significant' within the context of the SGC. The ceramic shield will save Jack O'Neill's life; Hammond will commit millions of dollars and Janet Fraiser's life to the rescue of an 'insignificant' 'Red Shirt'. These examples demonstrate that the demand for redefinition of terms that Bregman's own defamiliarising presence reveals cannot take place from within Bregman's point of view. This perspective must, therefore, either be discredited, as are those of Kinsey and Woolsey, or it must be rehabilitated and realigned.

The introduction of Woolsey in the second episode, as I note above, is key to this realignment. Sent by Kinsey to investigate the mission that results in Janet's death, Woolsey asks more or less the same questions that Bregman asks, questions about accountability and the consequences of the SGC's actions. However, while there is a complex relationship between the 'objective' point of view and Bregman's, and while we are constantly asked to look through Bregman's camera, Woolsey's video camera in the interrogation room is blind: never in the course of the episode do we see events through this lens. Therefore, this perspective is never made 'real' or visible to us, and Woolsey's camera comes to represent a silent mockery of the notion of documentation as he badgers SG-1 and suggests that, on the grounds of economics, where a wounded airman's value is measured against the budget's bottom line, their acts of heroism and the core values they stand for are imprudent, excessive and unacceptable. In a remarkable turn that neatly illustrates the realignment of forces in the visual–ideological field, Hammond suggests that Woolsey conduct his investigation in front of Bregman's camera. Threatened with exposure, Woolsey reminds him that '[t]his investigation is classified' and backs up his assertion with force, promising to put Hammond in a 'cold, *dark* place until the end of time' ('Part 2', 718, my emphasis). His authority is not ratified through a solicitation of our point of view, but only through a kind of violence grounded in carefully policed *blindness*.

By contrast, Bregman's point of view ultimately falls into line with the authoritative perspective of the 'objective' view. In one of the final scenes of the episode, Bregman tries to give the tape back to Daniel, but Daniel decides to let him keep it. Daniel confesses as he hands over the tape: 'I owed her … a lot more than I ever gave back' ('Part 2', 718). When he returns the tape, Daniel is not handing over the 'Truth' but is, rather, communicating his desire for *this* truth to be authorised, treated reverently in a way that shows *what Janet meant to him*. Truth may be a relative question and it certainly does depend on your point of view. So, in this case, then, the merit of that point of view is essential because representation is a dangerous tool that demands the utmost vigilance, skill and responsibility.[19] Bregman, it seems, has passed the test; their incommensurate points of view have somehow been reconciled. This reconciliation is clearly performed during Janet's eulogy, where the 'objective' camera turns from the scene and seems to 'enter' the lens of Bregman's documentary camera, which is filming the memorial service. It then 'exits' from the television in Hammond's office, where the rough-cut of the documentary itself is playing. In this way, the two perspectives are visually conflated, and the initially disruptive point of view has become a vehicle for the values of the 'objective' view, completing the process by which 'Heroes, Parts 1 and 2' adopt the consensus style. It is important to note that Jack, the un-disputed 'hero' of the series, only submits to his interview in the last scene of the second episode, *after* this realignment of perspectives has taken place, his presence finally ratifying Bregman's rehabilitation. The only word we hear of this interview is 'Okay' ('Part 2', 718).

As cinematic practice, 'the consensus style' does not embody specific values, but is rather a means of expressing values in a naturalised way by aligning some perspectives and ideas with the 'real' and excluding others. In the case of *Stargate SG-1*, Woolsey's inhumane emphasis on the dollar value of human life is discredited in the face of the episodes' insistence on the inherent value of the individual, regardless of broader political or economic considerations. In marking this progression from the political to a particular kind of personal focus, 'Heroes, Parts 1 and 2' can be located in a long lineage of such representations. Jan Johnson-Smith finds that such a progression characterises American television and film in the post-Vietnam War era: '[I]f Vietnam is a source of national shame and the location of America's first military defeat, in film history it becomes a location for pride in individual victory. Hollywood representations of soldiers post-Vietnam suggests [sic] that the USA has been fighting Vietnam on a personal level, creating a potential hero in everyone but simultaneously failing to address the real issues arising out of the war.'[20] Robert C. Cooper's comments on the topical nature of 'Heroes' reflect this trend. Noting that the episodes were being filmed when the United States was engaging in the Second Gulf War, he admits that there are apparent connections between the events on the world stage and the debates in which the episodes engage. That said, he concludes:

> Certainly, I know I never set out to make a commentary on *that*, although it's hard to make a show about the military without bleeding over into some of those issues. But one of my strongest feelings, having worked closely with the Air Force on the show for so long, was that whether you agree or not with what the decisions – decisions are being made by the powers that be – the people in the field, the soldiers are ... are ... have chosen to give their lives for all of us, for our freedoms ... *Stargate* is a metaphor, a wacky metaphor – it's science fiction; it's fantastic, certainly – but it's also about people who go out and risk their lives every day for the rights and freedoms of everybody on the planet including the United States.[21]

It is, then, these people who are the focus of the episodes, and whose values are elevated. Much screen time, for instance, is devoted to discussion of the personal lives of the 'Red Shirts', SG-13, where Col. Dixon talks at length about the trials of fatherhood, and offers his opinion on the interpretation of Wells' ultrasound photo of his unborn 'son' (who, Dixon correctly predicts with the confidence of much experience, is actually a daughter). And while Jack and Janet are also casualties, it is the 'insignificant' secondary character, Wells, whose wounding occasions the demonstration of the SGC's core value: no one is insignificant and that is why no one is left behind.

While Johnson-Smith identifies this personalising tendency in filmic representation as a product of the post-Vietnam era, Bernd Hüppauf demonstrates that it has a much longer history. He traces it back as far as the Crimean War and the early days of photography, but, for our purposes, his discussion of the photography of World Wars I and II is most germane. Representations of modern warfare, he argues, dramatised and responded to war's power to disintegrate individuality. Trench warfare and the destruction of both the landscape and traditional social order by the technologies of war removed the soldier from all the contexts by which his identity was constituted. War, in short, radically dehumanises, a consequence illustrated by aerial photography that represents the battlefield as a space of abstract engagement on a scale unable to capture or communicate the human element. In response, there is a concomitant construction in the media of the 'heroic' individual, the 'ace', the noble pilot who both 'puts a face' on the war and represents the values of the 'good guys'. Thus,

Hüppauf continues, there is 'a reinterpretation of the empty space of aerial photography in terms of individual experience and collective mythology [which] ... played a significant role in the process of maintaining a moral framework for war propaganda'.[22] The construction of the war 'hero', then, yokes the individual to the moral, the nationalist, the mythic.

In the staging of the film crew's responses to Janet's death, we can see both these trajectories: the inward focus on the individual and the outward focus on the mythic. In the screening room, we actually see very little of Daniel's footage. Rather, we see the reactions of the film crew, and the expressions on their faces (especially that of Tech. Sergeant James) are offered up as pure emotion, visceral responses to the horrible events that play out in front of them.[23] The reaction shots, a series of tight close-ups on Bregman, James, the sound man, Shep Wickenhouse (Chris Redman) and Col. Rundell, isolate each character from his context in such a way as to focus on individuated, psychological, emotional responses, thereby eliding the political context that characterises the first episode of the two-parter. The question is no longer whether the war and the secrecy of the programme are justified, but rather what the significance of *this* death is for *these* people. Thus, the events are personalised and depoliticised to the extent that Woolsey's investigation can be framed as a violation of Janet's memory, which is now assimilated to and synecdochically stands for the SGC's ethical position and military agenda. Within the footage, the tight focus on her face likewise decontextualises the moment: the scene could be taken from any modern war, anywhere on the planet, so that it can stand in for war in general, while, at the same time, the intimate perspective, the shot taken from Daniel's point of view of Janet's familiar face, personalises the notion of the conflict and its consequences. In this frame, then, which conflates the particular and the general, Janet becomes the 'mythic I'. The emotional power of the scene reflects and arises from what Torben Kragh Grodal refers to as the 'subjective mode', which shifts the focus of the scene from propositions, action and plot to the domain of affect and symbolism. The 'subjective mode' occurs when action is blocked and the emphasis falls on the creation of a feeling, whether that is fear or joy or relaxation.[24] In this case, Grodal's 'subjective mode' conflates the individual with her symbolic function as 'tokens of a type', that is, 'mother', 'American', 'human species'.[25] This broader participation in the 'type' sheds some light on the affective power of the montage that concludes Bregman's rough-cut of the documentary. The montage dissolves from a close-up of Sam reading the names of all those whom Janet saved in the line of duty to a series of images of unnamed SGC personnel in the field. The entirety is overlaid with a waving American flag. The intense personalising of the close-up and the list of names is coupled with the abstraction of nation and comradeship when individual (but unfamiliar and therefore generalised) faces stand for both 'America' and the SGC. 'America' is its brave, self-sacrificing soldiers. The question of the ethics of the war they fight is subsumed by this discourse.

In this way, the formerly defamiliarising perspective of the film crew falls into line with a larger pattern of association and value in the two episodes. Bregman despairs in the opening editing scene that his documentary is 'dull', a pastiche of 'talking heads' ('Part 2', 718), and this is not because he wants to entertain, but because, for him, the authenticity of the truth is found elsewhere than in the 'head'; rather, it is in the eye, in the body, the bodies of those on film and those who fulfil the role of witness. 'I believe you should speak only from your heart,' Teal'c advises Sam when her writing of Janet's eulogy stalls, caught in the eddy of Sam's inability to capture Janet in words. Urging Sam to find the truth about Janet in her 'heart', Teal'c rejects Woolsey's and endorses Bregman's understanding of how 'truth' is made into 'meaning'. It is made in the flesh. Sam's eulogy consists simply of a list of personal names.

In this way, 'Heroes, Parts 1 and 2' ultimately demonstrate, rather than resist, the consensus style. As Maltby concludes, 'By a concealed but false logic, it [the film in the consensus style] moves from the statement of a general issue to a particular manifestation of it, and from the resolution of that manifestation to the proposal of a general solution – a proposal that is never more than: if only we were all as much men of goodwill ... the problem would disappear.'[26] This is not to suggest that 'Heroes, Parts 1 and 2' are deployments of propaganda, but rather to note that they are part of a much larger discursive landscape wherein such representations struggle with the dehumanising effects of modern technological, military and social forces. The series as a whole engages with these issues in many forms, most notably posing its intense individualisation and privileging of the personal against the threat of ultimate depersonalisation represented by the Goa'uld, who reduce the human being to basic instrumentality by making human bodies into hosts. The monstrous Kull Warriors epitomise this instrumentality. Genetically engineered by Anubis, the Kull Warriors blend mentally undeveloped symbiotes with pseudo-human bodies consisting of only the barest essentials of human physicality required for combat. They are malformed, faceless drones, beings who exist solely as weapons of warfare.

In creating such characters, the series takes up a second motif that Hüppauf calls the 'grey warrior', the soldier as fighting machine who is the hardened, dehumanised product of the 'process of disintegrating the bourgeois ego and its meaningful psychological construction ...'[27] in the era of modern technological warfare. The Kull Warrior is both a frightening extrapolation from and a defensive displacement of the more terrifying spectre of the human soldier reduced to the status of the 'grey warrior'. Any long-time fan of the series will point to that spectre lurking, for example, in Jack O'Neill's stony refusal to discuss the 'death' of his friend and team-mate Daniel in 'Revelations' (522), or in the poignant fate of the duplicate SG-1 in 'Tin Man' (117), who are condemned to live eternal lives in robot bodies, working with tireless mechanical efficiency to repair a dying city. Thus, the series as a whole stages a debate between two powerful mythologies and offers the 'mythic I' as a bulwark against the dehumanising effects of modern warfare. In this light, 'Heroes, Parts 1 and 2', their adoption of the consensus style, and their reinforcement of the depoliticised perspective make a kind of strategic sense, even as they evade much of the political context that necessitates such a strategy in the first place. If the truth is a relative question and depends on your point of view, then, the episodes suggest, a choice must be made. In this struggle between the heroic 'mythic I' and the 'grey warrior', the hero wins.

Notes

1   All references to the episodes will be indicated parenthetically by episode number. See the Episode guide for further information.
2   John Corner, 'Visibility as truth and spectacle in TV documentary journalism', Ib Bondebjerg (ed.), Moving Images, Culture and the Mind (Luton, Bedfordshire, UK, 2000), p.147
3   Ibid., p.152
4   Graeme Burton, Talking Television: An Introduction to the Study of Television (New York, 2000), p.26

5   Ibid.

6   Richard Maltby, *Harmless Entertainment: Hollywood and the Ideology of Consensus* (Metuchen NJ, 1983), p.214

7   Ibid., p.190

8   Ibid., p.197

9   This is so unless such disorientation is the point of the scene, in which case the conventions will be broken to communicate that, for instance, a character has distorted perceptions due to strong emotion or drugs and so on.

10 It should be noted, however, that the full extent of this disruption is not realised because Bregman's camera shoots video and the 'objective' camera shoots film; therefore, the distinction between them is more clearly marked, reducing the disorientation that would be produced if the two perspectives were indistinguishable in terms of medium.

11 If you stand on your dining room table and look at your familiar home from that angle, you are engaged in a minor act of defamiliarisation: you see your furniture in terms of new spatial relationships; shadows fall in new patterns; colours contrast in new ways.

12 This moment plays off well against the scene on 666 where SG-13's anthropologist declares that 'Dr Jackson's gonna die when he sees this' (that is, the ruins of an Ancient city), and Col. Dixon replies: 'What, again?' ('Part 1', 717).

13 Murray Smith, 'Aesthetics and the rhetorical power of narrative', Ib Bondergjerg (ed.), *Moving Images, Culture and the Mind* (Luton, Bedfordshire, UK, 2000), p.157

14 Ibid., p.164

15 There are a number of episodes that raise the issues that Bregman does, but invariably the opposition is proven to be misguided or self-interested and the SGC's position ratified. See, for example, 'Disclosure' (617).

16 Maltby: *Harmless Entertainment*, p.191

17 And, as we have seen, the realm of representation is notoriously unstable. Bregman's most 'raw' footage, that of the rescue team and medics exiting the Gateroom, which he films secretly by holding the camera down at his side as he is being led away, illustrates this instability. As 'raw' footage, it seems to be *closest to the 'truth'*, but *at the same time* this footage is clearly *the most mediated*, the camera calling attention to its own peculiar point of view through the awkward angles, the unusual framing and so on.

18 Burton: *Talking Television*, p.107. I would add the caveat that 'clear' is not necessarily impartial.

19 In the audio-commentary to 'Part 2', Robert C. Cooper notes that Saul Rubinek was adamant that his character not be personally appealing; it was essential to him that viewers should only identify with him because

of the integrity of his point of view. Perspective cannot be escaped and so its intentions and integrity must be constantly tested.

20 Jan Johnson-Smith, *American Science Fiction TV: Star Trek, Stargate and Beyond* (New York, 2005), p.127

21 'Audio-commentary', 'Heroes, Part 2'

22 Bernd Hüppauf, 'Modernism and the photographic representation of war and destruction', Leslie Devereaux and Roger Hillman (eds), *Fields of Vision: Essays in Film Studies, Visual Anthropology, and Photography* (Berkeley, 1995), p.109

23 According to the audio-commentary, the actors began the scene expecting to see 'filler' footage on the monitors, but were in fact shown the actual scenes of Janet's death, which none of them had seen before. Their reactions, therefore, are at least in part 'candid' responses to what they are seeing, thus shifting the debate to a metadramatic level.

24 Torben Kragh Grodal, 'Subjectivity, objectivity and aesthetic feelings in film', Ib Bondebjerg (ed.), *Moving Images, Culture and the Mind* (Luton, Bedfordshire, UK, 2000), p.88. Such a shift can be elicited by any effect that limits our focus on or ability to perceive action in response to the circumstances presented: an empty space, distorted perception, unfocused images, rain, fog or darkness that limit our ability to respond to events, distorted perspective such as silhouette (pp. 92–96). All these effects and elements ask us to assess the visual image in terms of its symbolic value or simply to experience feelings related to that symbolic value.

25 'The individual persons needs [sic] to give up their individual actions in order to become part of a shared identity as humans. The viewers sheds [sic] tears when they passively give up their individual existence and give in to a participation in such sublime identity as species. Similar strong subjective feelings and autonomic reactions are often elicited in melodramas when persons incarnates [sic] social roles like "mother", "man", "woman", "American", and thus have to give up their free will in order to act as social symbols' (Grodal, p. 97). While I might debate the firmness of his distinction between 'free will' and 'autonomous response', Grodal's definition is a useful tool for reading the final movement of the episode.

26 Maltby: *Harmless Entertainment*, p.186

27 Hüppauf: 'Modernism', p.109

2

STARGÅTE SG-1: SELF-POSSESSED SCIENCE FICTION

DAVE HIPPLE

Agenda

The 'official' companion to *The X-Files*[1] points out: 'The crowded primetime marketplace [...], with millions of dollars riding on each project, tends to be built on replicating successes and not venturing down murky creative corridors.'[2] In 1997 (*Stargate SG-1*'s first year) a comment on *Babylon 5*[3] recognised another important principle for SF in particular: 'It takes a brave show to try to crack the stranglehold the *Star Trek* dynasty has on TV sci-fi.'[4] *Babylon 5* dealt with self-replicating SF expectations by going its own way, after a long search for a studio willing to allow the makers to follow their original vision. *Stargate SG-1* is certainly distinctive, but it also deploys stereotypes both to acknowledge forebears and to position itself as a deserving heir.

This discussion begins by considering the ways in which the *Stargate SG-1* pilot positioned itself as a television SF series amidst the traditions and expectations established by other products. It then closely examines two episodes from season one, reflecting upon the show's use of SF strategies to reinforce its storytelling. Next, *Stargate SG-1*'s self-construction is considered in relation to major SF icons, and to the film from which it was developed. The subsequent section examines a season five episode that uses a playful story to make serious points about Hollywood methods. Finally, *Stargate SG-1* is considered as a series/serial[5] of eight seasons and counting. As a mature show it now confidently plays games with history, as represented by its own narrative and its Hollywood heritage.

'Children of the Gods' – it's a television show

In 'Children of the Gods, Part 1' (101A)[6] Carter says, 'It took us 15 years and three supercomputers to MacGyver a system for the gate,' referring to the seven-year series *MacGyver*[7] in which Richard Dean Anderson (O'Neill) starred as a maestro of impromptu technical lash-ups. From the outset, *Stargate SG-1* portrays our own world of familiar entertainments (inscribing itself as, so to speak, 'less fictional' than those). This is not a unique strategy, of course. From 1993 *The X-Files* persistently used popular culture references to locate itself in our world. From 1997 so did *Buffy the Vampire Slayer*,[8] also mentioning *The X-Files* to position itself in turn. *Stargate SG-1* has gone beyond those shows, however, using the game of asserting its own authenticity as a springboard for discussing the industry within which this game is played.

'Children' foreshadows the development of this in several ways. A box of tissues is tossed through the Stargate as a signal to Jackson, and Major Samuels fears that 'the aliens' might intercept it. O'Neill replies, 'Well, they could be blowin' their noses right now.' These are not the relentless aliens of, say, *Independence Day*,[9] presented with awesome mystique, but a simple, pragmatic obstacle. Carter and Jackson later hypothesise multiple gate addresses, Carter already having upbraided O'Neill for perceived misogyny and failure to recognise her military rank, perhaps recalling the mere lip-service to gender equality in the original *Star Trek*:[10] 'I'm an Air Force officer just like you are, Colonel, and just because my reproductive organs are on the inside instead of the outside doesn't mean I can't handle whatever you can handle.' Jackson catches Carter's attention – 'Captain-Doctor, you're gonna love this' – and they begin a debate with all the style and cadence of the 'technobabble' for which later *Star Trek* series became justifiably notorious, but actually this dialogue plausibly uses the expanding universe model to explain irregularities in Stargate operation.

After loosely identifying its position as television narrative, this pilot hints at its self-awareness as product: Jackson promises to locate his abducted wife and bring her home in exactly one year – usefully signalling an exciting first season of adventures in an industry operating an annual production model.

'Solitudes' – it isn't about space travel

A promotional 'documentary' for *Stargate SG-1* includes an ad-libbed out-take from 'Solitudes' (118), where an apparently faulty Stargate traps Carter and O'Neill in an icy cave. Amanda Tapping (Carter) invokes Anderson's earlier series, illustrating *Stargate SG-1*'s infusion by its own television background:

> You spent seven years on *MacGyver* and you can't figure this one out!? We've got belt buckles … and shoelaces … and a piece of gum … Build a nuclear reactor, for cryin' out loud! You used to be MacGyver, MacGadget, MacGimmick … now you're Mr MacUseless![11]

This also reminds us that no rabbit-from-a-hat technical hand-waving is available here, a point firmly made in 'Solitudes' as finally broadcast:

> Siler [to Hammond]: That'll be 24 hours, General, minimum.
>
> Teal'c: Captain Carter and O'Neill do not have that long.
>
> Hammond [to Siler]: I'll give you half that.
>
> Siler: No, sir, it doesn't work that way. Twenty-four hours is the best I can do.
>
> Hammond [pauses]: Then you'd better get back to it.

This exchange is reminiscent of Scotty's legendary complaint in *Star Trek*, 'I can't change the laws of physics!' – Kirk must only insist that catastrophe is imminent to herald the immediate flouting of those very laws.[12] Not every statement is scientifically *perfect*, naturally: in 'Solitudes' the script misdirects us into wondering whether Carter's surmise (she and O'Neill must be near Earth) or Jackson's (they must be near the original line of travel) is correct. Carter's thorough-*sounding* analysis of possibilities is actually far from comprehensive, allowing the episode to trick the audience later on. Carter surveys the area and despairingly reports to O'Neill that they are stranded on 'an ice planet', the script (and a spectacular crane shot after she crawls to the surface) exploiting the audience's general experience of popular SF, where such unrelieved geographies are common. The ice planet Hoth, for example, is the striking initial setting of *The Empire Strikes Back*[13] – first sequel to *Star Wars*,[14] itself showcasing the *desert* planet Tatooine. It transpires that Carter and O'Neill have arrived at a previously undiscovered Stargate in Antarctica (Carter and Jackson were both correct, their apparently divergent theories a red herring): 'Solitudes' quietly recognises that SF can acknowledge realistic diversity as exemplified by Earth itself, and draws no further attention to Carter's narrow conclusion.

Ultimately, the traditional SF elements in 'Solitudes' act as a means of isolating Carter and O'Neill in order to tell a story that is centrally about mutual regard and team loyalty. This also applies to the SG-1 members and others searching for them from Stargate Command: the script's SF aspects are restricted to speculation, Carter and O'Neill eventually being located through traditional seismology thanks to Jackson's insight and loyal persistence.

Science fiction – strategic storytelling

Many 'definitions' of SF fail through aiming to isolate what it is 'about', with easy counterexamples always available.[15] Such definitions often arise from generalised assumptions drawing mainly on populist examples from the 'space opera' end of the genre (not widely respected for sophisticated narrative to start with). Attempts to say that SF is 'about' aliens, technology, the future or space travel collapse in the face of, for example, books (and films) such as *The Handmaid's Tale*[16] or *Flowers for Algernon*.[17] Both novels were widely acclaimed (each won a major SF award) and their respective films are generally faithful to them, but neither comfortably suits traditional definitions: *Handmaid's* 'future' is terrain that emphasises a modern gender politics debate, and *Flowers'* advanced surgery facilitates contemporary social observations by Charlie Gordon as he develops from subnormal intelligence to supergenius, then regresses again.

It is more useful to note that an impressive instance of SF will tend to involve an absorbing human story, resonant for its contemporary audience, in an unreal but coherent setting whose invented elements serve to foreground that story. Ideally, those elements are sufficiently intriguing to provide entertainment in reasoned speculation on their further implications.[18] Thus, the isolation shown in 'Solitudes' is emphasised by our acceptance that the Stargate network might strand people in an inhospitable landscape many light-years from Earth with no obvious hope of rescue. We can most productively understand SF as a particular strategy for storytelling rather than merely the display of extraordinary novelty; and, whether or not the makers of *Stargate SG-1* have consciously theorised this, 'Solitudes' is a good example of the approach.

'Tin Man' – it isn't about aliens, either

'Tin Man' (117) followed 'Solitudes' in broadcast[19] and further exemplifies *Stargate SG-1*'s approach to science fiction. SG-1 arrive in a run-down industrial complex and commence routine exploration. Apparently stunned by some kind of weapon, they later awake to find themselves wearing unfamiliar uniforms. It gradually emerges that these characters (and Harlan, the complex's amiably eccentric sole inhabitant) are androids embodying the consciousnesses of their originals. This discovery involves imagery recalling the android Ash's unmasking in *Alien*[20] (O'Neill's 'blood' sample is white goo) and *The Terminator*'s[21] self-repair (O'Neill slices open his own forearm similarly, revealing a familiar pushrod arrangement). Both references help to locate the episode in a tradition of classic screen androids. Initially the plot resolves into the relatively straightforward conundrum of how these androids can locate their original bodies and decant their consciousnesses back into them, while also helping to maintain the derelict complex whose dilapidated power systems are necessary to their own operation. The script distracts us from what may actually have happened to SG-1's bodies, since the androids' behaviour generally mirrors that expected of our familiar characters. O'Neill, ever pragmatic, demands that Harlan return them to their real bodies, but Harlan simply maintains that '[t]he transfer is permanent'. 'I am sorry, but there is no way to do what you ask. Your bodies are all gone. It is all part of the process. *This* is what you are now. You will see: it is … *better*.' Harlan stresses 'better' with the expansive, apparently ceremonial gesture that normally accompanies his habitual greeting-cum-benediction, 'Comtraya!' The overall effect is to emphasise Harlan's geniality while also heightening the team's dislocation in this entire scenario. Harlan admits that he simply needs assistants (and friends) to help him shore up the crumbling complex.

O'Neill becomes resentful: 'I say we let the place fall down.' The others point out that this would condemn themselves along with Harlan, but O'Neill is not mollified: 'Oh, *please* ... Has it occurred to anyone that all we are now is *robots*!?' Debating the potential of their condition with Carter, Jackson notes that the human body is itself a machine – so the virtual immortality of their new bodies may indeed be 'better'. Teal'c seems increasingly unwell and wanders off, but when Jackson and Carter make to follow him a total systems failure threatens the complex. The script again drifts away from what could have happened to the original SG-1, drawing us back into the jeopardy of *these* characters.

The 'robot' team saves the complex, but Teal'c reappears and inexplicably attacks O'Neill, damaging his cheek in a fashion again reminiscent of *The Terminator*. Harlan disintegrates the Teal'c android and begins to create another (the first attempt was defective, not having accounted for his Goa'uld symbiote), leading to the revelation, we might think, of the episode's true thrust.

> Carter: If you can transfer our
> consciousness into these bodies, then surely
> you can reverse the process.
>
> Harlan: No, it is impossible.
>
> O'Neill [incensed]: Why?
>
> Harlan [reluctant]: I will show you.

SG-1 is *entirely* intact: the androids are not vessels for the original minds, but self-contained duplicates. The script has diverted us from this possibility, concentrating on what is only android-O'Neill's conjecture that return must be possible and should be sought energetically. Harlan seems as upset as anyone, apparently having agreed to send SG-1 home as soon as their android copies were satisfactory, and he has tried to protect everyone from the existential tragedy that now looms. The weight of this dawns on android-O'Neill: 'We ... can never go back ...' The androids cannot 'return' to anywhere, and their artificial bodies cannot leave Harlan's complex for any significant duration.

Android-O'Neill, devastated, leaves the room. O'Neill follows, and the ensuing exchange focuses the episode with poignant wit. O'Neill's defensive brusqueness merely irritates another instance of himself, but dry humour remains available and the result is a touching rapport within which both versions try to rationalise the fate of O'Neill's android counterpart. Part of the background of the whole *Stargate* story is the death of O'Neill's young son, and now something analogous is happening: 'They're all debating the meaning of life out there: both Daniels think this is all "fascinating"; the Carters are arguing already; Teal'c feels left out. You and I have a few things to talk about.'[22] 'Tin Man' could confuse critics accustomed to SF primarily as space opera. There is no spaceship, and only the briefest glimpse of a tiny 'ray gun'. It emphasises debate over action, and in part the denouement simply restores the status quo (the revived team returns home), while also leaving the androids' fate unresolved (seemingly permanently: they plan to obviate the security risk that they now represent by disabling their own Stargate). Yet the episode works well because it conforms to the understanding of SF suggested above. Here, the SF strategy has utilised a modified but comprehensible environment such that the story can bear down upon issues of subjective human identity. Jan Johnson-Smith likens SF to paintings that provoke 'an air of quiet observation' by positioning viewers as 'complex beings suspended between the minute and the immense of the universe', and suggests that '[t]he best sf seeks to provide just such thought-provoking scenarios, and instead of offering spectacle only as a delusional or phenomenological experience sf television uses it to provide a location for interrogation and analysis'.[23] This is not always true, but it is how this late sequence of 'Tin Man' works. Its spectacle is understated but effective, presenting us with an 'O'Neill' that we have followed for most of the episode and with whom we have sympathised, alongside 'the original'. Their difference is indicated only superficially: the android exhibits the unconventional uniform, and facial damage signifying his artificial construction. We accept the two characters as being equivalent, partly because these two instances of the resolutely down-to-earth O'Neill consider each other 'basically the same guy'.

The episode has manoeuvred us into concentrating on the immediate details of a story whose wider implications (the nature of personal identity, ownership of one's own life and freedom) are now firmly pushed forward. Their full exposure is deftly achieved through a conversation between two instances of an individual who habitually handles disturbing news with fatalistic irony, and the title 'Tin Man' reminds us of a popular external text that sharpens the episode's conclusion.[24] One favourite source of allusions for *Stargate SG-1* is the film of *The Wizard of Oz*.[25] There, the Lion and the Scarecrow respectively seek courage and intelligence, which the androids clearly possess in abundance. The Tin Woodman's plight is that, lacking a beating heart, he feels condemned to an eternally loveless, solitary existence.

Star Wars and Star Trek – ancestor worship

Stargate SG-1 displays knowing regard for its genre forebears, two of which receive particular attention for their influence on modern visual SF in general.

In 'Ascension' (503) Teal'c (the team's most truly experienced interstellar traveller) delightedly advertises an obsession with Star Wars. O'Neill has never seen it ('You know me and sci-fi.'), which astonishes Carter and works in Stargate SG-1's favour: celebrating the popular image of juvenile, escapist 'sci-fi' distances the show from it. Star Wars receives nods in other episodes, nevertheless. In '1969' (221) the team accidentally time-travel to that year, and when captured and interrogated O'Neill identifies himself as Luke Skywalker, Star Wars's hero. Two aliens challenge Jackson in 'Prometheus Unbound' (812), and he says, 'Name's ... Olo. Hans Olo,' calling upon Star Wars's maverick gunslinger Han Solo for inspiration in uncertain circumstances. Teal'c's blindfold combat exercises in 'Threshold' (502) strongly suggest Luke's early training with the Force. Star Wars might be taken lightly, but its significance to popular SF is affirmed.

'Ascension' also includes John de Lancie's first appearance as Simmons, inevitably (acknowledged by Peter DeLuise's commentary for 'The Fifth Man', 504) reminding us of his role as Q in Star Trek (initially throughout The Next Generation),[26] especially since Simmons is apparently above the law as SG-1's nemesis. This pays off in 'Prometheus' (611), when, now host to a Goa'uld and an even more daunting adversary than before, he is flushed into space and killed: not quite as omnipotent as his most famous persona.

Star Trek references abound in Stargate SG-1. In 'Redemption, Part 1' (601) O'Neill and Carter test-fly the new X-302 aerospace fighter, first executing a pre-flight checklist. After predictable, common-sense elements (navigation, oxygen, temperature, pressure control) it progresses to 'inertial dampeners'. Viewers knowing some physics (or SF) might infer that such a system mitigates the ferocious accelerations of space flight. O'Neill seems familiar with this notion, deeming inertial dampeners 'cool'; and he may have encountered it in *Star Trek* (where similar terms figure), because once engines are verified he asks whether the craft also has phasers.

Carter obviously understands this as a joke, so here the episode cheerfully positions this series above *Star Trek*. The world of *Stargate SG-1* is so recognisably ours that references to *Star Trek*'s clichés are taken for granted – 'beaming' and 'cloaking device' are available as shorthand to *Stargate SG-1* characters just as they are to us. *Star Trek* references are lightly ironic, however, alongside the serious business of test-flying this spacecraft. *Stargate SG-1* can, it seems, somehow be expected to offer more realism and seriousness than *Star Trek*.

In '1969' O'Neill identifies himself not only as Luke Skywalker but also as 'Captain James T. Kirk of the starship *Enterprise*'. *Star Trek*'s first three-year run ended in June 1969, but O'Neill's reference is lost on his American interrogator: *Stargate SG-1* slyly remembers that *Star Trek*, whatever its later standing, was initially cancelled for failure to attract an audience.

Stargate – monsters from ancient history

Intuitively the most obvious Hollywood candidate for reference in *Stargate SG-1* would be the original 1994 film *Stargate*,[27] but this is made difficult. Early on (October/November 1997, after season one), the film's co-writer and co-producer Dean Devlin declared, 'I hate [the series] with a passion so strong I cannot even type about it without steam coming from my fingertips!!!'[28] Jonathan Glassner (co-creator of *Stargate SG-1*) has also mentioned problems (interview probably early 2001):

> [Devlin and Emmerich] were constantly badmouthing *SG-1* in the press without ever seeing a lick of film we had shot, or reading our script or anything, and that really wasn't fair. And there was nothing we could do about it, because we didn't want to argue with them in the press.[29]

During his 2001 DVD commentary for the film,[30] Devlin goes out of his way to say, 'We [Devlin and Emmerich] have nothing to do with the television series. Let me clear that up right now: we have *nothing* ... to do ... with the TV series.'

This ill-feeling (apparently arising from a belief that the series usurped a likelihood of film sequels) discourages playful intertextual reference, but *Stargate SG-1* perseveres nonetheless. An early dig occurs in 'Politics' (120), which introduces Kinsey as an overbearing executive, fanatical about cost savings and derisive of Stargate Command's value:

> Jackson: Senator, we have reason to believe
> that the Goa'uld are about to launch an
> attack, in force, in ships.
>
> Kinsey: Then I think they'll regret taking
> on the United States military.
>
> O'Neill [aside]: Oh, for God's sake …
>
> Jackson [calmly to Kinsey]: Oh, you're
> right. We'll just upload a computer virus to
> the mothership.

Kinsey glares, knowing he's been insulted: Jackson suggests the much-ridiculed, preposterously successful tactic from *Independence Day*, a film, like *Stargate*, directed by Emmerich, produced by Devlin and written by both.

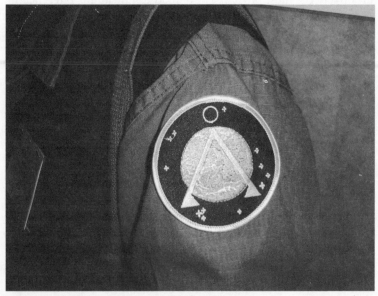

Earth glyph arm patch. Photo by Lisa Dickson, 2005.

The film's lead character is 'O'Neil', and in 'Secrets' (209)[31] O'Neill carefully ensures that his name is spelled correctly, to distinguish himself from 'another Colonel O'Neil, with only one "l". He has no sense of humour at all.' Again this appears to be a comment on the film's makers (and not on Kurt Russell, who played an extremely taciturn O'Neil'in the film but has been friendly towards the series).[32] Beyond that rather veiled final word on *Stargate* and related tensions, the series *has* made a point of using stories to examine the broad commercial Hollywood environment in which it is made.

'Wormhole X-Treme!' – self-reflexive television

'Wormhole X-Treme!' (512) introduces a fictional TV series that reflects the 'reality' of the Stargate programme. Martin Lloyd, earlier encountered in 'Point of No Return' (411), really *does* know about the Stargate operation but, having chemically suppressed his own memory, he now believes it to be his own original invention and serves as creative consultant for a television series based on the concept. This occurs within a science fiction show that can use the scenario to discuss itself.

After a brief sequence concerning an approaching ship, the episode's teaser erupts into bewildering self-parody. Three men and a woman wearing military fatigues enter the frame and take cover from incoming fire. In fact, the man seemingly in command *backflips* into view. *Stargate SG-1* characters have behaved oddly on many occasions, and several episodes have opened with teams other than SG-1, so the significance of this is not immediately obvious. What is unusual, though (except in *Star Trek* and its imitators), is technobabble about reversing the polarity of incomprehensible equipment.

Off-camera stage directions suddenly indicate that the scene is a studio set, although we cannot immediately understand why. Still, the episode communicates its self-awareness as TV SF, and we do at least know that we are invited to share *some* kind of in-joke.

After the *Stargate SG-1* credits, we see Hammond and SG-1 watching the *Wormhole X-Treme!* trailer. In ludicrously portentous tones it introduces 'four X-cellent heroes in an X-traordinary new sci-fi series', apparently caricatures of SG-1. The team leader ('wry Colonel Danning') mugs to camera and adamantly insists, 'As a matter of fact, it *does* say "Colonel" on my uniform!' and, 'Hey – it's what I do!'

before roughly kissing an exotic woman. 'Major Stacey Monroe' worries about the 'positronic field emitters', but thinks that she 'can compensate by generating a feedback loop'. 'Dr Levant', played by Raymond Gunne, is agitated: 'Dammit, Colonel, just because they're aliens and their skulls are transparent doesn't mean that they don't have rights!' 'Grell, the robot' burlesques Teal'c's already emphatic dourness.

Danning's 'wry' one-liners resemble O'Neill's in style, but are meaningless. DVD commentary confirms that he also recalls *Star Trek*'s Captain Kirk in *always* gripping women (including glamorous aliens) by the shoulders – and by the episode's end his shirt is ripped at the shoulder in classic Kirk style. Danning's remark about his uniform reflects O'Neill's in 'The First Commandment' (105), when subordinates question his plan: 'Does it say "Colonel" *anywhere* on my uniform?' he muses. (It doesn't.) By contrast, Danning really believes that his rank is advertised (it isn't) – so here even that joke fails. The real gag is that the makers of *Wormhole X-Treme!* could not know (even through Lloyd) of O'Neill's remark. Likewise, 'It's what I [or we] do' is regularly O'Neill's line, used, for instance, in three consecutive episodes of season eight: 'Zero Hour' (804), 'Icon' (805) and 'Avatar' (806). Danning's utterances, supposedly scripted for *Wormhole X-Treme!*, have context only in the framework of *Stargate SG-1*.

Wormhole X-Treme! is announced as 'sci-fi', a term frequently applied pejoratively to shallow material stereotypically emphasising ray guns, space battles and incomprehensible pseudoscience, with scant regard for human drama. If Major Monroe resembles Carter, her words also invoke those of any *Star Trek* engineer; and if technobabble is sufficiently emblematic of *Wormhole X-Treme!* to appear in its trailer then it is indeed 'sci-fi' nonsense.

'Raymond Gunne' is an old joke, abbreviating to Ray Gun. Like Jackson, his character is the team's archaeologist and linguist. His protest also recalls McCoy in *Star Trek*, frequently the emotional conscience of the hero team (mediating Kirk's impulsive physicality and Spock's cool rationalism), often opening with 'Dammit, Jim!' or 'Dammit, Spock!'. 'Grell, the robot' invokes *Star Trek*'s 'logical' characters, the obvious parallel being *The Next Generation*'s android Data but the lineage also includes Spock, Tuvok[33] and T'Pol.[34]

This introduction affectionately acknowledges the debt owed by televised SF to the original *Star Trek*. In simultaneously parodying itself, it suggests that some (but only some) SF shows have recognised *Star*

Trek's achievements but attempted to progress beyond it. It further implies that *Stargate SG-1* is far superior to *Wormhole X-Treme!*, and therefore also to the real series sent up here.

'Wormhole X-Treme!' continually satirises the Hollywood machine in general and television SF (including *Stargate SG-1*) in particular. Lloyd explains that series with 'X' in the title always do well, clearly referencing *The X-Files* and perhaps also *Mutant X*[35] (whose debut was imminent when this episode was made). While unconscious he mutters, 'The real money's in syndication.' This recalls the eventual success of *Star Trek* after failing on first broadcast, and also the resurgence of the franchise on TV when *Star Trek: The Next Generation* was released direct to syndication from the outset.[36] An imperious executive exhorts the crew to 'Make it go', spoofing Jean-Luc Picard's formulaic 'Make it so', from *Star Trek: The Next Generation*. When actors keep tripping over dead aliens, this refers to the near-ruination of a scene in 'The Fifth Man' (504) in exactly that way.

By these means and many others, 'Wormhole X-Treme!' problematises the notion of textual boundaries. Postmodernist responses are available,[37] but it is useful to note that the episode's involutions have a long heritage. Similar methods appear at the close of Shakespeare's *A Midsummer Night's Dream*, where the action seems complete but Puck remains on stage and invites the audience to regard the performance as a dream if they didn't like it: a character within the play discusses its qualities with us.[38] *Dream* blurs its own boundaries throughout, partly by presenting a play-within-a-play that interacts with its performers' world – just as *Wormhole X-Treme!* influences the *Stargate SG-1* world within which it is made: in one sense Lloyd's series is internal to this episode; in a second it is an identifiable example of TV SF in itself; so in a third it stands alongside and comments upon *Stargate SG-1*.

Routine experience gives us to expect discrete, bounded items neatly containing others, not boundaries disconcertingly overlapping like this. Something similar to Puck's coda begins when *Wormhole X-Treme!* technicians criticise a spaceship's arrival as a poor special effect that they can fix 'in post[-production]', when this can make no sense at their level of reality: for them the ship is real, but they doggedly regard it as an artefact of the show that they are creating, muddling the world of *Stargate* with that of the fiction within it. Again, this makes sense only at our level: we know that the ship is indeed a special effect, within the *Stargate* episode that we sat down to enjoy. The technicians then apparently control a fade that is real only at the level of making *Stargate SG-1*. The entire sequence confounds the fictional world where *Wormhole X-Treme!* is made, with that in which MGM makes *Stargate SG-1*.

The 'making-of' segment during the end credits of 'Wormhole X-Treme!' ostensibly describes the internal series but immediately disrupts any traditional relationship with it: 'Behind the Scenes of *Wormhole X-Treme!*' becomes truly frenzied. The really-real Christian Bocher addresses an unseen interviewer to trace a vertiginous lineage of characters:

> I'm Christian Bocher, portraying the character of Raymond Gunne, who portrays the character of Dr Levant, which is based on the character Daniel Jackson, portrayed by the actor Michael Shanks, originally portrayed by the actor James Spader. In the feature film.

Are you OK … ?

This might seem a witty conclusion where a performer smoothly indicates that the entertainment is over – but that cannot strictly be the case. The show is continuing, since the speech (like Puck's) is scripted, and Bocher is employed to deliver it, but the implied interviewer actually situates the audience as Bocher's confused addressee.

The sequence moves to an abortive campaign, by the performer playing the actor playing the character Danning, to persuade the *Wormhole X-Treme!* director to explain why he is now told, 'This isn't a real show.' (Ultimately he seems reassured to know that he is at least being paid real money.) The confused actor is played by Michael DeLuise – brother of Peter DeLuise, who both directs 'Wormhole X-Treme!' *and* plays the director of *Wormhole X-Treme!* We observe someone begging his brother to clarify, 'What plane of reality are we on right now?'

Having begun watching a show within a show, and spent 40 narrative minutes disentangling those two stories, we now have *real* actors talking to us about this complexity in their own right, or perhaps now 'appearing as themselves'. Again we must re-evaluate the episode: if it began as an elaborate narrative joke that we were pleased to understand, eventually it becomes a discussion of the multidimensional relationship between the writers, the actors, the producers, the studio and the audience. Like *A Midsummer Night's Dream* it exposes the fact that, while the audience's conventional position is 'outside the drama, looking in', the audience's presence is actually integral to whatever reality the drama itself may have.

Season eight – celebrations, blunders, games and impossible shapes

In one of the few scholarly comments from the early years of the series, Luke Hockley wrote that *Stargate SG-1* had 'emphasised special effects over narrative interest'.[39] This is surprising, because, although Hockley could not have seen the variety and depth of recent seasons, he should certainly have been aware of the early 'Solitudes' (118) and 'Tin Man' (117), and other solidly dramatic, un-'spectacular' episodes.

This is not to say that *Stargate SG-1* has always been exemplary SF. Season one also includes 'Emancipation' (103), a clumsily superficial tale of gender politics; and 'The Broca Divide' (104) relies upon a simplistic metaphor of contented and debased people living on the light and dark sides, respectively, of a planet – and upon the supposed triviality of *walking* back and forth between those hemispheres.[40] It quickly became more assured, however, and has acknowledged its own ability to fall short on occasion. 'Citizen Joe' (815) concedes that Joe's stories 'Holiday' (218), 'The Light' (418) and 'The Sentinel' (520) 'may have been a few small missteps' by planned standards – but use of the real episode titles transfers this observation to *Stargate SG-1* itself.

'Citizen Joe' provides many indications of the series' self-awareness. As with *Wormhole X-Treme!* (which, we learn here, was cancelled after one episode) we discover a character with privileged information concerning the Stargate: Joe unwittingly gains access to O'Neill's daily experiences, but compulsively writes them down in the belief that they are his own fiction. Joe's acquaintances perceive only a damaging obsession, but *we* know that his stories are real within the *Stargate* world. We might also recognise that his engagement with SG-1's activities reflects that of *Stargate SG-1*'s fans, most evidently in his devastation over the death of Daniel Jackson ('Meridian', 521) and delight at his reappearance ('Fallen', 701), culminating (when he meets SG-1 in person) in the statement: 'Doctor Jackson, can I just say, thank God you're back. Not that Jonas[41] was a bad guy, but after all you've been through you belong here with SG-1.' This recognises the furore among fans when Michael Shanks (Jackson) left the series, allegedly over dissatisfaction with his character's development. As has happened elsewhere,[42] some interpreted this as unconscionable treatment of Shanks by everyone from the studio to Corin Nemec (Jonas) personally. One result was the 'Save Daniel Jackson Campaign',[43] generating much mail, furious internet activity and advertisements in trade papers, such that the promotional documentary mentioned above[44] reserved space for segments where Nemec flatly stated that he and Shanks were never on anything but good terms, and Shanks expressed simple pleasure at being back. Joe's sentiments in this episode constitute the makers' direct, non-judgemental acknowledgment of fans' role in the presence and standing of their series.

Season eight closes with a two-part story in which SG-1 travel to ancient Egypt, 3000 BC, to recover a ZPM (a kind of super-high-tech battery). 'Moebius, Part 1' (819) introduces a number of elements pertinent here. This discussion primarily involves television, but *Stargate SG-1*'s SF background is broader: when Carter expresses anxiety that she may 'step on a bug and change the future' she undoubtedly refers to Ray Bradbury's renowned short story 'A Sound of Thunder'.[45] It becomes obvious that the team's mission *has* changed history, since in the new present-day the Stargate programme does not exist. Jackson and Carter are still scholars, but in junior posts, and we first see this downtrodden Carter rehearsing a protest to her boss: '... And just because my reproductive organs are on the inside instead of the outside doesn't mean ... *God*, that's horrible! Who would *ever* say that?' Well, we know. In *Stargate SG-1*'s very first episode a far more self-assured Carter would say exactly this to O'Neill. Those unfamiliar with early episodes can still easily interpret this Carter's evident frustration; others are rewarded with this reference to the beginning of the show that they have been following. In this new reality, Carter is brought into the project only because she is recognised in a message left by the 'original' SG-1 5000 years ago. Having no authority she is subordinate to Rodney McKay, a boorish, insecurely arrogant physicist who, in the established timeline, was greatly redeemed by experience as Carter's junior. Here his chauvinism and unoriginality go unchallenged, completing another link for those positioned to enjoy it. One attraction of the ZPM was that it could power communication to the Pegasus galaxy, destination of characters in the spin-off series *Stargate: Atlantis*,[46] whose first year ran parallel to season eight but which is rarely mentioned in it.[47] McKay's rehabilitation led to his being appointed lead scientist on the Atlantis mission, and such connections to established episodes and now the spin-off series foster an uncomfortable sense that the altered history presented here should somehow be 'fixed'.

The episode entitled '1969' played with a classic SF time paradox where SG-1 must delicately influence the past in order to preserve known history. In '2010' (416) SG-1 are manipulated by potential future selves, in order to avoid a catastrophic alliance. 'Window of Opportunity' (406) shows Teal'c and O'Neill hilariously reliving the same ten hours around 200 times, clearly patterned after *Groundhog Day*.[48] In a joyously contorted tale of time travel paradoxes, 'Moebius, Part 2' (820) goes much further. The 'new' team uses information left by the original SG-1 to travel to 3000 BC, and now includes Kawalsky, originally killed in 'The Enemy Within' (102). This is significant: the character (from the film *Stargate*) figured only briefly in the series; he reappeared in a virtual reality construct in 'The Gamekeeper' (204); and versions of Kawalsky and Carter arrived from an alternate reality in 'Point of View' (306). Part of this episode's playfulness is that he pops up yet again, here at the end of season eight. He dies again.

The 'new' Jackson becomes possessed by a Goa'uld and is killed by Teal'c (as in the simulation in 'Avatar', 806). This Teal'c is a new version of the Teal'c originally encountered in *Stargate*. The new O'Neill and Carter, accompanied by the new/old Teal'c, encounter the original Jackson, to learn that their own originals were captured and executed, and the four form a hybrid SG-1 from different timelines to repair the disruption that they caused in the first place.

Thus normality is restored. Or is it? In playing the SF game this episode does not set up jeopardy to provide a cliffhanger, as has occurred in previous seasons. Instead, the tiny (and purely visual) indication that there are now fish in O'Neill's previously barren pond suggests what we might call an 'intellectual cliffhanger'. We know (but the characters don't, in what is essentially a third timeline similar to the first) that the world of *Stargate SG-1* is now not *quite* as it was before – but Hollywood's industrial production model requires us to wait until season nine for this to unfold.

Conclusion – still travelling

Stargate SG-1's makers were aware of the long shadow cast in visual SF by popular entertainment typified by *Star Wars* and *Star Trek*. Rather than resisting related stereotypes (the approach of *Babylon 5* and, more recently, *Firefly*,[49] for example), from the beginning they used them ironically to establish their series' character. From season one this facilitated stories employing the strategies of classic SF literature, and opened up scope for occasional examination of the commercial context in which *Stargate SG-1* itself exists. By season eight the series is maturely positioned as respected SF, and can use that to be ambitiously playful about expectations of its tropes as a television series.

Notes

1   *The X-Files*, executive producer Chris Carter (Fox, 1993–2002)

2   Brian Lowry, *The Truth is Out There: The Official Guide to The X-Files* (London, 1995), p.10

3   *Babylon 5*, executive producers Douglas Netter, J. Michael Straczynski (Warner Brothers/Babylonian Productions, 1993–1998)

4   Roger Fulton, *The Encyclopedia of TV Science Fiction* (London, 3rd edn 1997), p.38

5   Briefly, a TV *series* uses certain common elements to unite numerous episodes into a whole that will retain a continuing audience. It can use simply a consistent approach and style with a variety of settings and characters, as with *The Twilight Zone* (executive producer Rod Serling; CBS 1959–1964). A *serial* focuses its attention on a continuing story, generally using constant or at least recurring characters. The original *Star Trek*, for example, fell somewhere between the two: it had ongoing characters, but episodes could be viewed in any sequence and remain comprehensible. *Stargate SG-1* has maintained a consistent setting and story continuity from the beginning, and threats to or apparent transgressions of that very continuity provide the impetus for many later episodes.

6   All references to the episodes will be indicated parenthetically by episode number. See the Episode guide for further information.

7   *MacGyver*, executive producers Jerry Ludwig, John Rich, Henry Winkler (ABC, 1985–1992; two TV movies, 1994)

8   *Buffy the Vampire Slayer*, executive producer Joss Whedon (Warner Brothers/UPN, 1997–2003)

9   *Independence Day*, written by Dean Devlin and Roland Emmerich, directed by Roland Emmerich (20th Century Fox, 1996)

10 *Star Trek*, executive producer Gene Roddenberry (Desilu/Paramount, 1966–1969)

11 *Stargate SG-1: The Lowdown* (John Murphy, New Wave Entertainment Television), first broadcast 13 June 2003. Commercially released as a bonus feature on the *Stargate SG-1 Volume 31* DVD, also part of the *Stargate SG-1 Season 6* set (though perhaps only in Region 2 releases of both).

12 This occurs in *Star Trek*, 'The Naked Time', John D. F. Black, Marc Daniels (Desilu, 29 September 1966), the fourth episode broadcast, and Scotty's first appearance in the series proper (immediately following the second pilot, 'Where No Man Has Gone Before', broadcast as the third episode and briefly featuring Scotty). A 30-minute engine restart is managed in under eight minutes, thanks to Kirk bringing a distraught Spock to his senses sufficiently for him to remember an experimental 'antimatter intermix' formula. This having been accomplished, a completely unexpected side effect is that the *Enterprise* is hurled three days into its own past, obviating the original problem entirely.

13 *Star Wars Episode V: The Empire Strikes Back*, written by Leigh Brackett and Lawrence Kasdan, directed by Irvin Kershner (20th Century Fox, 1980)

14 *Star Wars*, written by George Lucas, directed by George Lucas (20th Century Fox, 1977); later reissued as *Star Wars Episode IV: A New Hope*

15 Interested readers may wish to consult an extensive selection of attempted definitions, collected by the prolific SF scholar Dr David Lavery at Middle Tennessee State University: 'Toward a definition of science fiction' (accessed 7 July 2005, http://mtsu32.mtsu.edu:11090/305/Accessories/305OnlineSFDefinitions.html).

16 Margaret Atwood, *The Handmaid's Tale* (McClelland and Stewart, 1985); film: Harold Pinter, Volker Schlöndorff (HBO Studios, 1990)

17 Daniel Keyes, *Flowers for Algernon* (Harcourt, New York, 1966); films: *Charly*, Sterling Silliphant, Ralph Nelson (Selmur Pictures/Robertson Associates, 1968); *Flowers for Algernon*, John Pielmeier, Jeff Bleckner (CBS, 2000)

18 Darko Suvin's influential model of 'cognitive estrangement' in SF privileges this element of intellectual play, but in doing so it downplays the primary significance of *story*: see Darko Suvin, *Metamorphoses of Science Fiction: On the Poetics and History of a Literary Genre* (London, 1979). The thinking here is that 'SF-ness' occurs when a human story that could be told otherwise is accentuated by the appropriate deployment of non-real elements.

19 The DVD releases have reversed this sequence.

20 *Alien*, written by Dan O'Bannon, directed by Ridley Scott (20th Century Fox, 1979)

21 *The Terminator*, written by James Cameron and Gale Anne Hurd, directed by James Cameron (20th Century Fox, 1984)

22 O'Neill to android-O'Neill in 'Tin Man'.

23 Jan Johnson-Smith, *American Science Fiction TV: Star Trek, Stargate and Beyond* (London, 2005), pp.6–7

24 The android doubles reappear in 'Double Jeopardy' (421, first broadcast 16 February 2001), which largely disregards the main concerns of 'Tin Man'. They also 'die' rather arbitrarily, which retrospectively diminishes the existential tragedy of 'Tin Man' but, ironically, confirms its original power.

25 *The Wizard of Oz*, written by Noël Langley, Florence Ryerson and Edgar Alan Wolfe, directed by Victor Flemming (MGM, 1939)

26 *Star Trek: The Next Generation*, executive producers Gene Roddenberry, Rick Berman, Michael Piller, Jeri Taylor (Paramount, 1987–1994)

27 *Stargate*, written by Dean Devlin and Roland Emmerich, directed by Roland Emmerich (MGM, 1994)

28 Online chat session: 'SCIFI.CON 2.0: Dean Devlin chat' (accessed 7 July 2005, http://www.scifi.com/transcripts/scifi.con2.0/DeanDevlin.html)

29 Joe Nazzaro, *Writing Science Fiction and Fantasy Television* (Titan Books, London, 2002), p.124. Associated information suggests interview probably early 2001.

30 *Stargate, Director's Cut*, written by Dean Devlin and Roland Emmerich, directed by Roland Emmerich (Momentum Pictures, 2001)

31 Of course, within the history of *Stargate*'s world the two differently spelled characters played by Russell and Anderson are actually equivalent: Anderson's character is the same one who, as played by Russell, visited Abydos in the film. The invention in 'Secrets' of what must be a quite distinct character complicates the intertextual joke.

32 Anderson's own website includes pictures following Russell's visit to the set on 28 April 2000 (accessed 7 July 2005, http://rdanderson.com/updates/images/kurt.jpg).

33 *Star Trek: The Next Generation*

34 *Enterprise* (more recently known as *Star Trek: Enterprise*)

35 *Mutant X*, executive producers Avi Arad, Jay Firestone, Adam Haight, Peter Mohan, Gary L. Smith, Rick Ungar (Tribune/Fireworks Entertainment, 2001–2004)

36 Traditionally a series would first be broadcast by a network that had part-funded its making, and which would profit first from selling advertising during that initial airing. At a later date the *studio* where it was made would be able to lease it to other networks in the syndication market, frequently after having actually lost money on making it for the first run.

37   Jacques Derrida's concept of 'invagination' is relevant here, and is usefully explored in David Metzger, *The Lost Cause of Rhetoric: The Relation of Rhetoric and Geometry* (Carbondale, 1994) pp.14ff. The relevant text is viewable online at 'PRETEXT, a Re/INter/VIEW with David Metzger', *PRETEXT, REINVW, Metzger, 1* (accessed 7 July 2005, http://www.pretext.com/ptlist/metzger1.html).

38   Shakespeare, William, *A Midsummer Night's Dream* (ca 1600), V, i, pp. 425–440; cited edition is the Signet Classic Shakespeare New York, 1963)

39   Luke Hockley, 'Science fiction', Glen Creeber (ed.), *The Television Genre Book* (London, 2001), p.31

40   The terminator (the twilight band between day and night) is far too broad for this. Consider the time it takes for full daylight on Earth to become full darkness. Each hour represents 1/24 of the Earth's circumference – about 1700 km.

41   Jonas Quinn (played by Corin Nemec) was a member of SG-1 during Jackson's absence in season six, also a historian and academic but quite a different character.

42   Something similar occurred when Jeffrey Sinclair (played by Michael O'Hare) was supplanted as the central character of *Babylon 5* by John Sheridan (played by Bruce Boxleitner).

43   Campaign archive: 'Daniel Jackson is out of Stargate SG-1', *Save Daniel Jackson | Home* (accessed 7 July 2005, http://www.savedanieljackson.com/history/home/home.shtml)

44   *Stargate SG-1: The Lowdown*

45   Much anthologised; originally appeared in *Collier's Magazine*, 28 June 1952.

46   *Stargate: Atlantis*, executive producers Brad Wright, Robert C. Cooper, Joseph Mallozzi, Paul Mullie (MGM, 2004–present)

47   In this season, other than being seen to take shape in early episodes, the Atlantis mission serves mainly as misdirection in 'Prometheus Unbound' (812), when it is the intended target (never reached) of a mission led by Hammond.

48   *Groundhog Day*, written by Danny Rubin and Harold Ramis, directed by Harold Ramis (Columbia Pictures, 1992)

49   *Firefly*, executive producer Joss Whedon (20th Century Fox, 2002)

3

'WAY SMARTER THAN YOU ARE': SAM CARTER, HUMAN BEING

STEPHANIE TUSZYNSKI

> Carter: Theoretical astrophysicist.
>
> O'Neill: Which means?
>
> Hammond: It means she's smarter than you are, Colonel.
>
> – 'Children of the Gods, Part 1'

Female characters in science fiction or fantasy shows have long been a ripe target for scholars, becoming even more prominent in the years since Buffy and Xena became well-known cultural icons. These characters are especially useful for scholars as a means to examine cultural attitudes towards women, as well as the construction of gender in our society. Writers like Sherrie Inness have productively delved into female characters from film and television and explored changes (and the lack of changes) over time in cultural conceptions of 'toughness'.[1] Unfortunately, much of the writing on these characters is ultimately negative, emphasising the employment of stereotypes for female characters created by the mostly male producers of television. While there is much truth in these writings and much to be gained in breaking down the stereotypes and the underlying misogyny that certainly does appear in some shows and films, automatic dismissal of a female character based on one facet of that character benefits no one. For example, many scholars are trapped by the Freudian binary of 'active male/passive female', which frequently dismisses a female character who is active as 'phallicised'.[2] Often it seems that simply being beautiful is enough to undermine whatever heroic actions a female character takes and to turn her into something less than a hero, less even than a fully developed character.[3] This negation via beauty is a rather serious problem because it sets up every female character to be read as a failure, since it is unlikely that films and television will ever produce an ugly heroine. To examine every female character on the basis of whether or not she is a flawless feminist icon is to pre-condemn every character because a character without flaws would be nothing more than an empty shell. However, if we acknowledge that no female character can ever be entirely free from the cultural stereotypes that produce her and therefore will never be ideal, perhaps we can take some pressure off the characters – and those who analyse them – and instead find a more productive approach.

In her analysis of Ripley from the *Alien* movies, Elizabeth Hills points out the limitations of the feminist and psychoanalytic approaches to heroines, and called on scholars to find new ways that work outside a binary of male versus female.[4] My aim in this chapter is to take a more holistic approach by examining Samantha Carter of *Stargate SG-1* as a fictional character with both strengths and weaknesses. This is more a textual analysis than a theoretical one, looking at the character's history in terms of her narrative development as a character – and as a *female* character. I will review the basic facts of Carter's history over the first eight seasons of the series in terms of how Carter is positioned, with particular emphasis on certain familiar tropes (stereotyping the female character as a damsel in distress, as a love interest, etc.), and discuss how Carter sometimes fits and sometimes defies these stereotypes. I will also examine how the show actually presents her visually to the audience as the main female cast member. My ultimate goal is to evaluate Carter as a well-rounded (i.e. imperfect) character and consider what this means for science fiction and fantasy television and the related scholarship. My hope is that this kind of approach might provide a new perspective on female characters in science fiction and fantasy that can coexist alongside more traditional approaches, to balance out some of their overwhelming negativity.

The television series *Stargate SG-1* began its eighth season in July 2004. Samantha Carter is one of the five central characters of the series. Originally a captain in the United States Air Force, she was promoted to major at the beginning of season three and then to lieutenant colonel at the start of season eight. She is a pilot and a combat veteran who flew in the First Gulf War. In addition to being the second in command of Stargate Command's flagship team, she is also a theoretical astrophysicist with a Ph.D. in quantum mechanics and the foremost expert on alien technology on the planet. She is played by actress Amanda Tapping, who is 5' 9",[5] with blonde hair and blue eyes. While not quite matching the proportions of Lucy Lawless (*Xena*),[6] Tapping is much closer to Lawless' body type than, say, Sarah Michelle Gellar's (*Buffy the Vampire Slayer*) pre-adolescent, waif-like physique.[7]

The introduction scene in the series pilot, 'Children of the Gods' (101A),[8] provides a great deal of information about the character. Although she was working on the Stargate project at the time of the original 'mission' (meaning the theatrical film on which the series was based), she was not part of the team that went through the gate. Carter is rather obviously a strategic addition created to include at least one female character among the five men who were regular cast members – a reminder that the business and marketing side of the television industry cannot be ignored when analysing content. However, she is not a sidekick but a fully functioning member of a team.[9] When confronted by the chauvinistic attitude of the men in the room, she remains calm, but she is not afraid to push back when harassed: 'Is that tough enough for you? Or do we have to arm wrestle?' Given the prevailing culture of the US military, Carter would necessarily have had to develop skills to handle sexism from her fellow officers.[10] The show is careful, however, not to generate this prejudice from Carter's new commanding officer, Colonel Jack O'Neill (Richard Dean Anderson), but rather locates it in two secondary characters. O'Neill, the typical wise-cracking alpha male often found in science fiction and action adventure, has a 'problem' not with women but with scientists. His reluctance to accept Carter on the team influences the dynamic between the two characters over the first season; many episodes contain a subtext of Carter working to win the respect of her new superior. During the first mission in 'Children of the Gods', Carter bonds with her fellow intellectual, Dr Daniel Jackson (Michael Shanks), the two of them going off in a rapid, highly technical conversation about the Stargate system that leaves everyone else in the room staring in bafflement. One of the recurring motifs of the series is Carter rattling off a complicated explanation only to have to translate it into simpler language for her colleagues (including Jackson). This serves as a subtle reminder that Carter is truly smarter than almost everyone around her, at least in certain ways.

One thing that would be immediately apparent to any feminist scholar in discussing this character is, of course, her name. Carol Clover, in her discussion of the 'Final Girl' phenomenon, points out that female characters in horror movies who survive the carnage frequently have gender-neutral or masculine names.[11] Carter is almost always referred to as Sam – when addressed by her first name, at least. In fact, during the introduction of the character in 'Children of the Gods', after she salutes O'Neill and says, 'Captain Samantha Carter reporting, sir,' another character sarcastically points out, 'But you go by "Sam", right?' O'Neill almost always refers to her as 'Carter', largely because the relationship between them is bounded by the difference in their ranks and to be overly familiar would be inappropriate. The only people who routinely call her 'Sam' are Daniel Jackson, her father, Jacob Carter, and Janet Fraiser – the only other recurring female character, who is also the only female friend Carter is ever shown spending time with. To the other people around Carter, she is a rank, either 'Captain' or 'Major' depending on the season. Her full name, 'Samantha', is generally only used by male characters positioned as romantic interests for her. This is an interesting shorthand for the relationships in her life. The viewer can tell without having to think what kind of relationship exists between any character and Carter by what they call her. Additionally, the fact that it is her gender-neutral nickname that is employed by her career military father and her male colleagues supports the Final Girl trend. Carter is not seen by her male colleagues as a woman but as a member of the team, who, while biologically remaining female, is treated as an equal and not as a sexual or romantic object. Only romantic interests and men outside the social structure in which she lives see her as a woman, signified by their use of her full, feminine name. This becomes significant in the discussion of the early episodes of the series.

The first stand-alone episode of the series, 'Emancipation' (103), provides more insight into Carter. As the other new character besides Teal'c (played by Christopher Judge), the alien soldier who has switched sides in the war with the Goa'uld, Carter needs to be fleshed out more for the audience.[12] There is a great deal to unpack in 'Emancipation'. This episode marks the only time the team travels to a world so overtly patriarchal. Coincidentally or not, it is also one of the only worlds populated almost entirely by people of Asian descent.[13] This is the only team story where one, and only one, member of the team is required to change clothes in order to fit in – Carter is made to change into a dress supposedly to avoid causing a problem with the locals (this turns out to be false; the motive for her new clothing is mercenary). Taking her out of uniform and putting her into an ornate gown has the visual effect of reminding the viewer that Carter (despite her name, perhaps) is different from her team-mates, and repositions her as a sexual object. Carter resists having to do this, and in her first appearance in the local garb she is full of complaints, although she is controlling her temper with humour: 'Daniel, find me an anthropologist who dresses like this and I will eat this headdress!' Her team-mates' reactions in this scene are particularly problematic. Jackson stutters incoherently, Teal'c stares (the character was the antithesis of verbose in the first season) and, worst of all, O'Neill takes off his hat and addresses her as 'Samantha' – he only uses her full name twice in the entire series and both times are within the first four episodes.[14] Given that Carter was shown in the pilot wanting to prove herself to O'Neill, having him treat her not as an equal colleague but as a woman only feeds her anger. The show displays a good deal of self-reflexivity in having Carter aware that her power is being contained, literally and figuratively, by the traditional clothes. She will not regain her equanimity until she is back in uniform, although she never surrenders her ability to take action, no matter what her clothing indicates about her role.

Carter is kidnapped and sold to a powerful and misogynist warlord. Unsurprisingly, she wants to fight back but is constrained by her surroundings. Her team-mates discover what has happened and immediately begin searching for her, only to learn of her abduction and the danger she is now in. O'Neill decides to purchase Carter's freedom as the most expedient way to get her released; the warlord who now 'owns' Carter will rape her (or attempt to) as soon as night comes. One of the most obvious differences between male and female action heroes is that rape is far more commonly shown happening to women in fiction, films and television. The threat of rape can hang over a female character much more effectively, and therefore can automatically mark a female action heroine as being more vulnerable than a male counter-part simply because she is female (despite the fact that male same-sex rape is hardly impossible).[15] 'Emancipation' is a rare case where sexual rape is presented as an explicit, imminent threat in the *Stargate* universe. Possession by a Goa'uld symbiote marks a kind of physical and mental violation that lacks a sexual component, at least after the extremely eroticised sequence in 'Children of the Gods' where Sha're, Jackson's wife, is taken as a host. Being violated by a Goa'uld symbiote and rendered a prisoner in one's own body is often presented as the ultimate bad fate for anyone, male or female, which is perhaps why sexual rape is rarely brought up in the series.[16] With the threat of being violated by a Goa'uld hanging over the characters, the threat of sexual rape becomes almost redundant. Carter only faces this type of explicit threat one other time, in the second season episode 'Prisoners' (203); however, in that episode, which takes place in an alien prison, everyone but Teal'c is at risk. In 'Prisoners', the potential for male-on-male rape is treated as a distinct possibility as well, and allusions are made to time O'Neill spent in an Iraqi prison, raising the possibility that he either was himself raped or witnessed such acts. Interestingly, Carter is never actually sexually violated in the series, but both Jackson and O'Neill are, in the first season episodes 'Hathor' (113) and 'Brief Candle' (108), respectively – both occurrences involving mind-altering chemicals making them unable to consent.[17] After the second season, sexual encounters with other characters rarely happen, and never happen under duress or mind-altering influences again, perhaps because the danger of possession by a Goa'uld becomes far more immediate at the beginning of season two. In the second episode of the second season, Carter is taken as a host, although the purpose of her being taken is to introduce the Tok'ra, biologically identical to the Goa'uld with the significant difference that the Tok'ra (usually) do not take hosts against their will.[18] Carter's being taken as a Tok'ra host has the effect of further isolating her from her team-mates; until season six she is the only one who has been a host. In addition to being the only woman, she is now further marked by being a former host, in possession of some of the knowledge of the Tok'ra.[19] Her experience places a large share of knowledge on her shoulders. She now is not only the scientist but also has information that even Teal'c does not possess, all of which increases her value to the team, and simultaneously increases her isolation from them as well.

'Emancipation' seems to place Carter in the typical 'damsel in distress' position, down to wearing a cumbersome dress and helplessly requiring rescue by her male team-mates. This is not the end of the story, however. Carter's kidnapper was acting in an attempt to rescue the woman he loved, who happens to be the daughter of the warlord Carter was sold to (a 'Romeo and Juliet' subplot). Carter helps the girl escape but, after Carter is free, the team learns the girl has been captured and is going to be put to death. Carter insists on returning to save the life of the girl, which she does herself in single hand-to-hand combat with the warlord. Many of the later episodes' resolutions hinge on Carter's intelligence and ability to find solutions to complex problems. 'Emancipation' is resolved thanks to her physical strength and willingness to fight. It is worth noting that even when her power is physical, as it is in this episode, it is not sexual, a phenomenon I will discuss more later. This was perhaps a necessary step in the development of the character. Common conceptions of 'geeks' often portray them as intelligent but physically weak and unable to fight. Carter, as an Air Force officer, cannot be this way, and simply being proficient with weapons (like O'Neill, she carries a P-90 automatic rifle) is not enough for a woman in a field unit. Perhaps the physical combat serves to prove her status as a capable officer and 'one of the guys' as far as O'Neill is concerned. Carter does not possess superhuman strength or skill like Buffy or Xena, but she is a capable fighter. After demonstrating her ability to defend herself from physical attack in this very early episode, she can afterwards never be seen as just a helpless damsel in distress.[20]

Another episode from the first season is worth mentioning with regard to Carter's development. In 'Singularity' (114) Carter bonds with a young girl named Cassandra, the only survivor of an entire planet, who turns out to have been altered by the Goa'uld and turned into a living time bomb intended to destroy the Earth Stargate. This story is somewhat reminiscent of the Ripley–Newt relationship in *Aliens*, in that it positions Carter as a mother figure, once again contrasting her intelligence and rank (often masculine attributes) with a feminine role.[21] Positioning an active female as a maternal figure can have the effect of constraining her; maternal imagery is the antithesis of active heroines. A mother is someone who stays at home and takes care of children, not someone who carries an automatic rifle and battles aliens. Indeed, in *Aliens*, Ripley's positioning as a mother figure can be seen as encoding the character's actions in one of the few socially acceptable frameworks for female violence, namely a mother protecting a child, and therefore taking away her independence.[22] In a tense sequence at the end of 'Singularity', Carter is ordered to abandon Cassandra in an old nuclear facility. Believing that the bomb within the girl may not explode, Carter disobeys a direct order from O'Neill to leave – her affection for the child overriding her devotion to her duty and her maternal impulses therefore conflicting with her job. This would seem to support the idea that motherhood is not compatible with life in a dangerous occupation. However, Carter's decision to remain is actually placing her in more danger, and is presented as the correct choice. The character of Carter would never have been the same (would perhaps have been un-acceptable, particularly as a female character who would be expected to possess a parental drive, and be more open about showing it than a male character) had she abandoned a child in that manner.[23] Of course, Cassandra survives, and the close relationship between her and Carter

The well-appointed fan home. Photo by Lisa Dickson, 2005.

recurs in later episodes, including 'In the Line of Duty' (202) and 'Rite of Passage' (506). The latter episode indicates that Carter spends time with Cassandra every weekend she is on Earth, thus allowing Carter to remain in a motherly role without impairing the character's continued adventures in the series by turning her into an actual mother who would need to avoid dangerous situations because of her duties to her child, which have already been shown to be incompatible with Carter's duty to the Air Force and the planet. 'Singularity' is an episode that gives Carter the chance to try on the role of being a mother figure, but without constraining her into the limitations of that role permanently, because she cannot (supposedly) be a warrior and a mother simultaneously. Her skills and intellect are too valuable for the survival of the planet for the character to abandon her job.

Carter's great intelligence has not saved her from meeting her share of failures, or from making mistakes. While any number of episodes rely on her scientific mind to resolve complex problems, several episodes revolve around her not being able to find the answer. In 'Message in a Bottle' (207), Carter's scientific curiosity fails to recognise a possible threat and exposes O'Neill and the entire planet to a destructive alien organism. In 'Red Sky' (505), Carter bypasses some of the safety protocols on the Stargate's dialling programme and, in doing so, damages a star and nearly wipes out an entire planet of people. From season one, O'Neill has a tendency to look for the most pragmatic solution, for example in 'The Torment of Tantalus' (110), where it is O'Neill, not Carter, who suggests using the lightning from a storm to power the Stargate when the team is trapped – though it is usually up to Carter to make O'Neill's suggestions work.[24] The sixth season opened with a two-part episode, 'Redemption' (601–602), involving an attack on the Earth Stargate. Carter and an entire team of scientists, including her intellectual rival, Dr Rodney McKay, are unable to save the day. McKay is one of the few characters to ever look down on Carter. He specifically attacks her disregard for safety protocols and logic, a rare moment since most of the people around Carter never question her intellect.[25] The character, in other words, is far from infallible. While Carter has managed to escape some of the more common stereotypical constructions of female characters, such as damsel in distress or mother figure, a more fundamental stereotype is unavoidable when discussing her character.

Carter's combination of prodigious intelligence and physical strength brings up a long-standing cultural stereotype – brains versus beauty.

Women are often portrayed as either being beautiful and dumb or smart and ugly. On television 'ugly' often translates into wearing glasses and frumpy, unflattering clothing that are used to conceal the actress' beauty (since there are virtually no ugly actresses on fictional television series). In the season eight finale, 'Moebius' (819–820), this exact trick is used for an alternate-reality of Carter, though the wardrobe choice had perhaps something to do with concealing Amanda Tapping's pregnancy. Carter defies the brains versus beauty stereotype by being simultaneously beautiful and brilliant, but the series does not exploit her looks in the same way Lucy Lawless and Sarah Michelle Gellar were used as sexual objects by being put on display almost constantly, particularly while fighting. The cast of *Stargate SG-1* have perhaps the most boring wardrobe on television. Their standard attire is a black, long-sleeved shirt and green or blue cargo pants, with military-style boots. These uniforms are loose-fitting, unlike the clinging bodysuits found on *Star Trek*. On formal occasions, Carter and O'Neill wear Air Force dress uniforms. In the occasional episodes which show the team in 'street clothes', Carter favours jeans and a black leather jacket (she owns a motorcycle). Only in one episode of the first eight seasons was Amanda Tapping's body put on prolonged, deliberate sexual display in a provocative dress – the seventh season episode 'Chimera' (715), which revolved around Carter in a successful romantic relationship outside the SGC. In other words, the display was a part of the plot, and not done for (only) gratuitous reasons. One other episode that involved a direct, visual focus on Tapping's body was the second season finale, 'Out of Mind' (222), where a naked Carter is awakened by O'Neill. Her shoulders and bare upper back are clearly visible, and the show plays up the moment by having O'Neill pause for a moment before telling her to get dressed (there are other undertones to this scene, which I will discuss in a moment). In the roughly 170 episodes that have followed 'Emancipation' it has never been suggested that Carter is anything other than beautiful because, despite her boring clothes, it is obvious that she is. It is also obvious that her value is measured by her continuing ability to save her team-mates and the world, and not how good she looks doing it. Considering that television shows need to attract an audience, and pandering to the 'male gaze' by dressing women in skimpy outfits is hardly unheard of in science fiction and fantasy (Xena's all-over leather, *Star Trek*'s infamous miniskirts), it is even more remarkable that *Stargate SG-1* has been so careful not to emphasise Tapping's body or use it more to attempt to generate attention and ratings.[26]

Carter's combination of beauty and brains has attracted a number of male admirers but does not translate to a happy romantic life for the character during the first six seasons of the show. She has had two recurring love interests: Narim, a human from an advanced culture, who appeared in three episodes and is presumed dead after the Goa'uld destroyed his home world in the fifth season, and Martouf, a Tok'ra who is host to the symbiote Lantesh. Jolinar, the symbiote Carter carried, was previously his mate, although Martouf's feelings towards Carter develop specifically for her sake over time. Unfortunately, in the fourth season, Martouf is compromised by the Goa'uld and Carter herself kills him. While clearly fond of both these men, Carter never expresses an explicit attachment to either of them. Over the first six seasons, Carter has been the object of various men's affections, from an ascended Ancient who retakes human form to be with her, to Jackson ribbing her about a junior Air Force officer having a schoolboy crush on her. Like Narim and Martouf, several of these men have met an untimely demise, earning Carter the nickname 'Black Widow Carter'.[27] In the seventh season, in the aforementioned episode 'Chimera', Carter begins a serious romantic relationship with a police officer named Pete Shanahan, a man who has no involvement in the Stargate programme, which poses a problem because of the clandestine nature of her work. It is worth noting that Carter's team-mates are subject to the same restrictions due to their work, and none of them has been able to sustain a stable romantic relationship (although all three men have been married at some point in the past; Jackson and Teal'c are widowers and O'Neill is divorced). The nature of an episodic series means that, more often than not, romantic prospects are doomed to either die or be abandoned to preserve the dynamic of the central cast. The only way to introduce an element of romance that can be sustained is to create it between major characters, but this risks throwing off the basic chemistry of the show.

From their first encounter in 'Children of the Gods', *Stargate SG-1* clearly indicates the presence of a low-level attraction between Carter and O'Neill. This dynamic is somewhat overshadowed during the first season by Carter's attempts to prove herself to O'Neill, although the idea of sexual attraction between them is brought out early on in season one in 'The Broca Divide' (104), when Carter, while not in her right mind, violently attempts to seduce him. The series, though, is always conscious of the fact that O'Neill is Carter's immediate superior, and they are explicitly prohibited from any kind of intimacy because of Air Force regulations. Playing with this fact, two episodes, 'There but for the grace of God' (119) and 'Point of View' (306), delve into alternate realities to imagine what might have been if Carter had never joined the Air Force. The alternate-reality versions of Carter (identifiable by her long hair) are married or engaged to the alternate versions of O'Neill. In a neat piece of dialogue, though, the alternate Carter, after kissing the 'real' O'Neill, whispers in anguish: 'You're really not him, are you?' ('Point of View'). This moment suggests that the romantic bond is universe-specific. However, late in season three, the series begins to suggest that a romantic attachment is developing between the two of them. This 'unresolved sexual tension' dynamic is played up heavily during season four, particularly when O'Neill confesses in 'Divide and Conquer' (405) that he cares about Carter 'more than I'm supposed to'. Ironically this is the episode that ends with Carter killing Martouf. This thread disappears for long stretches in the subsequent seasons, although Carter's feelings seem to finally be resolved in season seven's 'Grace' (713), when a concussed Carter has hallucinations of the various men in her life and appears to let go of whatever hopes she had been holding on to regarding O'Neill, clearing the way for the introduction of Pete two episodes later.

The unresolved tension between Carter and O'Neill can seem rather arbitrary given how it comes and goes from the show's subtext. It also creates a problem for the character beyond the misleading trope of the 'Black Widow'. On the one hand, Carter's unresolved feelings for her 'boss' make her slightly more realistic. Any number of people have developed feelings for a co-worker who is out of reach for some reason. Unfortunately, falling for her commanding officer can have the effect of reducing the character's stature because it positions her as a love interest rather than an independent character, and as a typical irrational female falling for an unavailable man, which belies the massive intelligence Carter possesses. It would be easy to seize on Carter pining for O'Neill like a lovesick girl as a fatal flaw, an unforgivable weakness that degrades the character. To do so, however, would be to fall back into the all-or-nothing trap which I have been trying to avoid. One flaw does not negate the many strengths of a character, especially not when the problem is mined for genuine character development, as this particular situation was in season seven. Carter herself, in 'Grace', comments on the psychological reasoning that might be underpinning her feelings for O'Neill: 'As long as I'm thinking about you, setting my sights on what I think is unattainable, there's no chance of being hurt by someone else.' Much of the episode's personal development of the character addresses her loneliness and her realising that she deserves to be happy, if she is willing to take the risk. This is a set-up for Pete's arrival two episodes later, where Carter's 'flirty, girly' side is showcased for the first time.[28]

During season eight, Carter becomes engaged to Pete, only to end up breaking the engagement shortly before their wedding at the end of the season, in the episode 'Threads' (818). The reasons for her change of heart are not made terribly clear, although a strong feeling of disconnection is present as Carter contemplates living the typical suburban life with Pete while continuing her work in the Stargate programme. The two spheres seem unable to coexist for her. At the same time, the Carter/O'Neill relationship issue re-emerges. In her quest to resolve why she's having second thoughts, Carter seeks O'Neill out, only to learn that he is having a casual relationship with someone else. However, as Carter holds vigil over her dying father, O'Neill appears to comfort her. When she thanks him for being there, he tells her: 'Always.' With this scene, coupled with O'Neill's paramour breaking off their relationship because of his supposedly obvious feelings for Carter, the door seems to have been left open to pursue a genuine relationship between the two that rises above the subtextual longing that has been coming and going throughout the series. Would a genuine, official relationship ease the tension of Carter becoming 'just a love interest' or would it only further erode the character's position as a foolish, lovesick woman? The show stopped short of declaring such a relationship to exist within season eight. It remains to be seen what will occur during season nine, when O'Neill's character will be largely absent from the series.

Sam Carter is an Air Force officer, a pilot, a combat veteran, and the world's foremost theoretical astrophysicist and expert on alien technology. She is a statuesque blonde woman with blue eyes, a gender-neutral name, and a bad track record in romantic relationships, including an ill-advised attraction to her commanding officer. Despite actress Amanda Tapping's considerable physical attributes, her body has not been used gratuitously on the show. Carter is a character rich in history and detail, partly due to the fact that *Stargate SG-1* has been on the air for eight seasons and is still going. From the outset the character was more than a blank slate intended to fill the slot of 'token female character'. Carter was likely influenced by the female characters who came before, including Dana Scully of *The X-Files*, another female character who was overtly valued for her brains more than her (obvious) beauty.[29] Carter is also a far cry from the miniskirted or bodysuit-clad women of *Star Trek*, and neither is she a Buffy Summers. Carter represents a different kind of female character for science fiction television – intelligence that is respected by her male peers, compassion for others that sometimes serves her well and other times does not, physical strength that does not make her in any way masculine, all contained within a beautiful body that is not often displayed. I would never argue that Carter is a perfect character and should be the model for all characters in the future, but the balance of strengths and flaws is something rare for female characters. She is allowed to make mistakes, and to fail occasionally, just like her fellow team-mates, rather than having to always be perfect because she is 'the Girl'.

There is no way to categorise Carter as either 'good' or 'bad' in terms of feminist ideals or even psychoanalytic binaries, although no doubt long arguments could be made from either side. The key to looking at Carter, and, I believe, to examining other female characters, particularly in science fiction and fantasy television, is not to attempt to separate out the positive and negative traits and see which side weighs more. Neither is it to find a single weakness or stereotype in the character's development and use that problem as an excuse to condemn the character entirely. The key is to look at the character as a whole, including flaws. Carter, despite her almost inhuman capacity to solve immense problems in a babble of technospeak, is kept from being too perfect by several character traits which work to make her interesting. She has a sense of humour, and also a tendency to stick her foot in her mouth. She can also be relentlessly focused, for good or ill, and at the same time has been shown to have a nurturing side. As a character, then, Carter is well developed and contradictory; in a word, human. If we concede that there will never be a perfect female heroine, because perfect people are not interesting to hear stories about, we can abandon the quest for the idealised female role model and take a great deal of pressure off both the characters and the scholars who study them. Instead, we should evaluate female characters based on whether they are portrayed as individuals, with feelings and motivations, flaws as well as strengths, and whether they are developed respectfully as fully fleshed-out human beings.

Notes

1   Sherrie A. Inness, *Tough Girls: Women Warriors and Wonder Women in Popular Culture* (Philadelphia, 1999), p.2 passim

2   Carol J. Clover, *Men, Women and Chainsaws: Gender in the Modern Horror Film* (Princeton, 1992), p.50. See also the discussion of Ripley in Elizabeth Hills, 'From "figurative males" to action heroines: further thoughts on active women in the cinema', *Screen*, 40, 1 (Spring 1999), pp.38–50; see pp.40–49.

3   See Martha McCaughey and Neal King, eds, *Reel Knockouts: Violent Women in the Movies* (Austin, 2001) and also Jacinda Read, *The New Avengers: Feminism, Femininity and the Rape-Revenge Cycle* (Manchester, 2000)

4   Hills: 'From "figurative males"', pp.38–39

5   According to Tapping's Internet Movie Database profile, online (accessed 12 August 2005, http://www.imdb.com/name/nm0850102/)

6   *Xena, Warrior Princess*, created by John Schulian and Robert G. Tapert (Universal TV, 1995)

7   *Buffy the Vampire Slayer*, created by Joss Whedon (Mutant Enemy, 20th Century Fox Television, 1997)

8   All references to the episodes will be indicated parenthetically by episode number. See the Episode guide for more information.

9   A sidekick would be a female character who exists only to support the male lead and has little to no narrative purpose otherwise. See Inness: *Tough Girls*, p. 2.

10   Because Carter is white, any issues about her worth or power or lack thereof centre around her gender, not her ethnicity. In addition, she is from a military family, so class considerations are also not at issue either in the pilot or at any other time in the series.

11   Clover: *Men, Women and Chainsaws*, p.40

12   Teal'c's back-story was explained in the first episode after the pilot ('The Enemy Within').

13   The overwhelming whiteness of the planets in the Stargate universe is somewhat like the phenomenon of all these alien cultures being populated by English-speakers – both are highly unrealistic and largely a function of expediency for the series.

14   In the seventh season episode 'Grace' (713) O'Neill, as a figment of Carter's imagination, calls her 'Samantha' but it is not actually O'Neill.

15 An entire subset of horror films deals with rape and the so-called rape-revenge plot. Clover devotes an entire chapter, 'Getting even', to this phenomenon, pp.114–165.

16 It is yet another marker of Teal'c's difference from his companions that, as a Jaffa, he is immune to this threat.

17 While under the influence of an alien pathogen, Carter attempts to seduce O'Neill in the early season one episode 'The Broca Divide' (104), but she is subdued. This will be discussed later in more detail.

18 Narratively, Carter is the only one who can undergo this violation by a symbiote and be open-minded enough to believe the Tok'ra are different. Teal'c, as a Jaffa, is immune to becoming a host. O'Neill is too closed-minded; his dislike and distrust of the Tok'ra remain a constant throughout the series. In the early episodes, Jackson is still attempting to rescue his wife from the Goa'uld and shows signs of pathological hatred for the Goa'uld; he would also have been too closed-minded.

19 Carter and Teal'c, the woman and the black man, are after this point always in possession of a special kind of knowledge the two white men of the team do not have access to. An entire paper could be generated on this subject alone.

20 It is worth noting that a number of *Stargate* episodes revolve around one or two of the team members being somehow separated from the others and in need of rescue. This happens to every one of the four members of SG-1 regularly. Life-threatening peril is equal opportunity in the series.

21 Inness: *Tough Girls*, p. 109

22 A significant amount of work has been done on Ripley, much of it including the kind of essentialist debate about whether Ripley is a successful feminist icon or not. See Susan Jeffords, '"The battle of the Big Mamas": feminism and the alienation of women', *Journal of American Culture*, 10, 3 (Fall 1987), pp.73–84; Ximena C. Gallardo and C. Jason Smith, *Alien Woman: The Making of Lt. Ellen Ripley* (New York, 2004); and especially Hills, 'From "figurative males"', for a sampling of this discourse.

23 While Carter is shown as liking children and getting along with them, O'Neill's character, being a father whose child died young, is more often the person most likely to bond immediately with any children the team encounters, despite his being the team leader and definitely cast in the role of a warrior.

24 Part of this characterisation of O'Neill may have something to do with the fact that Richard Dean Anderson is the nominal star of the show.

25 In the second half of the two-parter, McKay admits he is actually jealous not of Carter's intelligence so much as her ability to think creatively in applying her intellect to problems.

26 The unisex nature of Carter's costume and the lack of sexuality could easily be turned against the character; an argument could be made that in denying the character any sexual expression the show is denying the character full expression. Such an argument would not hold up, in my opinion, because the lack of sexual expression is not limited to Carter. She is dressed the same as everyone else; her attire is not discriminatory either way.

27 Joseph Mallozzi, 'Production Diary: Chapter Two'. (accessed January 2005, <http://www.gateworld.net/articles/features/diary/chapter02. shtml>)

28 *Sci-Fi Lowdown: Behind the Stargate – Secrets Revealed*, directed by John Murphy (MGM, 2004)

29 *The X-Files*, created by Chris Carter (Ten Thirteen Productions/20th Century Fox Television, 1993)

4

'YOU KNOW THAT "MEANING OF LIFE" STUFF?': POSSESSED OF/BY KNOWLEDGE IN *STARGÅTE SG-1*

CHRISTINE MAINS

In 'Tangent' (412),[1] Daniel Jackson and Sam Carter hitch a ride with her father, Jacob, a Tok'ra ally, in order to rescue their team-mates Jack O'Neill and Teal'c, who face imminent death in the vacuum of space after a failed test flight of a human-modified Goa'uld spacecraft. Their conversation turns to the lack of wisdom of trying to push technological advancement too quickly. 'You can't just slap a USAF sticker on the side of a death glider and call it yours. Advancement like that has to be earned,' Jacob scolds them. Unfortunately, from Earth's perspective, their struggle to catch up to the technological level of both their allies and their enemies is constantly frustrated by the unwillingness of those allies to share such knowledge. A constant theme of *Stargate SG-1* has been the reluctance of aliens with superior technology to share with the human race, despite its desperate need in the face of an ever-growing number of hostile threats to Earth's survival; a related issue has been the methods by which the Stargate Command gains that knowledge. In times of crisis and threat, 'pure' knowledge leading to enlightenment, to the development of personal power, matters much less than instrumental knowledge which grants the user power over others. While *Stargate SG-1* never explicitly makes the connection between the SGC's fictional war with alien enemies and America's political war on terror, it is impossible to ignore the implications of the show's depiction of the ethical concerns surrounding the subordination of the pursuit of knowledge to military needs.

Because *Stargate SG-1* is set in the present day, in their war with the Goa'uld, who seek to enslave humanity, the SGC must rely on knowledge no more advanced than our own. But the enemy they fight has access to superior technology, making it necessary that the SGC acquire knowledge in order to defend themselves. They need to gather intelligence about enemy forces for military purposes, Jack's primary concern as team leader and, later, base commander; they need to pursue scientific discovery in order to progress technologically, Sam's purview as the all-purpose scientist/engineer. In the eyes of the SGC's military and political masters, intelligence and realising practical technological development is the kind of instrumental knowledge that seems worth the effort expended to achieve it. What seems less necessary is the gathering of 'pure' knowledge, to gain wisdom and enlightenment, a task left to Daniel, the social scientist and philosopher. His worth to the SGC lies not in his search for wisdom but in his proficiency with languages, enabling him to communicate with others and thus, hopefully, open the door to the kinds of knowledge valued by the rest of his team. Daniel's interest in seeking wisdom in Earth's past and from other cultures seems self-indulgent to those driven by the urgency of gaining instrumental knowledge that will prove useful against the enemy, a view which Daniel eventually comes to share.

In order to gain knowledge, the team travels to other worlds, encountering aliens both less and more advanced. Such First Contact situations provide an opportunity to comment on the difference between self and Other, on the ways in which people separate themselves into categories of friend or foe on the basis of skin colour, religion or nationality. In his discussion of First Contact in science fiction, Carl Malmgren describes 'two possible treatments of alien alterity: the Other-as-enemy and the Other-as-self'.[2] Given that the SGC is a military organisation waging war against a hostile force, the team's first response in any encounter is to decide whether the alien is a potential ally or another enemy. To make this decision, to gain at least this much if not more knowledge from the encounter, it is necessary to establish some means of communication. But there is a limit to the ways in which communication barriers can be overcome in fiction and on television. Although the need to find a way to communicate with the Other is an essential element of any narrative of exploration, episodic television, where problems must be resolved by the end credits, works against a realistic depiction of communication between human and alien. Daniel Jackson is a linguistic prodigy, but he cannot spend the better part of a one-hour episode translating. Despite this constraint, the show has made some gestures towards demonstrating the difficulty of communication. In 'The Torment of Tantalus' (110), an ancient ruin holds a version of the Rosetta Stone, a message carved on the wall in four alien languages and displayed as holographic representations of atomic elements, which Daniel theorises are used as the basic building blocks of communication. Daniel attempts to use gestures to communicate with the non-speaking aliens of 'One False Step' (219) and with the Unas, Chaka, in 'The First Ones' (408). Sometimes, even when the alien speaks English (a fact never explained within the show's universe, with an equivalent to *Farscape*'s translator microbes or *Star Trek*'s universal translator), an effort is made to acknowledge that it may be extremely difficult to understand the alien's world-view; although the monk on Kheb speaks English to Daniel and Jack in 'Maternal Instinct' (320), he speaks in what Daniel believes to be Zen koans, which frustrates Jack but intrigues Daniel:

> Monk: I only know a snowflake cannot
> exist in a storm of fire.
>
> Jack: What?!
>
> Daniel: Jack …
>
> Jack: No, you know me, I'm a huge fan of
> subtlety, but that's downright encrypted.
>
> Daniel: Sorry … ah, don't worry about him.
>
> Monk: The sun is warm, wind is wild,
> grass is green along the shores, here no bull
> can hide.
>
> Jack: Oh, I dunno about that.

Malmgren goes on to note: 'Communication between species suspends the "law" of Darwinian struggle; it allows the humanisation of the other.'[3] Given the military setting of most science fiction television, including *Stargate SG-1*, the problem of communication becomes even more urgent, with the need to negotiate peace treaties or at least ceasefires, to build alliances, to gain access to both intelligence about the enemy and scientific knowledge leading to technological advances. For the SGC, communication is further complicated by the fact that the enemy is extremely long-lived, as are potential allies; thus the information needed might be more likely found in the distant past than in the present day, meaning that direct experience of knowledge is impossible; short-lived human beings do not have the same access to methods for gaining knowledge about aliens as aliens have for learning about them, such as 'eons-long longitudinal study of life on earth' and 'direct access to the contents of the human mind through telepathy'.[4] The writers of *Stargate SG-1* have consistently made use of a means of knowledge acquisition that overcomes these barriers; possession of the human mind by alien life form or technology proves a method of communication that overcomes the language barrier and allows for a form of direct experience of the past. The 'notion of possession, of the mind taken over by a superior alien power, is probably one of the oldest concepts of human culture'[5] and a common theme in science fiction.

The most advanced technology discovered by the SGC belongs to the Ancients, the original builders of the Stargate network. Understanding even a fraction of the knowledge of such an advanced race would certainly benefit the SGC, and, fortunately, the Ancients have left some record of their accomplishments, carved into stone in ancient ruins and recorded in archives programmed to download information directly into the brain. In 'The Fifth Race' (216), Jack unwittingly receives such a download; he begins to speak words in an unknown language, and to demonstrate decidedly un-Jack-like levels of scientific knowledge, recording, in base-eight maths a formula for calculating astronomical distances, and drawing detailed schematics of the inner workings of the DHD. But Dr Fraiser discovers that the downloaded information is taking over Jack's brain, rewriting his hard drive, to use her analogy, with new and incompatible software. Eventually nothing will remain of Jack's own consciousness. Acquiring knowledge through possession is obviously too dangerous a method to use regularly.

Yet the SGC gains immeasurable advantages from Jack's possession of and by the knowledge contained in the archive. He enters new gate addresses into the database, addresses unknown to the Goa'uld. He creates a new dialling programme, which enables the gate to connect to extra-galactic addresses, and builds a power generator capable of providing sufficient energy for the longer trip. He also makes contact with the Asgard, once allies of the Ancients and still enemies of the Goa'uld; the Asgard become one of the SGC's staunchest allies, providing defensive shields and hyperdrive-capable engines for Earth's first starship, *Prometheus*. And Jack's second, more deliberate encounter with an archive leads to the discovery of an Ancient weapons outpost in Antarctica, and to the design of a weapon effective against the

Replicators. Jack twice undergoes possession, risking his identity and his life, to acquire knowledge without which Earth might have been destroyed.

Over the course of the series, most of the team members have been possessed by an alien force in order to facilitate communication between human and alien and thus avoid the inevitable destructive consequences of alien encounter with the Other-as-enemy. In 'Message in a Bottle' (207), Jack is taken over by a microscopic alien collective brought back through the Stargate inside an artefact; the inability to communicate has left the SGC on the brink of a self-destruct countdown. Through Jack, the alien is able to explain the history that Daniel has been unable to read in the symbols recorded on the artefact, and a compromise is reached guaranteeing the survival of both sides. In 'Entity' (420), Sam is possessed by an intelligent energy being that downloads itself into Sam's brain and explains that the SGC's initial probe caused irreparable harm to its society; it has travelled to the SGC to ensure such harm will not be repeated. While Daniel's attempts to communicate peacefully seem unsuccessful, the entity in Sam's body understands Jack's threats to completely destroy its world unless it releases Sam. A similar negotiation takes place in 'Watergate' (407) with what turns out to be intelligent water, which, although it does not speak while in possession of the human body, is still able to negotiate what Jack recognises as a hostage exchange. Enough communication takes place through the agency of possession for both human and alien to recognise the Other as, if not self, at least not an enemy requiring destruction.

All these acts of possession have been temporary situations benefiting the SGC, a fact that tends to stifle any concerns about the ethics of such practices. But, in each case, consent is neither asked nor given, and the potential harm to the human host causes at least some misgivings. In other, more disturbing instances, possession provides the means to invade the mind in order to dominate and control. The human-form Replicators of 'Unnatural Selection' (612) take over the team's minds, and are able to inflict pain in order to force them to reveal information that will aid the Replicators in their invasion of the galaxy; in 'Reckoning' (816–817), Replicarter, the human-form Replicator made in the image of Sam Carter, invades Daniel's mind, using the memories of his mentor Oma Desala and his time among the natives of Vis Uban in an attempt to manipulate him into revealing the Ancient knowledge buried in his subconscious.

Complete and permanent possession of the human host, mind and body, is the favoured method of the Goa'uld, the primary antagonist in the SGC's war, beginning with the history learned by Jack and Daniel in the original movie, *Stargate* (1994), that reveals the Egyptian god Ra to be a young boy possessed by an alien being. In the series pilot, 'Children of the Gods' (101), the act of possession is depicted as a rape; Daniel's young wife, Sha're, is stripped naked before Apophis and his servants, drugged into submission by the hand-device technology, and laid out on a table for the use of Apophis and the Jaffa female who carries his queen, a phallic-looking snake, in her belly. The snake slithers up Sha're's naked body to enter, forcefully, through the back of the neck, Sha're screaming in agony. While taking a human host may be a necessary and natural part of the symbiote's life process – in 'Crossroads' (404) it is revealed that the Goa'uld cannot otherwise communicate with each other – the visual imagery used, including the full-frontal nudity rarely seen on American television, encourages the viewer to see the act of possession as a violation of the human body, performed without consent or concern for the host. After the initial possession, Sha're is next seen 'using' her body to shield Apophis from attack, looking coolly and without recognition at her husband; her expression and actions make it clear that it is no longer Sha're in control.

Despite the Goa'uld's initial claim that 'nothing of the host survives', that the human host becomes nothing more than a shell, it is soon obvious that enough of the host's personality remains for the Goa'uld to gain information through possession. In 'The Enemy Within' (102), the only way for the Goa'uld who has taken possession of Kawalsky to know secure computer codes would be to have taken that information from his intact memories. Osiris, trapped in stasis for thousands of years, draws on enough of the memories of his new human host, Daniel's former girlfriend Sarah, to successfully mimic her, fooling her friends and colleagues in 'The Curse' (413). And in the alternate timeline created in 'Moebius' (820), Daniel Jackson is implanted with a symbiote for the explicit purpose of using Daniel as a spy. For the Goa'uld, the human Other is either 'a tool to be used' or, if not immediately useful, 'an enemy to be destroyed'.[6]

These kinds of experiences with the Goa'uld provide a rationale for the SGC's reluctance to communicate with them in an attempt to improve understanding and negotiate a peaceful end to conflict, a resolution that might open the way to sharing knowledge of Earth's history and of alien cultures. Even Daniel, supposedly the SGC's moral conscience, persists in seeing the Goa'uld as pure evil, as he tells Dr Weir in 'New Order' (801), when she suggests attempting diplomatic relations. And yet the SGC has gained tangible scientific and military benefits from being used by the Goa'uld, beginning with Sam Carter's possession in 'In the Line of Duty' (202). Without her consent, Sam is invaded by a symbiote evading pursuit. The symbiote uses Sam's body to pass undetected, at first, among her friends and co-workers; captured and confined, it uses Sam's knowledge of them in an attempt to manipulate them into giving it freedom. But the symbiote claims to be Tok'ra rather than Goa'uld, part of a resistance movement opposed, as is the SGC, to the Goa'uld System Lords. Tortured by its pursuer, it makes a conscious effort to save Sam's life as its final act, leaving behind in her mind its own memories of the Tok'ra resistance movement. Sam is left in possession of knowledge about a possible ally, and in 'The Tok'ra' (211–212) the team does manage to form an alliance with this technologically superior alien society which purports to share its goals of defeating the Goa'uld. Sam's possession by the Tok'ra benefits the SGC just as much as does Jack's possession by the Ancient archive; in both instances, the SGC gains allies whose aid often makes the difference between life and death for the team and for the planet.

It is difficult, however, to ignore the ethically troubling method of possession by which Earth has gained such valuable friends, whether Asgard or Tok'ra. The Tok'ra's claim to be different from the Goa'uld rests on the statement that they do not take complete control over the human host but instead share the body and mind equally with its original owner, asking permission before taking possession. They state outright that they do not ever take an unwilling host, preferring to die if permission is not given. But, even before they enter into an agreement with the Tok'ra, the SGC has proof that the Tok'ra claim of equality is, at best, overstated, if not an outright lie; Jolinar did not ask Sam's permission before taking possession of her. (This is not the only instance of a Tok'ra behaving as a Goa'uld; although an otherwise dying Jack does give consent to a temporary 'blending' with a symbiote in 'Frozen' [604], his body is used against his will to break into a fortress held by the System Lord Ba'al, leading to his repeatedly being tortured to death in 'Abyss' [606].) The Tok'ra's actions clearly demonstrate that, when they urgently require the use of a human body, they are willing to ignore the autonomy of the host, just as a Goa'uld would. Yet this evidence of their potential ally's questionable ethics, even the later evidence that the Tok'ra engage in torture to extract information ('Crossroads', 404), is not sufficient to overcome the SGC's desperate need for intelligence and technological information. On television as in politics, the ends justify the means.

Despite the circumstances of their initial meeting, both Sam's 'rape' by Jolinar and the Tok'ra's initial refusal to consider alliance because of the humans' reluctance to provide the only thing they have to offer in exchange – human hosts – the SGC does negotiate an agreement with the Tok'ra. Sam convinces her dying father, Jacob, a general in the USAF, to become a host, to agree to permanent possession of his mind and body in order to act as a liaison between the two sides. Jacob-Selmak becomes a recurring character in the series, a narrative embodiment of the difficult alliance. The Tok'ra do appear, mostly, to act in accordance with their claims, but Jack remains suspicious of their actions and motivations, and the alliance is often an uneasy one. The Tok'ra demonstrate the same perception held by the Goa'uld of humans as less than equal, as suggested by Anise's response to the SGC's concerns about her desire to use the team in an experiment ('Upgrades', 403). When General Hammond proposes delaying the experiment in order to allow Sam and Daniel to study the devices, Anise insists that she must 'begin human trial experiments immediately' and that, if SG-1 are unwilling to participate on her terms, she will 'find human subjects on another planet'. Anise sees the team only as 'subjects' to be used to further her own research, not recognising either Daniel or Sam as scholars who might be her equals in ability or curiosity.

Nor is this the only instance of the Tok'ra expressing a perception of human instrumentality similar to that of the Goa'uld. Tensions build to a crisis point in 'Death Knell' (716), when the Goa'uld Anubis attacks Earth's Alpha Site, where both Tok'ra and Jaffa have taken shelter; the alliance fractures because the Tok'ra have not been sharing information about their covert operations, in violation of their treaty. Jacob-Selmak learns that, despite his seat on the High Council, he has also not been kept informed. The Tok'ra question his loyalties, observing that what they have learned from blending with the Tau'ri – Jacob, Sam, even and especially Jack – is that the Tau'ri make poor hosts because their will has not been eroded by millennia of slavery. In other words, the Tok'ra imply that, despite their stated intention to treat symbiote and host as equals, they value the human host less than they do the symbiote, and prefer the host to be pliant and meek. (This is depicted on-screen by the scripting, directing and acting of scenes in which host and symbiote switch control of the body; the hosts of Lantesh, Anise and Garshaw are much more soft-spoken and conciliatory than their symbiotes.) Although he remains with the Tok'ra when they withdraw

Jack O'Neill: 'Magnets!': the well-appointed fan refrigerator. Photo by Lisa Dickson, 2005.

from the alliance, Jacob-Selmak, obviously concerned about the Tok'ra's ambivalent attitude towards Earth, eventually defies them to return with intelligence and technology to use against the Replicators and Anubis in 'Reckoning' (816–817). Certainly, the SGC could never have successfully advanced its war against the Goa'uld without the aid of the Tok'ra, but it is troubling that, to gain that knowledge, they are willing to ignore that the Tok'ra also perceive human beings in terms of use value, and to provide human hosts to the same alien race that they fight against. The Tok'ra's once-strong conviction that symbiotes and hosts must live in harmony has clearly been eroded by their millennia-long struggle, so that the difference between the Goa'uld and the Tok'ra, after all is said and done, is not much more than that between political rivals for power.

Not all forms of possession are necessarily evil, nor is the nature of possession decided only on the basis of tangible benefits accruing from the experience. Traditionally, literature 'posits both good and evil forms of alien possession'.[7] Most of the SGC's encounters with technologically advanced aliens involve what Malmgren, following Gregory Benford, terms 'anthropocentric' rather than 'unknowable' aliens;[8] that is, SG-1 attempts to communicate with aliens who are recognisably human. The Goa'uld and the Tok'ra are snake-like parasites, but what the team, and through them the viewer, see is a human body, speaking in a human voice, demonstrating human behaviours. But science fiction also attempts, at times, to depict the alien as truly alien, as unknowable or strange, to 'suggest the possibility of transcending those limits' that define what it is to be human, to envision the alien-as-God rather than as self or as enemy.[9] In *Stargate SG-1*, the unknowable alien with whom the team attempts to communicate is the Ascended, inhabiting a higher plane of existence. Ordinary mortals can become Ascended by freeing themselves of the burdens of human emotions and concerns, thus achieving enlightenment, understanding all the knowledge of the universe. In effect, the Ascended function as a collective spiritual force; in order to become a part of this collective, the human being must surrender individuality. In this sense, the Ascended are reminiscent of the Overmind of Arthur C. Clarke's *Childhood's End*, an entity which philosopher Stephen R. L. Clark terms the 'unity-in-diversity of Intellect' that is the destiny of the enlightened spirit.[10] Communication with the alien-as-God is as frustrating as is communication with anthropocentric aliens, and possession serves a similar function in removing or overcoming barriers to communication. But it does not necessarily imply the same ethical concerns. The Goa'uld enslave humans and kill those who are of no use to them, actions that code them as not only the villains in the narrative but also, because of their complete possession of human hosts against their will, as evil. 'But alien possession was not always horrible,' Koelb observes, continuing: 'Just as one could be taken over by an unclean spirit, so one could be overcome by a holy spirit.'[11] Daniel's interactions with the Ascended Oma Desala could be characterised thus, despite his eventual rejection of the pure knowledge she seeks to share with him.

While Sam the brilliant astrophysicist represents the use of scientific knowledge, Daniel is both the communicator – because of his linguistic skills – and the embodiment of the pursuit of knowledge for its own sake, knowledge that leads to spiritual enlightenment rather than technological progress. In other words, Sam usually functions as the Engineer, harnessing knowledge communicated by aliens to serve human purposes, while Daniel is the philosopher, the lover of wisdom and seeker after truth. In 'The Torment of Tantalus' (110), Daniel is so excited about the opportunity to learn more about the secrets of the universe, 'that meaning of life stuff', that he is willing to risk being stranded alone, unable to share his new knowledge or even to continue the search for his wife. In order to have discovery and exploration become part of the SGC's mandate, he fights Air Force administration, and in 'The Other Side' (402) he opposes his own team-mates when their desire for advanced technology leads them to choose sides in another planet's war without ascertaining the facts. He points out to General Hammond: 'We're about to turn the tide of a world war that we know nothing about. Against an enemy that we know nothing about! Is that the right way to go about getting their technology? Yes. But is it the right thing to do?' Facing certain death from radiation poisoning in 'Meridian' (521), Daniel finds his mind possessed by the vision of Oma Desala, Mother Nature, a powerful alien. While his deteriorating body, wrapped in bandages and unconscious much of the time, lies in the infirmary, Daniel's self resides in a world created by Oma within his mind, reflecting on the choice she offers him between death and ascension, where he will be able to pursue all the knowledge of the universe, a temptation for Daniel at any time but particularly at this point in the war, when he feels his contribution has been insufficient to make any real difference.

Over the years that the SGC has been fighting against the Goa'uld, Daniel has come to share his warrior colleagues' view of knowledge as a tool to be valued for its contribution to victory or at least survival, rather than an end to be valued in its own right. This has been a lesson that Daniel has been slow in learning, one that he has struggled against in the face of overwhelming personal losses. By the time of Oma's offer, Daniel is no stranger to having his subconscious mind taken over; in 'Forever in a Day' (310), Sha're is able to use the mind-powered hand-device of Amonet, the Goa'uld possessing her, to tell Daniel about her child, a Harsesis carrying all the genetic memories of his Goa'ulded parents and thus a potential source of intelligence vital to the SGC. Driven by the SGC's prioritising of intelligence-gathering over exploration and discovery, Daniel pursues the Harsesis in order to gain an advantage over the Goa'uld, but eventually recognises, in 'Maternal Instinct' (320), that Oma has far more power than he does to keep the child safe. At this point, Daniel is torn between his passion for knowledge about life and what comes after, and his awareness that the SGC needs the information in the child's mind, but he chooses to leave the child behind. 'I thought we needed that kid,' Jack says, but accepts Daniel's decision.

After another year of fighting the Goa'uld and an encounter with a new enemy, the Replicators, Daniel's priorities change. He has lost both his wife and his former girlfriend to the Goa'uld, and the SGC is beset by enemies within its own ranks who believe in acquiring technology no matter what the cost to other worlds or to other countries on Earth. In 'Absolute Power' (417), the child, Shifu, his growth artificially accelerated, seeks out Daniel in order to learn about his mother; Daniel takes the opportunity to ask him about his Goa'uld knowledge, which Oma has helped him to suppress. Daniel is well aware of the danger posed by the possession of such knowledge, that the Goa'uld's genetic memory is the reason why, as Teal'c says, 'all Goa'uld are born evil'. Daniel himself, during the briefing in which the team discusses Shifu as a source of information, acknowledges: 'We'd be flooding his mind with the thoughts of a thousand Hitlers.' Nevertheless, fearing the destruction of Earth and hoping that Oma can help Shifu to forget again, he does ask for the knowledge, and in response Shifu places Daniel into a dream state during which Daniel experiences being possessed by the same knowledge that Shifu is suppressing. In his dream, the knowledge does bring him power, not only technological power to defend against and defeat the Goa'uld, but also political power, as he becomes a villain worthy of James Bond, complete with a secret underground bunker, responsible for the murder or mistreatment of his friends in his pursuit of world domination. The knowledge of the Goa'uld corrupts him as it has corrupted them, transforming him into his enemy. Shifu tells him: 'Oma teaches the evil in my subconscious is too strong to resist and the only way to win is to deny it battle.' The Ascended, perhaps as a result of their own ancient wars (hinted at in *Stargate: Atlantis* and the ninth season of *Stargate: SG-1*), refuse to allow the knowledge that they gain through enlightenment to be put to actual use. But Daniel finds it increasingly difficult to accept this lesson, given the struggle for survival waged by the SGC on a daily basis and his own losses and failures.

When Oma offers him the choice between death and ascension, she is really asking him to decide between remaining an individual or becoming possessed by the collective mind of the Ascended, to choose between instrumental knowledge and pure knowledge. 'The universe is vast, and we are so small. There is really only one thing we can ever truly control,' she tells him, 'Whether we are good or evil.' Forgetting that Oma rarely speaks so clearly, thinking that Oma refers to the intentions behind one's actions and perceiving his own actions against the enemy Goa'uld to be based on his good intentions, Daniel believes that he will be able to do more to aid the SGC in its wars. Confusing or conflating pure and instrumental knowledge, he does not realise that, once he gives up control of his body and is assimilated into the collective mind, he will be unable to act upon the knowledge he gains. The Ascended do not interfere in the affairs of mortals; those who do are punished, as is shown in 'Ascension' (503), 'Threads' (818) and the *Atlantis* episode 'Sanctuary' (114). Unable to keep from intervening in his team-mates' battles, Daniel decides that enlightenment has too high a cost. Possessed of all the knowledge of the universe, possessed by the collective wisdom of the Ascended, Daniel can no longer choose knowledge for its own sake over information of use to the SGC. He chooses action as a warrior rather than inaction as a philosopher, and as a consequence loses possession of that knowledge when his memories are removed by the Ascended.

Changed more by years of battle than by his single year among the Ascended, Daniel continues to pursue information necessary to defeat the Goa'uld no matter what the cost. In 'Resurrection' (719), hoping to defuse a bomb, Daniel confronts Anna, a human/Goa'uld clone created by an NID scientist named Keffler in an attempt to extract the Goa'uld genetic memory. To access the necessary knowledge, Anna will have to risk becoming the Goa'uld, who has already used her body to commit murder. Daniel tells her about Shifu, who taught him that 'it was wrong to seek [Goa'uld knowledge] for any reason', but then immediately asks her to do just that. Anna rightly accuses him of sounding like Keffler, a man who justifies his actions by reminding Daniel and Sam that '[t]he Goa'uld are a terrible threat to us all. Anna is a device, a conduit to the knowledge that could level the playing field, and I think we all agree that if killing one person could save millions, billions of innocent lives, you would have no choice. You would do it.' While SG-1, the heroes, never knowingly and deliberately pursue such a course of action, they do benefit from the actions of Keffler and other NID operatives, just as they benefit from the ethically troubling acts of possession which they undergo.

Daniel's search for enlightenment, like Sam's pursuit of scientific advancement, is subordinated to military needs. Both forms of knowledge serve to support the growth of military power, despite ethical concerns. As the years go by, Sam functions less as a scientist and more as a soldier; Daniel becomes less the team's conscience and more Action Jackson, a fighting man. In consequence, the most important result of possession, becoming the Other if only for a brief time, communicating with the alien to discover the Other-as-self[12] so that shared understanding becomes possible, is never fully realised by the SGC. Acts of possession by aliens serve to transform Jack, Daniel and Sam into the Others with whom they attempt to communicate, albeit temporarily. But both Jack and Daniel lose the knowledge they gain, and neither Jack nor Sam fully accepts what they learn from being Tok'ra. Because military needs take priority over scientific or philosophical interests, the knowledge gained from the experience of possession is valued only for its tangible benefits. Shared understanding would further the conversion of Other into self, would humanise an enemy who must remain an enemy, must be perceived as evil, in order that the war continue.

And continue it must, for both narrative and cultural reasons. Narrative context plays an important role in television science fiction, demanding continuing conflict, an enemy for the heroes to fight; peace cannot be considered until the closing minutes of the final episode. As for the cultural context, there has always been a need in America to define good guys and bad guys, to demonstrate support for a strong military and to depict an enemy against which America can define itself, to 'reflect and influence US national fears and desires', as Floyd Cheung observes in his analysis of the film on which the series is based.[13] While the parallels between the real world's war on terror and the fictional world's war against the aliens are not as overt as in *Battlestar Galactica* (2003), it would be naive to claim that no such connection exists. Speaking of the relationship between science fiction and politics, Jutta Weldes observes, 'A long history of fantastic enemies and sophisticated high-tech wars ... renders desirable a future of militarised security seemingly attainable through advanced weapons and information warfare.'[14] The tension between the desire to understand the Other-as-self and the fear of the Other-as-enemy, evident in *Stargate SG-1*'s reliance on possession as a means of communication, reflects this reciprocal relationship between science fiction television and real-world politics. The lesson that Daniel and the SGC do not learn, that knowledge valued only to defeat the Other rather than to increase understanding of the Other, is a lesson that needs to be learned by those who give unquestioning support to America's wars.

Notes

1   All references to the episodes will be indicated parenthetically by episode number. See the Episode guide for more information.

2   Carl D. Malmgren, 'Self and Other in SF: Alien encounters', *Science-Fiction Studies*, 20, 1 (March 1993), p.25

3   Ibid., p.21

4   Paul Rice, 'Metaphor as a way of saying the Self in science fiction', Robert E. Myers (ed.), *The Intersection of Science Fiction and Philosophy: Critical Studies* (Westport CT, 1983), pp.138–139

5   Clayton Koelb, 'Inspiration and possession: ambivalent intimacy with the alien', George E. Slusser and Eric S. Rabkin (eds), *Aliens: The Anthropology of Science Fiction* (Carbondale IL,1987), p.157

6   Malmgren, 'Self and Other in SF', p.25

7   Koelb, 'Inspiration and possession', p.160

8   Malmgren, 'Self and Other in SF', p.16

9   Ibid., p.17

10 Stephen R. L. Clark, *How to Live Forever: Science Fiction and Philosophy* (London, New York, 1995), p.158

11 Koelb, 'Inspiration and possession', p.158
12 Malmgren, 'Self and Other in SF', p.25
13 Floyd D. Cheung, 'Imagining danger, imagining nation: postcolonial discourse in *Rising Sun* and *Stargate*', *Jouvert: A Journal of Postcolonial Studies*, 2, 2 (1998) (accessed June 2004, http://social.chass.ncsu.edu/jouvert/v2i2/cheung.htm)
14 Jutta Weldes, 'Popular culture, science fiction, and world politics: exploring intertextual relations', *To Seek Out New Worlds: Exploring Links between Science Fiction and World Politics* (New York, 2003), p.4

5

SAM, JARRED: THE ISIS MYTH IN OPERATION

JO STORM

Samantha Carter was the main reason I started to watch *Stargate SG-1*. While I was interested in the deployment of myths and their science fiction flavour, mostly I identified with her character. At first glance, Carter seemed like a perfect postmodern fit for subversiveness; in a traditionally male job, she gave orders, could shoot a weapon better than anyone on her team, rode a motorcycle and did not need a man to complete her. In fact, she seemed to spurn men's advances. However, as a feminist and a critical thinker, I had to ask myself: how subversive *was* Carter? As a female character entering the realm of television legend with the announcement of the series' ninth season, how did Carter compare to another, mythological, figure who enacted strong feminist ideals and whom we also meet in the series?

As many of the stories of *Stargate SG-1* are based on mythology, particularly that of ancient Egypt, it is not surprising when the Egyptian goddess Isis and Carter 'meet' in the fourth season episode, ironically named 'The Curse' (413).[1] A clay *canopic* jar is found, its seal broken: inside is the Goa'uld Isis. The *canopic* jar holds the alien parasite in 'stasis', allowing for an immeasurably long life, but because its seal is damaged the Goa'uld within has died. Daniel Jackson, the Egyptologist, makes passing reference to Isis as 'a consort of Osiris' ('The Curse'). It is clear to the audience that Isis' death is not really the thrust of the narrative, except as a plot device to anger her partner Goa'uld, Osiris. Later, Dr Fraiser (who, until her death in season seven, is the only other regularly recurring female character in the series) remarks that Isis' body has been 'remarkably preserved. She could have died yesterday' ('The Curse'). This statement is telling in a show which contains its female characters in culturally defined areas. Even the female figure of the goddess is, in the series, reduced to a container.

Unlike the fictional figure of Isis, in Egyptian myth the goddess looms large. She is the sister/wife of Osiris, part of the original *ennead* (ruling gods), and participates in many myths and stories. She battled for supreme knowledge against the Sun god Ra, exacted revenge on her brother Seth, and eventually eclipsed Osiris in terms of worshippers.

Both Isis and Samantha Carter represent autonomous, agented women who refute conventional figures and give female viewers role models on which to base their lives. However, on closer inspection, Carter is revealed to be a broken or jarred version of the syncretic Isis, contained and framed by contemporary hegemony, making her a false, failed feminist model. In reality, Carter serves to reinscribe hegemonic practices, maintaining conventional female roles as consumers and helpers.

Carl Olson argues that, in monotheistic Western culture, only the figure of Mary can be seen as a goddess figure. He notes that 'we are disposed to conceive of the divine in masculine terms and images',[2] which suggests that one of the basic paradigms of Western ideology, the Madonna/whore figure, may have come about because of the absence of syncretic goddesses. In contrast, ancient Egyptians did not consistently link a specific trait with a specific gender (e.g., aggression conceived as masculine). Isis does not come from either a lineage of 'mother figures' (deities who were figurations of the Great Mother), or from a monotheistic pattern. Carter, however, is much more involved in the Western duality of the Madonna/whore dyad. She is seen as a role model in her professional life, but this is sharply contained and separate from other aspects of her life, particularly her sexual life, as opposed to Isis, who embodies many facets simultaneously and whose sexual nature is never concealed.

According to one Egyptian myth, when Seth murdered and dismembered Osiris, Isis searched for the disparate pieces, put them back together again, and through personal knowledge (in some versions a magical spell) brought Osiris back to life. Another version of this myth involves Isis reviving only Osiris' sexual organs, in order that she may become impregnated with Horus (the living god), who would exact revenge on Seth where she could not.

While the frank sexuality of Egyptian texts can shock people today, they show how Isis moves very fluidly from a role of mother/concubine to a ruler in her own right. Carter, however, has been set up within the confines of canon and now must always be presented within that paradigm, however dualistic and separatist it may be. For instance, it is not until the seventh season of the series that Carter gets a personal life in the form of Pete Shanahan, and the viewing experience is almost a bipolar one, going from the vacuum of the character's love life to a life that is both alluded to and seen on a regular basis.

It is not only the characters of ancient myth (Isis) and contemporary legend (Carter) that present similarities. Like *SG-1*, the Egyptian *ennead* is team-like in that in many of its stories the gods depend on each other for validation and cooperation. Contemporary script writers for television work as teams, starting with an idea that is pitched, then expanded, refined and remoulded to serve the show's best interest. The show's best interest is to sell advertising. Ancient Egyptian myths and mythemes were told in much the same way. Long-lasting stories were 'pitched' at festivals and temples, with each story developing particular characteristics valuable at the time – location, local kingship and didactic message. From such historical roots scholars have been able to trace the movement of goddesses such as Isis from their Egyptian home to newer places of worship, still using the same syncretic model to make her more appealing to her new audience.[3] Her story was told and refined by priests as well as laypeople and professional storytellers – male and female.

But, unlike Isis, Carter's canon is not told by men and women. Of the 173 (at the end of season eight) episodes, only 16 are credited as having been written by women. While this is not to suggest that simply because one is a woman means one necessarily writes from a feminist background, a prime opportunity to redress un-balanced narrative strategies as they pertain to female characters has for ever been lost to *SG-1*. The story of Carter's life is still primarily told by men, while, in her many forms, Isis has been a role model for women.

Similarly, female fans' strong and emotional response to Carter suggests that segments of this contemporary audience identify with her as a site of resistance, despite the overwhelming patriarchal hegemonies within the show. Carter becomes the terrain onto which women dream. But, as Christine Scodari points out in her piece on resistance measures perpetrated by *SG-1* fans, the 'particular adjustments or the motives behind [adjusting commercial texts] are not always resistive'.[4]

In effect, while Isis was both resistive and syncretic because she carried multiple human traits, moving fluidly between her status as a role model, warrior and mother, in all these guises she enacted autonomy, lived sexually and did not shy away from emotive contact. Carter, in contrast, enacts autonomy only when it is constructed in collusion with the male (usually sexualised) gaze: take as an example the fantasy that the human form Replicator, Fifth, constructs of Carter in tight jeans and sheer nightgown in the episode 'New Order, Part 2' (802); while Carter is indeed acting autonomously in that situation, resisting Fifth's forced fantasy, she is still dressed as he wishes her to be dressed, still has the hair he wishes her to have, and is still stuck in his fantasy. Furthermore, Carter harbours an impossible affection for her superior officer for seven years before finally allowing herself to become intimately involved with someone, and shies away from emotive contact unless it serves to embody the emotive content of the rest of her team. In 'Paradise Lost' (615), it is Carter who displays the fear and anxiety over Colonel O'Neill's disappearance for the rest of the team; in 'Singularity' (114) it is she who first becomes emotionally implicated in Cassie's plight; in 'Meridian' (521), while Jack and Teal'c deal with their grief over Daniel's departure silently, it is Carter who exhibits the clear emotional repercussions of losing someone they all loved. In none of this is Carter a site for or of resistance to the traditionally hegemonic and patriarchal discourses at hand.

Additionally, while on the surface Carter transgresses some aspects of the traditional helper female common in Western narratives in episodes such as 'Foothold' (314), 'Nightwalkers' (605) and 'Space Race' (708), in which she takes a lead role in the action, these examples are conspicuous more by the absence of O'Neill than by Carter's resistive measures. Compared to the confrontational attitudes of Jack and Daniel in 'Scorched Earth' (409), or Jack and Teal'c in 'Cor-ai' (115), or even Jack and his commanding officer ('Learning Curve', 305; 'Redemption', 601), Carter's acts of resistance to the hegemonic discourse of patriarchy are more by omission than confrontation. For example, when she is held in a room at the SGC in 'The Fifth Man' (504) she conspires with Janet Fraiser to hack into the facility's mainframe in order to prove the team's sanity, going behind General Hammond's back with subterfuge rather than direct confrontation.

Compounding the sheen of Carter's apparent autonomy, Colonel O'Neill presents himself as the underdog, giving way to his team-mate's superior intellect, seeming to vest authority and agency into her role. However, this mytheme has been demonstrated as another way to cloak the limiting of female autonomy.[5] In the final analysis, O'Neill is Carter's direct superior, and, unlike Teal'c and Daniel, her refusal to follow orders is subject to military law. Daniel Jackson flaunts his non-military status in 'Enigma' (116) to free refugee survivors from the NID; Teal'c point-blank refuses orders as well ('Cor-ai'); O'Neill himself is seen either disobeying orders for a greater cause such as the continuation of the SGC in 'Shades of Grey' (318), or because they go against his personal ethos ('Learning Curve'). But, after eight seasons, Carter has never disobeyed a direct order in a move that has not been tacitly approved by the rest of her team, and O'Neill in particular. In 'Singularity' (114), her decision to remain with Cassie, rather than representing a resistant act, is authenticated by the entire team's decision to stay put also; in 'Ascension' (503), it is not until Jack says, 'Major Carter was working with the approval of her superior officer. [...] I authorized her to collect as much information as possible,' that Carter's actions are justified in the eyes of General Hammond, the Pentagon and the audience.

Like the Isis of the *SG-1* universe, Carter is already contained in a 'jar' – the boundaries of which are policed constantly – and while her contribution is always necessary, it also always limited. Any power that Carter possesses – linguistic, sexual, personal – is curtailed and contained. Jack routinely diverts power from Carter with language; in 'Exodus' (422), he belittles the magnitude of what she's about to attempt, blowing up a star: 'Well, they say the first one's always the hardest.' O'Neill contends often enough that Carter is smart, but simultaneously places this knowledge in a derogatory context, as in 'Redemption, Part 1' (601), where he expresses his support of Carter's intelligence and ability to come up with solutions with the flippant, crass phrase 'Well, you do have a penchant for pulling brilliant ideas out of your ... butt'. Also, these pronouncements ring hollow if Carter demonstrates any form of insubordination (he firmly reminds her of her duty when she expresses hesitation over their actions in 'Unnatural Selection' [612]). Jack also, and paradoxically, quips and pokes fun at Carter's professional life, remonstrating with her for not taking a vacation: 'It's always something, isn't it?' ('Sight Unseen', 613).

In this way, singular lines as well as underlying narrative structures within episodes serve to police the boundaries of Carter's power. Some convenient revisionist mythmaking on the part of the writers in the episode 'Seth' (302) sets up what could have been an extremely empowering scene as another routine moment in the military life. Originally, the Egyptian god Seth was also a member of the *ennead*, a powerful god who killed his brother Osiris, which led his sister Isis to exact revenge. Jackson relegates Seth to an 'enigmatic leader' of a minor cult with 'about 50 followers' ('Seth'), drastically reducing his threat potential. Later, Carter, now armed with the knowledge and power of the Tok'ra, kills Seth with an alien hand-device, a device that she alone can wield. Up to this point, killing a Goa'uld (a deified figure) has been viewed as incredibly hard. In 'Seth', the leather-coated Seth is maniacal, ineffectual and dies easily. The camera cuts to a close-up of Carter's horrified face after the killing, but O'Neill's response is typically laconic: 'Hail Dorothy,' he says, invoking a 'girl power' theme that's often seen in the late nineties–early millennium. The episode, which could have been an excellent example of Carter's agency and power, is reduced to intertextual flippancy in one sentence. O'Neill stuffs Carter back into her jar once she's done what's needed.

This incident illustrates the dichotomy that Carter's character presents. She is by all accounts a fully empowered woman, as is the goddess Isis; but where Isis was continually portrayed as living up to her full potential as a woman – she is at once wise, maternal, sexual – Carter is not. The inscriptions of her potential are there, signing the outline of a fully integrated life; there is no reason why she should not be able to fulfil that potential. The constrictions placed upon her by a television universe that is male-dominated and rigidly, hegemonically hierarchical in nature see Carter firmly contained, in body as in language.

To the ancient Egyptian, the power of language was inherent in words and the pictorial representations that hieroglyphs represented. Hieroglyphics were seen as divine words, and could mean either an image or a phonetic sound. Both image and word 'were thought of as potentially alive'.[6] One of the best-known stories regarding Isis is that of 'The Secret Name of Ra'. Isis, after viewing the god Ra crossing the heavens each day, concluded that she too wanted the ultimate power this god wielded, so she fashioned a snake from some of his spittle and set the snake in his path. When it bit him, Isis approached Ra and said she would cure him, but only after he gave her his secret name. Secret names held a great deal of power; as Ra was the most powerful god, his secret name would grant Isis an all-knowing status. At first Ra refused, but as his death grew imminent he told her. The story of Ra's secret, or true, name was used to remind the Egyptian that words carried power.

Placing this metaphor in the contemporary setting of *SG-1*, we see that each time Carter gets close to finding her true name she is invaded and/or thwarted. 'Death Knell' (716), with its ominous ring, in season seven was hailed as an excellent 'Sam' episode, one that exemplified her courage, strength and resources. Close examination of the episode reveals that, once she is truly alone, Carter is completely silenced, facing off against the equally silent Super Soldier. The silence imposed on Carter by her enemy's own silence (and by extension the silence imposed on her by the camera) comes in stark contrast to the effect yielded in similar episodes such as 'The First Ones' (408) and 'Paradise Lost' (615). In the former, Daniel is taken captive, and, although he is in jeopardy throughout the whole episode, he continually maintains speech, both into his tape recorder or in an attempt to establish dialogue with his captor, who responds, albeit incomprehensibly. In the latter episode, Jack is stranded on a planet with the pesky Colonel Maybourne, up against unseen dangers. The two men manage to co-habitate, and, although communication breaks down, it is eventually re-established. In neither case do the male characters lose their words. We also see this mytheme of words as power operating brokenly in Carter's buried memories of Jolinar, although these 'secret words' are blunted, disregarded or only taken out of their box as a last resort; in addition, we see the theme of silenced Carter in other episodes such as 'Entity' (420).

One of the reasons Carter appeals to women viewers is because she is a reflection of the postfeminist ideal – that is, a model of a woman with agency and power who doesn't need to prove it constantly. Like the Egyptian gods and goddesses of old on whom much of the mythology of the show is based, she is a syncretism of masculine- and feminine-identified traits. On the surface, Carter (with the masculinised 'Sam' as her name of choice on the show) is emancipated, autonomous, in control of feminised traits such as emotion; however, she is still easily identifiable linguistically, visually and sexually as traditionally feminine, reflecting current hegemonic practices. Not only do her sartorial choices reflect these practices (she wear skirts and make-up where this is not rigidly required by the military), but Carter also lives out the emotional lives of the whole team. Her relationship with Pete Shanahan is explored in all its resonances and nuances, from its beginnings to its end, passing through first kiss, first sexual contact, engagement and finally break-up. Although the male members of the SG-1 team have been involved in relationships, never are theirs explored to such an extent or in such detail. The in-depth treatment we are given of Carter's relationship makes it seem that *that* is what is important to the character, that *that* is what she prioritises, as opposed to the men, whose relationships have always been glossed over, and rapidly subsumed by their work.

Carter's outward appearance is another example of this normative pressure in action. Military code does not stipulate that women wear skirts or make-up,[7] but Carter's dress uniform is always a skirt. I do not want to recreate what Susan Kray asserts is 'adopt[ing] masculinist assumptions about female human nature'[8] by belabouring sartorial themes. Rather, I want to point out that, in terms of functionality, skirts and make-up serve as markers in a general, gendered way to ensure that, whatever else Carter *is*, she is womanly in all the traditional, socially constructed acceptable ways. This narrows the focus of what is and is not acceptable for Carter to *do*, because of the limitations set up which resonate with that image. It is acceptable for Carter to argue: it is not acceptable for Carter to argue and then not back off because of the normative roles that such sartorial subtexts denote; the glass ceiling, the household woman of the fifties, the hierarchical positioning where men are directors while women carry out those directives. In *SG-1* this positioning is doubly achieved (and authenticated) through the use of institutionalised power, the military.

With her agency canonically constructed and plausibly validated, Carter is placed in a fantasy relationship, constructed by viewers, with the protagonist O'Neill, and all her struggles are seen primarily through this relationship. In her book on gender and sexuality in popular cinema, Yvonne Tasker notes the 'overrepresentation of the figure of female prostitute [...] and its polar counterpart, the nun. Whoopi Goldberg skirted both these stereotypes comedically in the feature film *Sister Act*.'[9] At that time, *SG-1* was in its second year, and episodes such as 'In the Line of Duty' (202) and 'The Broca Divide' (104) suggest that this kind of limiting role was as much on the small screen as it was on the big screen. Ancient and current narrative tendencies also lean towards a feminisation of evil.[10] We see this in operation in the series as well, where despotism and malevolence combine with sex and pleasure in the goddess Hathor ('Hathor', 113), who signs the way to the femme fatale, an apt representation of Tasker's model. In *SG-1*, Colonel O'Neill characterises Hathor as the goddess of 'sex, drugs and rock 'n' roll', making her illicitness seem transgressive and alluring by positioning it historically with the sixties, but his comment also belies the suspicion that women are always connected with the dangerous, subversive and violent, an anxiety that is often sublimated into the narrative of the

Stargate Magazine asks the question. Photo by Lisa Dickson, 2005.

pregnant woman, her power thus subverted by the traditional constructs of motherhood – piety, submissiveness and domesticity.

Carter evades this family storyline of pregnancy, but at the cost of all her sexuality as well. Isis is regenerative, not only of family – also of herself. Whereas Carter is caught in the 'all-work, no-play' thread, Isis not only works but also plays, and has sexual relations. For Isis, they are not exclusionary roles; they are for Carter. She is either working or a sexualised being, but never both at the same time. When Carter's sexuality is acknowledged, it is in a predominantly male space; her sexualised performance of that role is firmly established in episodes such as 'Emancipation' (103), where she is forced to assume a subordinate role in a 'primitive' culture, wearing a dress and being threatened with rape and physical violence. 'The Broca Divide' again enforces that narrative of institutionalised rape. When confronted with women who are being raped she responds with anger, but is told by Daniel Jackson that 'that's how […] males probably had sex'. When she refuses to stand by this opinion, she is physically detained by O'Neill. These groundings in mythic male landscape make any later attempts at moving from this position doomed from the start. It is no wonder that Carter has a much vaunted 'black widow syndrome'.

Carter's 'black widow syndrome' is the performance of a kind of perverse femme fatale. We've already seen more traditional versions of this trope in Hathor and Anise; Carter's postmodern version has the same 'she's deadly' motif, but instead of inhabiting the space of sex-as-a-weapon, it inhabits the space of sex with someone other than O'Neill. Carter has amassed an impressive list of men that she meets who then die – often (although not always) in the same episode: Jonas ('The First Commandment', 105), Narim ('Enigma', 116), Martouf ('Divide and Conquer', 405), Ambassador Joe ('2010', 416), Orlin ('Ascension', 503), and Aiden ('Forsaken', 618). Any attempt Carter makes at pursuing a sexual relationship results in the hapless man's death. Although these deaths are never *directly* attributed to her, the implicit message is very clear: Carter is not allowed sexual relations.

For seven seasons this trope held firm. The only sexual relations Carter ever alludes to are within the context of an unbalanced hetero-sexual coupling, hinted at in season one's 'The First Commandment' (105). In it Carter reveals she has a 'soft spot for the lunatic fringe', implying not only that it was her fault she was in a less than ideal relationship, but that she'd do it again. O'Neill, Daniel and Teal'c, in contrast, all have stand-alone episodes that deal with a sexual liaison ('A Hundred Days', 317; 'Need', 205; 'Family', 208). Even when Carter gets a life and gets laid ('Chimera', 715), her suitor turns out to be a stalker, and much more time is devoted to Carter's agonising over her inability to tell Pete Shanahan 'everything' than over the sexual union itself. Season eight also sees the (now cleared) stalker engaged to Carter, re-iterating the ideology that women who have sex must form a long-term commitment with their sexual partner. O'Neill, in comparison, leaves his lover Laira in 'A Hundred Days' (317) after suggesting that he would live out the rest of his life with her when it looks as if there will be no rescue. This narrative of a higher calling is seen in all three men (Daniel, Jack and Teal'c all leave their respective partners to continue to fight the Goa'uld), with no repercussions. In fact, in 'A Hundred Days' it is hinted that Laira may be pregnant. Such desertion of women by men is cursorily looked at in the episode 'Family', which deals with Teal'c's estranged wife, but by and large it is a subtext of legitimising abandonment.

Carter's dismissal of emotional entanglements also seems to reverse traditional narratives, but inspection of the context tells us otherwise. In 'Divide and Conquer', for instance, she is the one who assures O'Neill that their feelings for each other never need 'leave this room' ('Divide and Conquer', 405), but closer analysis suggests that the statement is a mask for several concerns that Carter has. Her job, her future and her reputation are always at stake. The pressure to perform in 'the boys' club' of the military, not to mention living up to her father's ideals, leverage an intense pressure on her. Carter doesn't refuse emotional entanglements because she wants to, but rather because she cannot afford not to. In 'Forsaken' (618), when talking to Aiden Corso, she acknowledges these background pressures:

> Carter: You can call me Sam, that's my first name.
>
> Corso: Sam. It's pretty.
>
> Carter: Not really. It's short for Samantha.
>
> Corso: Even prettier. What does it mean? Samantha?
>
> Carter: My father wanted a boy.

In addition, this type of statement helps to shape Carter's sexual life by always containing it through refusal of advances. Like the dead Isis found in the *canopic* jar, Carter is relegated to 'consort' without the need to engage in sexual contact at all; Carter's use of sexual self-discipline cloaks her lack of sexual agency. It is also a false ideal; in the series, Carter's sexuality is restrained *until* it is performative – that is, when it is constructed for the male gaze, which Laura Mulvey has argued to be the primary discourse of the camera.[11]

Explicit use of performative sexuality on the part of Carter is seen in early episodes such as 'The Broca Divide' (104) and 'Emancipation' (103), as well as later episodes such as 'The Other Guys' (608), 'Space Race' (708), and 'Avenger 2.0' (709). Both 'The Other Guys' and 'Avenger 2.0' use weak narrative strategies of fantasy and homoerotic bonding to parody or counter the message that Carter would *actually* do these things. Felger, a nerdy scientist, indulges in fantasies which figure Carter as the sexual object. In 'Avenger 2.0', the inclusion of Colonel O'Neill in these daydreams further lends an authenticity to the 'rightness' of such fantasies; O'Neill is the leader of the team and Felger's hero, and, therefore, his wishes must be acceptable. Carter's sexuality is developed only to the degree that it can be easily thrust back into a space where it is performative. In season eight's 'New Order' (802), Carter is shown in a long-term relationship with a single man, but all her masculinised traits are subsumed into a more traditional epitome of womanhood as it exists in Western narratives – long hair, tight jeans (with camera shots clearly showcasing Carter from behind), and waking up in a skin-tight white dressing gown ('New Order, Part 2', 802). Later we learn that she is in fact in yet another sexual fantasy of a man, Fifth, another 'nerd' whose emotional life is so arrested he tries to consume Carter's affection as the rest of his race consume metal. Although this can be read as a parody of the stereotypical science fiction viewer, the parody is still constructed *for* that viewer. Fifth is never seen naked or in revealing clothing, is constantly threatening violence, manipulates Carter to get what he wants, and finally, when thwarted, goes off to make a Carter clone to serve him properly.

Like the Egyptian goddess Isis, Samantha Carter has multiple aspects which are invoked on separate occasions for vastly different reasons. Carter performs daily operations in conjunction with her job as a member of SG-1 and the military. She also functions as a hero model for viewers as a female in a dangerous, physically and mentally taxing job. Unlike Isis, however, Carter fails to fully integrate her various aspects and is consistently contained by a limiting narrative structure. She is, in effect, a failed version of syncretic models such as that of the goddess Isis. While Carter represents, cursorily, varied threads with a post-feminist outlook, holding autonomy, sexuality and power on equal footing with men and aliens, closer examination reveals that she is a reification of these feminist pillars in terms of the hegemonic culture that *SG-1* is still aiming for – men aged 25–44.[12] This is despite evidence that *SG-1*'s demographics are across the board rather than exclusive,[13] and in direct opposition to statements made by writer and executive producer Joseph Mallozzi: 'Our writing is not geared toward a specific demographic. The fact is, while, for instance, *Star Trek*'s core audience is males 14–35, our core audience appears to be women 30–45.'[14]

A rounded, serious but fun-loving female character with Carter's intelligence, skills and human relations can only be a positive role model for young women; there is no reason for her not to embody the potential she so clearly purports to have. Carter could be all she seems on the surface to be, but it will take revision of the narrative structures underlying the series, and careful interweaving of the character's many fascinating, realistic threads. The crack in the seal is there; but until our significations of female characters like Samantha Carter represent living, breathing figures whose multiple sites of autonomy, sexuality and power are fully realised and integrated, and not perfectly preserved specimens seen through the lens of a hegemonic, consumerist fervour, then, like the Isis we meet in 'The Curse' (413), these characters will remain for ever jarred. Slight movement by the newer series *Atlantis*, aimed at younger audiences, may offer a glimmer of hope – let's just make sure it's not making the *canopic* jar clear instead of breaking it wide open.

Note: The author wishes to express gratitude to Eliza Bennett, Professor Priscila Uppal and Professor Sharon Davidson for their assistance in the editing of this article.

Notes

1   All references to the episodes will be indicated parenthetically by episode number. See the Episode guide for more information.

2   Carl Olson, *The Book of the Goddess* (Prospect Heights IL: 2002)

3   Friedrich Solmsen, *Isis among the Greeks and Romans* (Cambridge MA, 1979)

4   Christine Scodari, 'Resistance re-examined: gender, fan practices, and science fiction television', *Popular Communications*, 1, 2 (2003), pp.111–130

5   Rhonda Wilcox. 'Lois's locks: trust and representation in *Lois and Clark*', Elyce Rae Helford (ed.), *Fantasy Girls: Gender in the New Universe of Science Fiction and Fantasy Television*, (Lanham MD, 2000)

6   Geraldine Pinch, *Egyptian Myth* (New York, 2004)

7   Richard E. Brown, 'Dress and appearance of Air Force personnel', *US Air Force* (accessed 3 July 2005, http://www.e-publishing.af.mil/pubfiles/af/36/afi36-2903/afi36-2903.pdf)

8   Susan Kray, 'The things women don't say', Gary Westfahl (ed.), *Science Fiction, Canonization, Marginalization and the Academy*, (Westport CT, 2002), pp.37–49

9   Yvonne Tasker, *Working Girls: Gender and Sexuality in Popular Cinema* (New York, 1998)

10 Margaret Malamud, 'Pyramids in Las Vegas and in outer space: ancient Egypt in twentieth-century American architecture and film', *Journal of Popular Culture*, 34 (Summer 2000), pp.31–47

11 Laura Mulvey, 'Visual pleasure and narrative cinema', Jessica Evans and Stewart Hall (eds), *Visual Culture: The Reader* (London, 1999)

12 Chris Dillabough, 'MGM runs *Stargate SG-1* DVD campaign on Virgin.net', *New Media Age*, 18 September 2003, p.11

13 Sci-Fi Channel, 2005. 'Press release from February 8', *SG-1 Atlantis.com*, online (accessed 3 July 2005), http://sg1-atlantis.com/index.php?p=220 #more-220)

14 Joseph Mallozzi, 'Joseph Mallozzi's Q&A with H/C list members', *SaveDanielJackson*, online, 12 January 2002, (accessed 3 July 2005, http://www.savedanieljackson.com/history/episoderedux/jmallozzi.shtml)

6

STARGÅTE SG-1 AND ATLANTIS: THE GODS OF TECHNOLOGY VERSUS THE WIZARDS OF JUSTICE

MICHAEL W. YOUNG

Ancient epics and romances often tell us both of powerful, divine creatures, often seen as gods, and of the intermediaries between the omnipotent and common humanity, the wizards or shamans. For the Greeks, Mt Olympus was home to the pantheon of immortals, but they were often vain and capricious gods. While they often would take on mortal form to walk and scheme among the people, the gods also sent messengers and protectors, such as the oracle at Delphi or the semi-divine heroes, such as Hercules/Heracles, Theseus and Perseus. They were extraordinary humans, like the courageous Odysseus, in the full sense of beyond the ordinary. In another of our culture's popular myths, King Arthur of the Britons had Merlin as his teacher, mentor and sorcerer. Merlin's powers allowed him to change into the form of other species, to twist nature to his will, and extended even over time itself. It is the human, and humane, legends of the wizards and heroes that we still celebrate, not the selfish, power-hungry gods. Still, all these great heroes, and even the gods themselves, could be overthrown, even destroyed. In the end, Merlin, like the Olympian gods, fades into the shadows of history.

Today, our fascination with magic and the supernatural is alive in our literature, cinema and television. While we no longer have entire cultures built on superstition, this new form of magic and wizardry is a very twentieth- and twenty-first-century concept, one probably born out of our scientifically affected lives. This trend has been growing since the Industrial Revolution and is reflected in the works of the first great science fiction writers, Jules Verne and H. G. Wells. Those early epics gave us technological wizards like the brooding but fantastical

Captain Nemo, with his many futuristic inventions, especially the ultra-modern ship, the *Nautilus*. Today, this is the generation of Harry Potter, the Jedi Knights from *Star Wars*, the film versions of J. R. R. Tolkien's *Lord of the Rings* and the intergalactic mysteries of *Star Trek* and *Babylon 5*. The television series *Stargate SG-1* and *Stargate: Atlantis* continue this long and popular tradition. In these two series, there are two major categories of wizards and 'gods', those of Earth and those from the cosmic 'elsewhere'. Each category can then be organised into heroes and villains.

Leading the villainous categories, and appearing first in the original feature film *Stargate*, only identified by name in the *Stargate SG-1* series' first season, are the Goa'uld. They are a parasitic race bent on conquering all known planets in the galaxy and they live within human 'hosts'. They have deliberately used stolen technology to appear as gods to the inhabitants of the planets they conquer. Adding to the mythological quality of these villains is the fact that they bear the names of many Earthly gods from many cultures, although primarily they are those of ancient Egypt. Their names include Ra, god of the sun, Apophis, god of the night, Ammonet, Hathor, Heru-ur, Sokar, Seth, Cronus, Nirrti, Osiris, Ba'al, Mot, and the most powerful of them all so far, Anubis, lord of the dead. They operate in a loose confederation of Goa'uld, the System Lords, in an unending campaign to conquer and dominate space – while occasionally trying to destroy each other and each other's armies in order to accrue more individual power. Their nature as parasites is total and complete. They live off the body of another, always an unwilling victim, and they conquer and enslave by taking over the inventions and discoveries of others. These are the intergalactic Bad Guys.

Primary among the Good Guys are the four main members of Stargate Command's (the SGC) flagship group of explorers, diplomats and warriors: SG-1. All four original members of SG-1, Colonel Jack O'Neill (who is later promoted to general), Capt. (later promoted all the way up to lieutenant colonel) Samantha 'Sam' Carter, Teal'c, and Dr Daniel Jackson, are heroes, warriors and wizards. Each has the unique, classic qualities of extraordinary humans and their synergism is a major reason for their success in their fictional world and with audiences around our world.

They work in the lower levels of the ultra-secure Cheyenne Mountain base, taking orders from, in the first seven seasons, General

George Hammond. In effect, it is their wizards' lair in which they gather and analyse the mysteries of the universe. The centrepiece of all their power, of course, is the Stargate, which, as shown in the 1994 feature film, was discovered decades before during an archaeological dig in Egypt. It is only when a brilliant but unconventional scholar, Dr Daniel Jackson, is able to clearly translate the hieroglyphics on the stone covering the Stargate that the Air Force's special unit is able to travel across the galaxy. In the film, Daniel and a group of soldiers, lead by Colonel O'Neil, arrive on a desert planet called Abydos, named after a sacred city of ancient Egypt. It is populated by the descendants of Egypt who were brought through the Stargate to serve their Goa'uld master, whose base is a full-sized replica of the Great Pyramid. In the climax, Ra is killed, the inhabitants are set free and Jackson chooses to stay with them and his new wife, Sha're.

We learn in the second season of the television series that these symbiotes, as they are most politely called, are not inherently evil. In fact, our heroes gain vital allies in the Tok'ra, whose name means those against Ra. These are symbiotes who follow the peaceful teachings of their great queen Egeria, do not use the sarcophagus (technology that unnaturally prolongs life), and who 'blend' only with willing hosts who are able to retain their personalities, unlike the helpless victims of the Goa'uld. Carter becomes host to a Tok'ra, Jolinar, for a brief time but she retains many of the symbiote's memories, including her deep feelings for another Tok'ra, Martouf. This leads to a very romantic, tender, though tragic subplot within the Tok'ra stories, not conceivable with the selfish Goa'uld. Sam's father, Jacob, also blends with a Tok'ra leader, Selmak, and establishes another long-term, emotional storyline,

Jack O'Neill is the archetypal North American frontier hero. He is simply spoken, fearless, ready to settle a dispute with his modern-day version of a six-shooter, and quietly cares for the local schoolteacher, though a very twenty-first-century one, in Carter. He carries the biggest gun, metaphorically, in this sheriff-of-the-cosmos analogy. Jack is not worried much about diplomacy or politics but in a straightforward sense of justice. He is the team's obvious leader, such that other cultures often defer to him as if he is some sort of sovereign. Instead of trying to rule over anyone the way the Goa'uld feel is justified, though, he tries to teach each new civilisation justice, fairness and freedom. This role as deliverer and sources of law and order is one often only awarded to supernatural beings. Ironically, if there is a famous wizard from literature who O'Neill most closely resembles, it is probably Prospero from Shakespeare's *The Tempest*. While not a king, or even a deposed one, O'Neill goes beyond being an ordinary human to one who through experience, education (O'Neill twice gains the knowledge of the Ancients through their depositories while Prospero has his books) and what he takes from his opponents (in Prospero's case it was from the witch Sycorax while for O'Neill it is usually a zat'ni'katel energy weapon or commandeered Goa'uld ship) becomes the bringer of order out of corruption and chaos.

Teal'c, the rebel Jaffa leader, is a wonderful counterpoint as a hero and user of technological magic. The Jaffa are a warrior race, bred by the Goa'uld to not only fight their battles and dole out punishment to their slaves, but to be living incubators for the Goa'uld young. These larva forms of the Goa'uld 'snake', as O'Neill likes to call them, provide the Jaffa long life, health and healing powers. Teal'c's was the First Prime, the highest ranking of Apophis' Jaffa, but gave up that authority, and his family, to free SG-1 in the first episode, 'Children of the Gods' (101B).[1] Despite being the most fearsome of warriors, Teal'c has a very courtly manner. His strict Jaffa code of honour and action are like those of a Knight of the Round Table. He comes to a foreign land, from a place where he was first among warriors, to pledge himself to the service of another warrior. In effect, he is Lancelot from the Arthurian legends.

Teal'c is also in many ways the teacher of warfare and a source of information about the many new worlds SG-1 visits. This is often the duty of a wizard or divine being who has pledged to help the more human heroes of epic tales. This is true for Merlin, Gandalf of *Lord of the Rings*, Yoda and Obi Wan in *Star Wars* and Dumbledore and most of the Hogwarts faculty in *Harry Potter*. O'Neill is specifically introduced to Master Bra'tac, the over-one-hundred-year-old warrior and teacher of Teal'c, as being his former student's 'apprentice'. These two Jaffa are the *sensei*, or ultimate martial arts masters, of warfare and weaponry. They often are there to explain and operate the highly techno-logical weapons SG-1 encounters in its adventures. They also are the keepers of many important Jaffa legends, such as that of the planet of Kheb in 'Maternal Instinct' (320), that lead SG-1 and Bra'tac to meet Oma Desala, their first acquaintance among the very powerful and almost god-like Ascended. Here, they also find the Harsesis child, whose parents are Apophis and Sha're/Amonet, who, in their joining, have given the child all the knowledge of the Goa'uld and a tie to Daniel through his late wife.

Samantha Carter is another of their wizards/shamans, but of science and technology, not magic. She does not use incantations or devices which simulate divine powers but the logic of mathematics and the poetry of physics. It is the heroes' technology, as with the Goa'uld, that is magical to many of the races they meet. She is the diviner of truth about time and space, the mysteries of evolution and mechanics, sophisticated traps, inventor of escapes, and one who envisions the possibilities of the future. Her training is both as an astrophysicist and as a pilot/special operations officer. While beautiful (men routinely fall in love with her, only to then meet some horrible death), Sam wants to be one of the team, one of the guys. Sam, along with Daniel, is also the team's moral compass. Her sense of duty is equal to her compassion. That is established in a very early episode, 'Emancipation' (103), where she literally fights hand to hand in order to gain equal rights for the women of a planet. Trained as both scientist and warrior, she is able to still show her heart to everyone but O'Neill, who outranks her. Theirs is an affection forbidden by the rules.

Daniel Jackson is described by O'Neill in the very first episode as a 'geek' who sneezes a lot, but he is also a classic hero and, eventually, someone with the most amazing powers. His unconventional academic scholarship leads him to the SGC and then on a totally unplanned adventure. The other three chose the warrior's life but Daniel has to become one. Initially, he is a wizard, not of technology but of language and beliefs. While Sam bridges the relatively primitive Earth science to alien technology and spaceships' hyperdrives, Daniel bridges cultures, religions, dialects and has even bridged life and death. Often, he is their most effective diplomat because he is able to divine alien languages and customs.

But not all Earthlings are good and honourable. We see the greed to gain power and an arrogant misuse of authority similar to that of the Goa'uld in several recurring characters. One of the first, and most meddlesome, is Senator, later Vice President, and even later Goa'uld host, Kinsey, who consistently invokes what he hypocritically argues is humanity's right to be kept safe by simply cutting off the dangers on the other side of the Stargate. At the same time, however, he is involved in a plot to usurp the vast technological resources found through the gate. Often in league with Kinsey are the NID, a secret government agency (so secret, in fact, that even the show's writers don't know what the acronym stands for). It is supposed to be a department within the United States military but its members, notably Colonels Harry Maybourne and Frank Simmons, who also ends up as a Goa'uld host, frequently operate as if they are above the law and the elected government they are sworn to protect and obey. Often, SG-1 is as busy fighting fellow humans as they are the Go'auld.

The SG-1 team is often thought of by inhabitants of more primitive cultures as messengers of the gods or gods themselves. This began with the teams' first trip to Chulack. In fact, the very first people SG-1 meet on Chulak ('Children of the Gods', 101B), who seem by their robes and staffs to be some order of monks or priests, immediately assume they must bow to them because they came through the Stargate, the chaapa'ai, as it is called by the Goa'uld. Only the gods and their ordained servants, it seems, are thought able to use the device. The Goa'uld have been very careful to keep the peoples on these different planets at a low level of technological development. Most of the time, the team finds a colourful but stagnant culture, one still wearing the dress and following the customs of the time and place from which they were kidnapped by the Goa'uld to live on these new home worlds. Because of this forced transportation by what must have seemed to be supernatural means, the Stargate, the inhabitants of these many worlds have been conditioned to view any traveller through the gate as a god. As we shall see, O'Neill and his team routinely dismiss any notion they are more than travellers and explorers, what we might call wizards instead of gods; this distinction is one of their essential moral or heroic choices and leads to many of their successes.

There are lessons taught in the series for those who suddenly gain power and influence, like that of a wizard or deity. In one of the first episodes, 'The First Commandment' (105), the leader of another SG unit, and former lover of Sam's, Captain Hanson, has gone mad, making himself the despotic ruler of primitive people they discover on an alien planet. He makes them work in an old Goa'uld mine and brings his twisted justice with a swift fury. The character is very much like Kurtz in Conrad's *Heart of Darkness*.[2] Instead of bringing the glories and prosperity of modernity such as technology or medicine or education, he becomes a tyrant who relies on the helplessness of a less advanced people. Just as Conrad's tale can been seen as a cautionary one about the morality of colonial rule, this episode set a standard of caution regarding the dangers of the power of technology. In the end, the horror of Hanson's mad delusion of godhead leads to his own crushing death. When SG-1 reveals that he is a false god, the people of the planet rebel. En masse, they carry and drop him into the means of execution Hanson had arranged for O'Neill's team, to be thrown into a horizontal Stargate, knowing a closed shield on the other end of the wormhole would smash any traveller.

The two *Stargate* series do praise the initiative, bravery, intelligence, compassion and, most of all, the potential of the human race. We will discuss soon, in episodes such as 'The Fifth Race' (216), how the great and ancient races of order and justice all come to see the possibility that humanity will mature into their equal. These may be, as Abraham Lincoln called them, 'the better angels of our nature'.[3] But the two series also warn us not to abuse the power we acquire or fall victim to our own greed and ambition. We are not gods but we have the promise of being faithful wizards, servants of morality and justice, if we are not blinded by our pride, what the ancient Greeks called hubris.

In 'The Broca Divide' (104), when SG-1 reaches the planet designated by the SGC's computer as P3X 797, the inhabitants, who, as their Minoan dress and architecture suggest, seem to be stuck in the Greek Bronze Age, refer to the team members, especially O'Neill, as 'my lord'. As in 'The First Commandment' this population knows of the power of the Stargate and so assumes that anyone from another world must be a powerful being from their legends. O'Neill and his peers continually ask Councillor Tuplo and his people, who all seem to live as if nobility themselves, to see the visitors as only other humans there to meet and help them. Thanks to the SGC's chief medical officer for the first seven years, Doctor Fraiser, the team realises that the use of a powerful antihistamine can cure a long-time plague, one that sent 'the Touched' evolving backwards into a Neanderthal state. In the happy ending, SG-1 are again greeted as heroes, as if they are gods, and O'Neill again tells Tuplo to not kneel to him. Unlike Hanson, O'Neill and his team are liberators, not tyrants.

The reverse of being treated as god-like or royalty was shown early in the episode 'The Nox' (107) about an apparently primitive and simple-minded rural civilisation of the same name. The team arrives at the same time and with the same purpose as Apophis, who is hunting for a legendary animal, the Fenri, which has the power to become invisible. The team sets an ambush in the woods for the Goa'uld and his guards, but it fails. It is such an utter failure that all of SG-1 is killed. That is not the end of the story, though. Instead, our four heroes' bodies disappear before Apophis can celebrate. They have been taken by the Nox, who heal them so completely, SG-1 feel they must have died and gone to heaven since there is no trauma or pain.

Despite this seeming miracle, SG-1 immediately see themselves as the technologically and militarily superior race to the Nox and so try to protect a small family who live in the woods and who seem indifferent to the Goa'uld and dismissive of the team's armed force. The Nox, when they speak of how the young take so long to learn a lesson, are not referring to Nefrayu, the child in their family, but ironically to SG-1. The team's relatively minor hubris is finally made clear when the Nox show that their power to heal, and even to hide a flying city from view, is much more powerful than that of any Goa'uld or SG unit. We find out in a later episode, 'The Fifth Race' (216), that the Nox were part of an ancient and mighty alliance that included the Asgard, the Tollan, the Furlings and the Ancients, also tantalisingly referred to as the 'Gate Builders'.

The planet of Cimmeria is home to two of the most important episodes concerning another of the series' adaptations on our own

Convention dealer's table. Photo by Lisa Dickson, 2005.

world's mythology. In the initial season's 'Thor's Hammer' (109) is the first encounter by SG-1 members with the race named the Asgard, whose name comes from the home of the most powerful Norse gods. Primary among the Asgard characters throughout the series is Thor, the Norse's god of thunder. The writers mix images of tall, epic warriors and the mighty halls of Nordic kings with the stories of the short, thin, large-eyed, grey Roswell aliens popular in entertainment and tabloids for the last few decades. During the next season, in 'Thor's Chariot' (206), they first meet O'Neill's 'buddy', Thor, face to face and see the power of the Asgard when Thor's ship appears suddenly, travelling vast distances within moments, and vaporising a Goa'uld mothership and its Jaffa with quickly moving beams. The Asgard are benevolent, if powerful, technological 'gods' who protect rather than enslave peoples they believe as yet too simple to understand their science.

In season two, the 'Spirits' (213) are the native creatures of PXY 887 who liberated the descendants of a kidnapped indigenous North American people, the Salish, from the Goa'uld. They have taken the form and roles of the Salish's gods, such as a wolf named Xe'ls, to integrate themselves into the newcomers' society. Their land has a supply of critically needed trinium that the humans want to mine. The sin of vanity again shows itself in our heroes. The SGC is willing to lie to the Salish, whom they see as primitive, about what the mining is going to do to their environment. The Spirits catch them in these lies. O'Neill and Daniel must prove themselves trustworthy to these false but protective 'gods' in order to save the SGC from destruction. It is nearly another case, like Hanson's, of pride going before the fall.

Late in season four is yet another lesson in the dangers of knowledge and power. 'Absolute Power' (417) tells of Daniel's request to gain the knowledge of the Harsesis, now apparently a grown child, who was last seen as an infant in 'Maternal Instinct' (320). As a sort of gift, the child gives Daniel an opportunity to see what this information would bring, even to a good man such as Daniel. We see him suddenly able to construct massive defence satellites that are to be weapons platforms to destroy any new Goa'uld invasion fleet. Being the only one with this knowledge, Daniel goes from explorer to emperor of technology, running the entire programme and keeping his finger on the trigger. Even as his friends desert him, Daniel is confident in the righteousness of his action, believing himself infallible and all-powerful. When the Russians protest against the unilateral launching of these weapons, Daniel casually uses the satellites to vaporise Moscow. It is only when the world is turned upside down that Daniel realises it has all been a vision supplied by the child in order to teach Daniel a lesson. Perhaps that recurrent theme of placing others before self is one reason why so many of the *Stargate SG-1* episodes have references to the 1939 film *The Wizard of Oz*. The motif fits very well. All Oz's acquired powers are only to serve the people, not to rule them. Yet, when it comes to fulfilling Dorothy's simple wish to go home, his magic is not as powerful as the love in a little girl's heart.[4]

In 'Red Sky' (505), in season five, the people of Katal worship the Asgard as gods, specifically Freyr, who has been protecting this planet the way Thor has Cimmeria. The locals call their sun 'the Eye of Odin', referring to the god known in Norse mythology as Thor's father. To them, SG-1 must be Freyr's elves, who come, not as friends, but as a test from their god. When Carter disables a safety protocol in the dialling device, allowing them to reach the planet, their wormhole goes through the sun and causes its spectrum to shift. This places the inhabitants of Katal in mortal danger, or, as they call it, Ragnarok, which Daniel translates as Armageddon. SG-1's arrogant misuse of technology nearly leads to a Judgement Day. This is about as close to crossing the moral and technological line, as Hanson did in 'The First Commandment' (105), as the team ever steps. Carter and the SGC scientists had become arrogant with their new knowledge and, hungry for new achievements, disregarded the standard Stargate safety protocols in order to gain the glory of connecting to a previously unreachable world. It is only after repeated, humbling efforts to fix their own mistake, and perhaps with some secret assistance from the Asgard, that the people of Katal are saved.

In the episode 'Menace' (519), we finally learn the source of a deadly threat to the Asgard. These are the Replicators, which first appeared in 'Nemesis' (322) at the climax of season three. They look like small toy spiders but they have the power to overwhelm and consume whole civilisations in their unending drive to build more of themselves. This combination of abilities and single-minded appetite for technology and minerals make them a formidable nemesis, a self-ordained god made of – not simply using – technology, that nearly consumes the Asgard.

On a deserted world, full of great buildings and art but no people, the team, in 'Menace', finds what appears to be a beautiful, sleeping girl. They awake her and discover she is actually a very sophisticated android, but with the emotional maturity of a child. Reese comes back to the SGC for observation but becomes impatient with everyone but Daniel. While locked in a laboratory, Reese begins building some 'toys' she wants to show to Daniel, obviously hoping for approval from him. They turn out to be Replicators and the story of how this artificial life form became mother, or perhaps god, to the Replicator race is finally discovered. The team is able to stop the Replicators attacking the base but Reese dies in the process. They will begin to evolve, though, in future seasons. By the time of 'Unnatural Selection' (612), they have begun to build humanoid forms, and by 'New Order' (801–802), at the beginning of season eight, a humanoid duplicate of Carter has been manufactured. She will soon take over all the Replicators in the universe and, towards the very end of season eight, nearly destroy all organic life in the universe. She and Reese are would-be gods created out of technology, not simply those which use technology. While the Replicator Carter is a different kind of villain, she is easily as evil as the Goa'uld. She and her kind may be warnings to our own scientists to calculate the consequences of playing with power.

Late in season eight is the two-part story called the 'Reckoning' (816–817), which stands as a climax to the Replicator storyline. Led by the Carter double, they are about to recreate the universe in their image. When confronted by Daniel's accusation of being evil and destroyers of civilisations, the Carter Replicant scoffs because of her belief in their right to create their own version of existence. This latest and most menacing evolution of Reese's toys is a would-be god who believes in its dogma of reproduction at the cost of all other life and technology. It has become, for the moment, the most fearsome of all the would-be divine Bad Guys in the *Stargate* pantheon. At this point, they parallel the Borg of *Star Trek: The Next Generation* as technology that has placed itself above life.[5] Ironically, the Replicators' main opponent at this time is not SG-1 but the Goa'uld, whose much older claim to being omnipotent creatures is under what might be a final attack by these voracious machines. Of course, this is science fiction and dead 'gods' have already come back to life a few times in this series.

In 'Meridian' (521), the next-to-last episode of season five, Daniel sacrifices his life to save the people of Kelowna from a powerful explosion of naqadria (an element not found on Earth but which is essential in building and powering Goa'uld and Ancient technology) and is transformed by Oma into one of the Ascended, literally becoming a shining light that floats up and through the cement ceiling. During the next season, Daniel appears, literally, in three episodes, each time there to care for others as a sort of guardian angel. In 'Full Circle' (622), he is willing to use his new god-like powers to fight Anubis in an attempt to save Abydos and its people. He is stopped at the last possible second by Oma, who knows that the Ascended do not permit their powers to be used to interfere with the lives of the corporeal. He does not let his new power cut himself off from humanity, as do the would-be god/ villains. Instead, he remains a defender of others. This motif of the self-sacrificing hero being taken body and soul is a popular way to add to a hero's mythology. Besides the obvious religious parallels, it is used at the conclusion of the *Lord of the Rings* as Frodo, Gandalf and the Ring bearers go across the Sea to the Undying Lands; in *Babylon 5* as John Sheridan was taken by the First One, the original living being, Lorien; and in *Star Trek: Deep Space Nine* when Captain Sisko goes to live, for at least a little while, with the Prophets.[6] Daniel's willingness to use his Ascended powers to help, or interfere, is enough to make the Ancients send him back to his human friends without powers or Ancient knowledge, though he does get to star in the series again.

In season six's 'Frozen' (604), SG-1 meet their first non-Ascended Ancient face to face, a woman named Ayiana, who looks surprisingly human but has survived being buried in the ice of the Antarctic for millennia. It takes a great deal of effort by Jonas Quinn, Daniel's one-season replacement, to communicate with her. As they are finally establishing clear connections, though, it is discovered that she is making all the humans in this isolated research facility very ill. Ayiana is able to cure the humans but at what seems the cost of her own life. Later, we learn the Ancients were dying of a plague. It is also a storyline that leads to the sequel series *Stargate: Atlantis* and the epic battle over Antarctica at the end of season seven in which the most powerful of all Goa'uld, Anubis, is apparently killed.

In season eight's 'It's Good to be King' (813), Jack's old nemesis, friend Col. Harry Maybourne, has been appointed King Arkhan the First of a planet because his ability to translate Ancient text is perceived as evidence of his divine power as a seer. All Maybourne (who had been exiled there so he would not face criminal punishment on Earth for conspiring to steal SG-1's technological finds) has done is read a stone obelisk left by an Ancient who had been experimenting with a time ship.

With that information, Maybourne has assumed power, like that of a wizard, because he knows of natural disasters that the time traveller had seen and left a sort of galactic post-it note. He does, though, stand up to the invading Jaffa and help O'Neill and SG-1 fight. Maybourne proves himself to be a good sovereign who cares for his adopted people. He has given up his selfish ways to be more of a truly heroic Stargate wizard.

Towards the end of season seven of *Stargate SG-1*, more of the groundwork was laid for the sequel series. Perhaps it would be better to call it a paralleling series since the two shows' production and storylines will overlap for at least a few years. *Stargate: Atlantis* is a journey to the site of another of the Earth's legendary myths, the lost city of Atlantis, whose story goes back at least to the time of Aristotle. This science fiction journey can only be accomplished using the *Zero Point Module*, or ZPM, a power source found by SG-1 and used to activate weapons in Antarctica that save Earth from Anubis' fleet ('The Lost City', 721–722). On their arrival at Atlantis in the faraway Pegasus Galaxy, a brand new, larger team of explorers discovers a recording of one of the last Ancients, who appears in a heavenly aura. She both welcomes and warns them. A plague was killing their race but they also were losing a long war with a horrible enemy. This makes the clearly superior and almost divine Gatebuilders or Ancients, later referred to as Atlantians, very vulnerable and very human. They had survived only because the entire city was hidden beneath a sea. When the explorers arrive, the last of the city's ZPMs uses up its power, and the city, now without its protective shield, rises to the surface. Now the Ancients' home of Atlantis is not a magic cave or temple, but a storehouse of technology, such as the Puddle Jumper ships. They have no other operating weapons, though, and not enough power to 'gate' back to Earth. The Ancients are not magical or divine but only technologically advanced. These fabled wizards of technology, like our own today, have very human limitations.

The more we learn about the Ancients, the more we see that they have parallels to powerful races in other recent science fiction television: the Q Continuum of *Star Trek* and the Vorlon of *Babylon 5*. The Q, who are mainly represented by the character Q (which was the name they all shared), are boorish and condescending towards Star Fleet's finest.[7] The Vorlon are a purposefully mysterious race, which uses its telepathic powers and million-year-old technology to affect the evolution of hundreds of other, younger races across the galaxy.[8] Perhaps, though, the closest parallel for the Ancients is in Tolkien's elves. They are warriors, priests, poets, artisans and magicians. They understand that power is simply a generational matter, that their time will end, and someone else, contemporary humans, will then have the chance to grow and lead. The Ancients are sometimes called the first evolution of humanoid life on Earth and so they seem to greet the Stargate heroes, as will be discussed using two specific episodes later, as if the humans are their children, and even, potentially, peers.

The Wraith, on the other hand, are the new Bad Guys preying on humans in the Pegasus Galaxy. Unlike the Goa'uld, they do not claim, at least not yet, to be gods, per se. One of their leaders, though, tells Major Sheppard that they are superior to humans and so their 'cullings', when whole planets are ravaged using ships and technology to gather populations to serve as food, are no more evil than humans raising and butchering farm animals for sustenance. Their way of survival is to literally use their hands to draw the life out of a victim, aging and shrivelling them to death slowly, as if an appetizer, or sucking it out quickly like a meal for a hungry wolf. Sheppard, who has many of O'Neill's qualities, such as bluntness and a tendency to act on instinct, immediately joins the fight to protect both his team-mates and any other innocent people. His last name, which invokes the traditional, especially Christian, image of a lone guardian of the helpless, is probably not a coincidence. Like O'Neill, Sheppard possesses a rare gene that has descended from the Ancients and allows him to instantly use much of Atlantis' amazing technology, such as the Puddle Jumper ship. He is, like the SG-1 team members, a wizard.

In 'Sanctuary' (114), the team from Atlantis meets the beautiful high priestess of Athar, named Chaya. The people of this planet, Proculus, have never known, or at least cannot remember, a Wraith culling, prompting Major Sheppard to ask if there is something that can help to protect Atlantis or if refugees may come to Proculus for asylum. The requests are denied but Sheppard continues to pursue Chaya, hoping for a different answer. Finally she admits that she is an Ascended Ancient, and prefers the term Atlantian, who protects their planet from the Wraith as punishment for using her powers to protect the people of the planet many years before. As with Daniel's attempt in 'Full Circle' to defend Abydos while Ascended, that kind of interference, even in defence of the helpless, is forbidden. It seems, though, that this series continues to comment on the lack of wisdom in that rule. On another level, though, Chaya seems quite taken with Sheppard, and the show ends with her sharing herself with him in a whirl of light. Sheppard is a bridge between the evolutions of these wizards of justice.

In 'Before I Sleep' (115), an Atlantian named Janus has given Dr Weir, a skilled diplomat, a measure of immortality when he keeps her alive for 10,000 years in order to keep her team and Atlantis alive. In this story of alternative timelines, the team's original arrival in the city came too late for the three ZPMs to have enough power for Atlantis' shield and the city did not have an automatic failsafe to send it to the surface in case of a failure. In the original timeline, all but Dr Weir died, and, via additional time travel in an attempt to escape the flooding waters, she became a witness to the Atlantians' last days there before escaping back to Earth. Through technology, the city is given a chance at immortality and to change history using the added failsafe that sends the city rising to the surface when the catastrophe begins to recur. Being able to alter the fates is the kind of thing only a divine creature might be able to accomplish. Weir, then, is also a bridge from one generation to the next in the continuing battle against these would-be gods of oppression.

But not everyone in Pegasus recognises the link from the Atlantians to Shepherd and Weir. In 'The Brotherhood' (116), Major Sheppard's team finds a civilisation on Dagan that worships the Atlantians, or Ancestors, as they are called. Through a study of ancient Dagan texts, left in tatters after centuries of Wraith cullings, they search for a desperately needed ZPM that this planet's inhabitants had promised to keep safe for the Ancestors' return. It has even acquired a holy name, the Potentia. When the people discover their visitors are not the original Atlantians, they take the Potentia back by force to await the return of the Ancestors, in a classic creation and salvation archetype. Their religion-like faith about the Atlantians would seem to have been tested by the outsiders and found strong enough to keep the sacred Potentia safe. For them, it will be their duty to keep it safe until there is a second coming of the Ancestors, who would then reward them. Sadly, they have not recognised that Weir and Sheppard and their team *are* the second coming of Atlantis.

The two *Stargate* series are full of hope and painful lessons. While some ultimate force keeps allowing the Good Guys to win despite the heavy odds, the heroes must deal with both would-be gods and the temptation to take on supernatural roles for themselves. In this galaxy of the Stargates, there is still morality and spirituality, but the magic is more from chemistry and physics, more circuit boards and wormholes, than fire, ice, wand or potion. In simple terms, it's good to be the wizard.

Notes

1   All references to the episodes will be indicated parenthetically by episode number. See the Episode guide for more information.
2   Joseph Conrad, *Heart of Darkness* (New York, 1993)
3   'First Inaugural Address', 4 March 1861
4   *The Wizard of Oz*, based on the novel by L. Frank Baum, screenplay by Noël Langley, directed by Victor Fleming, perf. Judy Garland (MGM, 1939)
5   *Star Trek: The Next Generation*, 'Q Who', written by Maurice Hurley, directed by Robert Bowman (Paramount, 1989)
6   *Star Trek: Deep Space Nine*, 'What you leave behind, Part II', written by Ira Steven Behr and Hans Beimler, directed by Allan Kroeker (Paramount, 1999)
7   *Star Trek: The Next Generation*, 'Encounter at Farpoint, Part I', written by D. C. Fontana and Gene Roddenberry, directed by Corey Allen (Paramount, 1987)
8   *Babylon 5*, 'Secrets of the soul', written by J. Michael Straczynski, directed by Tony Dow (Warner Brothers, 1998)

7

GENDER ROLES, SEXUAL IDENTITIES AND THE CONCEPT OF THE OTHER IN *STARGÅTE: SG-1*

SABINE SCHMIDT

The 'concept of the Other' plays a key role in such diverse scientific fields as gender studies, psychosocial development, ethnology, cultural anthropology, and its subsidiary in the political sciences, xenology. One aspect is essential to all these theoretical concepts: the deeply embedded binary structure of the Other versus the self. Throughout history it has created a lot of very influential supplementary oppositions – foreign versus familiar; wild versus civilised; female versus male; nature versus culture; emotion versus rationality; colonised versus coloniser – coupled with a hierarchical perception placing the self always as superior to the Other. Thus it served, simply put, as an important part in the process of creating group identities based on, for instance, race, nationality or religion.[1] The emergence of increasingly multicultural, multi-ethnic societies, cultural studies in the wake of Homi Bhabha's theory of 'hybridity',[2] and postfeminist gender studies have recently resulted in a more egalitarian outlook but the basic binary structure still remains intact.

In Western culture and history, since the early age of Greek philosophy, women have been assigned (and for several millennia also endorsed) the role of the inferior 'Other'.[3] So, it can be argued that even these days preconceived notions of gender roles and gender boundaries, as well as specific ways of dealing with a variety of sexual identities, are a sure indicator of the inner development of a society, a culture.

In *Stargate: SG-1* distinct gender differentiations enhance the omnipresent distinction between 'self' and 'Other' – that is 'Earth' and 'alien' – and provide the audience with a familiar background from which to relate to the main characters and also the central storylines. This analysis will first focus on Samantha Carter as the only woman in the SGC flagship team, then will turn to the relationship and dynamics of SG-1, and the perception and assessment of alien societies, qua cultural differences and questions of sexual identity.

'I can't figure out how to feel like one of the guys with these guys'

> Carter: I'm an Air Force officer just like you are, colonel. And just because my reproductive organs are on the inside instead of on the outside doesn't mean I can't handle what you can handle.
>
> O'Neill: Oh, this has nothing to do with you being a woman. I like women. I've just got a little problem with scientists.
>
> Carter: Colonel, I logged over 100 hours in enemy airspace during the Gulf War. Is that tough enough for you? Or are we going to have to arm-wrestle? (101)[4]

When Sam Carter, captain in the US Air Force, F-16 fighter pilot, Desert Storm veteran and theoretical astrophysicist, is transferred to Stargate Command in the show's pilot 'Children of the Gods', the tall blonde has to overcome the deep-rooted prejudices of her commanding officer – and she does so by standing up to him, by openly confronting and provoking him without being openly disrespectful. Colonel Jack O'Neill, former Black-Ops specialist, seems to have a problem with a woman being assigned to his team and he definitely has a problem with her being a scientist. This potentially antagonistic relationship is further charged by Carter's obvious beauty, emphasised by her form-fitting dress uniform and sparkling blue eyes.

Concerning the male and female main characters, the show thus relies on and reproduces a behavioural pattern familiar from other shows of the 1980s and 1990s, such as, for instance, Detective Sergeant Rick Hunter (Fred Dryer) and Detective Sergeant DeeDee McCall (Stepfanie Kramer) in *Hunter* (1984–1991) or Chris Lorenzo (Rob Estes) and Rita Lee Lance (Mitzi Capture), the first pairing of detectives in *Silk Stalking* (1991–1999), one of the most successful police shows ever: initial antagonism turns into friendship and trust, and finally is enhanced by sexual attraction and even love.

O'Neill's attraction to Carter becomes evident in 'Divide and Conquer' (405), during a lie detector test, although the signals are there almost from the beginning. For her part, Carter takes much longer to admit to his sexual appeal (see 'Grace', 713; and 'Threads', 818). And that's as far as they go; including the fact that O'Neill and Carter were engaged/married in the two alternate realities they come across ('There but for the Grace of God', 119; 'Point of View', 306). The dynamics of their relationship are basically governed by military regulations and the hierarchical command structure, providing both of them with a security blanket that is conveyed by the use of rank instead of first names even in their private interactions – a restriction none of them adheres to when addressing Teal'c or Jackson.[5] The non-fraternisation rule efficiently keeps them apart but it also is the reliance on these behavioural patterns that helps O'Neill to overcome his initial misgivings against his new second-in-command. He only begins to trust her when Carter, at the beginning of season one, in 'Emancipation' (103), defeats the misogynist Mongol chieftain Turgan in hand-to-hand combat. In other words: he begins to trust her when she proves her worth and abilities as a soldier, not as a woman or a scientist.

* * *

As a soldier Samantha Carter is reluctant to show emotions of any kind; though there are occasions when her stoic resolve crumbles and she proves to the audience that, after all, she's only human, for instance after Daniel's ascension (see 'Meridian', 521; and 'Revelations', 522). 'Singularity' (114), written by Robert C. Cooper, directed by Mario Azzopardi (MGM, 1997), offers particular insight into Carter's emotional make-up: Carter's relationship with Cassandra, the lone survivor of a world destroyed by the Goa'uld, Nirrti, illustrates her nurturing and protecting qualities. The alien child quickly forms a bond with the blonde captain; she doesn't let her out of her sight and seeks constant physical contact; and by returning to the presumably dying girl she openly defies her CO's orders.

The whole episode thus is part of an effort to make her into a more complex and complete personality by bestowing her with these stereotypically 'female' traits.[6] Under normal circumstances, however, she is able to channel her feelings, her anxieties and her enthusiasm, in activity, especially in research and technical invention, such as when her invention of a 'particle beam generator' allows O'Neill to return to Earth after being stranded on the planet Edora ('A Hundred Days', 317).

There is (of course) a psychological explanation as to why Carter is so reluctant to show emotions and vulnerability: her familial situation and upbringing. Samantha's mother died when she was still in her teens; because of her affiliation with the Air Force, she's estranged from her brother; and her father, an Air Force general, comes across as emotionally cold or at least aloof, illustrated when he wants to get her to apply for NASA by emotionally blackmailing her with his lymphoma ('Secrets', 209).

But, more than an unconscious reaction or a deficiency, Carter's reluctance to show emotional vulnerability is a conscious choice and a conscious effort on her part, a strategic career decision. There only are a few women at the mountain base and most of them are non-combatants, working in the infirmary or the science departments.[7] As one of the couple of women serving in combat units Carter is in a position where she has to prove herself every day. So, her stoicism is part and parcel of succeeding in an androcentric environment such as the US Air Force, where the stereotypical, centuries-old notions of presumed gender boundaries still abound.[8]

* * *

Carter's physical beauty is another part out of the arsenal of stereotypically 'female assets' the creators of the show use to add another layer to her personality: the ability to inspire sexual desire in men – an ability even made stronger by the fact that she seems unaware of it. The show also goes to great lengths to ensure that the continuous storyline holds not even the hint of any other than heterosexual relationships by supplying the lead characters with a series of (potential) 'significant others'. But it seems that every one of these relationships is doomed; their partners either get killed, are taken over by the Goa'uld or have more important off-world obligations – one only has to think of Daniel Jackson's wife Sha're or Ambassador Joseph Faxon, who sacrifices himself to save Carter's life in '2001' (510). In other words, they are removed from the equation before they can affect the balance and relationship dynamics of the team.[9]

Colonel Jack O'Neill is undoubtedly not the only one attracted to Samantha Carter. It seems as if every single male alien they encounter, especially those of technologically advanced races, falls for her: Narim of the Tollans ('Enigma', 116; 'Pretense', 315; 'Between Two Fires', 509), the Ancient, Orlin ('Ascension', 503), and the Tok'ra Martouf/ Lantesh, who falls in love with her as he once had been in love with her former symbiote, Jolinar ('Tok'ra I and II', 211–12; 'Jolinar's Memories', 312; 'The Devil You Know', 313; 'Divide and Conquer', 405). The human-form Replicator Fifth is literally obsessed with her, to the point that he creates, like a second Pygmalion, an exact copy of Carter ('The New Order II', 802), down to her memories and thought patterns but minus her sense of morality and duty.

The storyline with Fifth and the replicated Carter also marks one of the moments when her duty as a soldier conflicts with her other character traits, such as moral standards and civil responsibilities. Although she was only following orders when leaving Fifth behind in 'Unnatural Selection' (612), she holds herself responsible for his actions and ultimately for the actions of her 'evil twin': 'But the fact is she learned betrayal from Fifth. And he learned it from me' ('Gemini', 811). Carter takes responsibility for what she does, be it with Fifth or when a gating accident threatens to destroy the Asgard-protected planet Katal ('Red Sky', 505). However, her responsibilities as a member of the Air Force, in this case as in many others, outweigh and overrule every other obligation.

So, to Samantha Carter being a soldier is far more than a job or a role, it also is an integral, if not the dominating, part of her personal identity.[10] The confidence she showed during her first encounter with O'Neill is born out of this self-perception. The same goes for her scientific mind and intellectual brilliance.[11] She has an innate grasp of alien technology. Her abilities save the world on an almost regular basis: she blows up a sun ('Exodus', 422), manipulates hyperspace to manoeuvre an asteroid right through the centre of the earth ('Fail Safe', 517). She builds a bomb out of a naqada reactor ('Scorched Earth', 409), uses another one to power up a stranded alien spaceship ('Forsaken', 618), or writes a 1000-page book on wormhole physics ('Upgrades', 403). Over the years, even O'Neill comes to depend upon her ingenuity, although he uses every chance to either cut her explanations short or to dumb them down.[12]

* * *

Samantha Carter: beautiful woman, compassionate human being, brilliant scientist, tough soldier – stereotypically male and female roles, she fulfils them both with equal grace and thoroughness; it thus is impossible to reduce her to only one of them. So, although as the only woman in SG-1 she should be the perfect personification of the 'Other', the analysis made evident that she is not. The heterogeneous make-up of the flagship team, combining a formerly retired Black-Ops specialist, a civilian scientist and an alien warrior, reduces her biological 'Otherness' to just one among many and at the same time gives her the opportunity in indulge in the core elements of her personal identity, being a scientist and a soldier. This, however, doesn't mean that SG-1 is completely lacking in traditional 'feminine' behaviour.

'Danny Boy' and 'T-Man': dealing with aliens

'Unless we want to give ourselves a bad reputation, I think we should avoid shooting the first people we meet on a new planet' (Daniel Jackson, 'Children of the Gods', 101B).

The task of making first contact with the cultures and people they meet when stepping through the Stargate usually falls to Doctor Daniel Jackson, due to the fact that he speaks 23 languages. More than just doing the talking he also acts as a mediator in times of conflict. He has a genuine interest in finding non-violent solutions, especially against the odds. In 'Scorched Earth' (409), his talking saves an entire civilisation, and in 'Enemy Mine' (707) he brokers a peace treaty and mining agreement while saving the lives of Colonel Edwards and his men.[13] Jackson also serves as the voice of reason and humanity, especially in discussions with O'Neill, and thus as a moral compass for the SGC as a whole, for instance in 'The Other Side' (402).

As an archaeologist by trade and for the love of it, he counts among his duties to put the civilisations and cultures they encounter into perspective by comparing them to similar phenomena in the history of Earth, for the 'alien' cultures, having been transplanted from Earth to other planets some time in the past, in most cases are not really 'alien'. It is more like a parent–child relationship, with the visitors from Earth usually being the more technologically advanced in the role as the 'parents', scolding the 'child' for not following the rules. In accordance with his conciliatory nature, Jackson tries to respect the traditions of these cultures; he tries to see things from their perspective, to put himself in their place – not unconditionally but to a greater degree than, for instance, O'Neill.[14]

The leader of SG-1 upholds his own set of moral standards and friend–fiend concepts and expects other people, be they off-world or Earth-based, to act accordingly. In this regard Colonel O'Neill acts like a cultural anthropologist of the nineteenth century – using his own values and experience as a yardstick in order to judge the Other, in good old American military tradition. He's not fussy about what methods he chooses to get things done in order to keep his friends from harm, or, as he says to Hammond: '[O]ne day I may ask you to buy back my soul.'[15] But O'Neill also is not willing to pay every price, as his final decision to return to Earth empty-handed rather than to help the Eurondans commit genocide proves ('The Other Side', 402).

* * *

Jackson's psychological make-up is as ambiguous as Carter's. He seems to completely lack a military mindset, although over the years he learns how to fight and use weapons. He appears to be the embodiment of intellectual curiosity, emotional intelligence and peaceableness – that is, possessed of qualities in Western culture usually associated with women, with 'femininity'.[16] Regardless of whether he is confronted with living persons, Goa'uld fossils, or ruins, his enthusiasm to learn more about them rivals Carter's love for technical and astronomical discoveries. At times he gets so carried away that he would willingly risk his own life and the lives of this team-mates, just for the sake of research, as in 'The Torment of Tantalus' (110). What in Carter is tempered by a sense of duty and military discipline, in Daniel Jackson is allowed to run almost unchecked.

In other areas he also shows few inhibitions and tends to fall prey to his emotions. When he and Carter are sent to retrieve a Goa'uld larvae to study, he destroys the whole reservoir despite her warnings: 'If we kill them when they are as vulnerable as they are right now, we'd be no better than the Goa'uld' ('Bloodlines', 111). After only a few sessions in a sarcophagus he lets his friends suffer in a naqada mine while he enjoys life in the royal palace and the good graces of Princess

Shyla ('Need', 205). Jackson's hallucinations in 'Absolute Power' (417) show that he's capable of typical Goa'uld behaviour; he incarcerates Carter, delivers Teal'c into the hands of Apophis and uses the defensive satellite grid to destroy Moscow and take over Earth. More than any other member of SG-1 Daniel Jackson easily falls prey to the lure and temptations of power, thus taking on the part of the stereotypical easily influenced and manipulated 'woman'. This impression is further enforced by O'Neill's often patronising and indulging attitude concerning his 'space monkey's' lack of discipline and protocol.

As they did with Carter and O'Neill,[17] the creators of the show offer a psychological explanation for his behaviour: he witnessed his parents' accidental death when he was only eight years old. Having grown up in foster care he has serious abandonment issues and a need for harmony and assent. His self-esteem gets a further blow from the unanimous rejection of his theories in the academic world. On Abydos, however, he is regarded as a saviour and hero.[18] In other words: Daniel Jackson takes on the role of the 'Other', be it by fate or deliberately – and only the unique, family-like relationship with his team-mates balances his 'otherness', integrating it and him in a new 'self'.

The golden boy: dealer's display of *Stargate Magazine*. Photo by Lisa Dickson, 2005.

* * *

A similar process can be observed with Teal'c. By defying 'his god' he sets himself apart from the rest of his birth society; he becomes the Shol'va, the traitor, the 'Other'. The SGC and SG-1 give him the opportunity to realise a lifelong dream: to fight for the freedom of his people. Over the seasons he becomes the figurehead of the Jaffa rebellion, thus initiating the formation of a new community with a new sense of 'self'.

At first sight, the former First Prime of Apophis appears to be the epitome of stereotypically male 'virtues'. He's courageous, honourable, rational, selfless and loyal. He's a great warrior. He's a loving father and husband who still has the inner strength to put the freedom of his people above his family. An attentive observer of other cultures, especially Earth traditions, he is usually not guided by preconceived notions of conduct, as his acceptance of Carter and Fraiser indicates – or, at least, as long as his own traditions are not concerned; then he tends to get 'short-sighted'. Fuelled by a need to preserve his traditions even during his stay on Earth, ironically it is his adherence to centuries-old Jaffa rules of conduct that threaten his mission time and again.

For example, like many others of his fellow rebels he wants to believe in Kytano/Imhotep, the Goa'uld posing as the charismatic and ruthless leader of the Jaffa rebellion ('The Warrior', 518). Kytano touches a chord in Teal'c due to his alleged adherence to Jaffa traditions and values, to Jaffa pride and beliefs, especially his continued promises concerning the afterlife in Kheb. He thus conveys a sense of belonging that effectively breaks the unity of SG-1 and puts O'Neill, Jackson and Carter in the role of the 'Other'.[19] Teal'c's determination to avenge Shaun'auc's death nearly kills him twice ('Exodus', 422; 'Enemies', 501; '48 Hours', 514). He also has a hard time accepting Ishta, the leader of the women Jaffa rebels, as a warrior in her own right because it does not conform to traditional Jaffa society, which tends to be hierarchical and segregated.[20]

In contrast to Daniel Jackson Teal'c easily integrates in the military structure of the SGC; his core identity and sense of self, his individuality, remain basically untouched by his new experiences.

* * *

Every member of the flagship team qualifies in at least one aspect as the 'Other', but together they present a united front to friends and foes alike. Individuals become a team, more than a team; they act as the embodiment of the 'Earth-self', an intricate set of binary oppositions, alliances and opponents, hierarchies and democracies – a 'self' that like any other tends to define itself not by what it is but by how it differs from others, from the 'Other', and once again the differentiation between the sexes and gendered behaviour comes in handy.

'Oo yo wolin wolin we tayil' / 'The enemy of my enemy is my friend'

It's an unsurprising biological fact that virtually every culture of Earth origin SG-1 visits has two sexes, male and female. The majority of the cultures they encounter are unequivocally patriarchal. This, however, does not preclude the existence of a number of strong female characters, to name but a few: Jackson's wife, Sha're, Travell, the spokeswoman of the Tollans, the Cimmerian Gairwyn, or Hadrizar, the blind leader of the Encarans. All of them not only act out of self-preservation but are guided by a strong sense of commitment and community. They act for the good of their group and in accordance with the rules of their respective societies. When Sha're incites the rebellion of the younger generation against Ra (*Stargate*, 1994, movie), she wants to free not only Daniel Jackson from captivity but also her people from slavery. In contrast, Linea ('Prisoners', 203) stands outside any societal structure, even on the prison planet Handante. She is feared but not respected or integrated. In contrast to Samantha Carter, her intellectual brilliance is not harnessed by a sense of belonging; instead of protecting and creating she turns to destroying. One would be tempted to say that it is legitimate to challenge and even transgress bourgeois gender boundaries as long as it does not also challenge the structure of society as a whole.

* * *

Gender differentiation to a certain degree also exists in truly 'alien' civilisations and races, with the exception of the small, white-striped beings on PJ2-445 ('One False Step', 219).[21] The Nox have the classic two sexes, and seem to live in typical family units with a man, Anteus, at the head of it. They are, as Jackson puts it, 'definitively more advanced than anything that has evolved on Earth' ('The Nox', 107), technologically as well as spiritually. Just like the Tollans, they follow a non-violence policy and are rather reluctant to interact with other, less developed civilisations, but still help the members of SG-1 on numerous occasions, for instance, among others, in 'Enigma' (116) and 'Pretense' (315).

The shape shifters guiding and protecting the descendants of a tribe of 'central coast Salish Indians' in 'Spirits' (213) also have two sexes, although neither their names nor their behaviour show gender differences. In their need to shield Tonani's people from nefarious outside influences they go as far as wanting to destroy the SGC and are not bound by any treaty agreements with the Goa'uld as are the Asgard concerning planets such as Cimmeria, Katal or Earth.[22]

The little grey beings from the planet Halla[23] match the most widespread rumours concerning 'alien' life forms; Roswell comes to mind. To guide but not unduly influence the inhabitants of the protected planets, they choose the big, burly Norse gods to represent themselves – which proves the show's strange sense of humour – conveying a sense of community, honour, equality and pride.[24] The Asgard reproduce by cloning and apart from their height and slightly different facial structures there are no visible differences between them. In addition, all the Asgard that SG-1 comes in contact with are named after male Norse gods[25] – and yet there is a faint possibility to differentiate between the sexes: the voice.

When O'Neill in 'The Fifth Race' (216) travels to the Asgard planet Othala to have the knowledge of the Ancients removed from his brain, he also speaks with two of the Asgard. There is a slight inflection in their respective voices that, coupled with their differences in height, could help with sex determination. The differences become more evident when comparing Carter's dealings with Thor ('Small Victories', 401) and her interactions with Heimdall ('Revelations', 522), not least by choosing a man's voice for Thor (Michael Shanks, aka Daniel Jackson) and a woman's voice (Teryl Rothery, aka Doctor Janet Fraiser) for Heimdall.[26] Thus, after a long evolutionary process, and at first sight asexual, the Asgard as they appear to the audience are still easily sexually discernible. The same doesn't go for the 'evil' aliens SG-1 encounters.

* * *

The Replicators, the nemesis of the Asgard, were created by a 'female' android named Reese as a toy, a very independent toy. Their one and only goal is to reproduce at all costs; to do this they absorb technology, preferably advanced technology, to help their further development. They mostly appear in the form of, to quote Jack O'Neill, 'nasty techno-bugs' ('Nemesis', 322), with the ability to communicate and band together to form whatever structure they want to be. In the next stage of their development, however, they pattern themselves after their creator and take human form, including sex differences, with a man (First) followed by a woman (Second) followed by a man (Third) and so on, thus perpetuating the biblical belief of Adam preceding Eve ('Unnatural Selection', 612). They mimic human form in their quest to emulate their creator and thus emphasise the human knowledge that 'evil', that the 'Other', can take on the outward appearances of familiarity, of the 'self'.

Immune to conventional weaponry, they are even more dangerous than their less advanced brethren. Their ultimate goal has not changed but has been turned into a drive for the conquest and destruction of the universe by Carter's evil Replicator doppelgänger. 'Replicarter' disposes of Five, her creator and prospective mate, because she sees him and his unchecked feelings for Carter as weak. Her thirst for power and destruction is all-encompassing and accentuates the notion of women as the Other, thus calling to mind the mechanical woman Hel in Fritz Lang's neo-romantic science fiction film *Metropolis* (1927).[27]

The incarnation of evil is a role generally taken on by the Goa'uld and their actions speak for themselves. For millennia they took human beings from their homes and enslaved them in every way imaginable, making them believe that the Goa'uld are gods and thus to be worshipped, taking possession of their bodies, imprisoning their minds – and yet, they are neither male nor female. As Martouf/Lantesh explains to Carter, the 'symbiote does not have a gender' ('The Tok'ra I', 211). Most of them, however, have a predilection which shows in their choice of either a male or female host. Jolinar, the Tok'ra Carter was blended with, is always referred to as a 'she' because she preferred female hosts, whereas Selmak, the symbiote of Carter's father, Jacob, first is called 'she' but later her denomination changes to 'he'.[28]

Unfortunately, it isn't always this straightforward. On more than one occasion Apophis speaks of 'his queen', thus implying that there are indeed sexual differences between the Goa'uld larvae. This view is corroborated by Hathor, who calls herself 'the mother of all gods': she and others like her create the larvae. To avoid rejection she needs to incorporate the DNA, 'the code of life' of the species intended as hosts ('Hathor', 113). In contrast, the Tok'ra Malek explains to O'Neill that 'symbiote queens are able to fertilise their own eggs', some sort of parthenogenesis without the necessity to take special precautions to ensure compatibility ('Cure', 610).

The one thing a Goa'uld queen obviously does not need to procreate is another Goa'uld, thus efficiently cancelling the traditional excuse for sexual intercourse and the interaction between the sexes. They even have control over the knowledge and other character traits they pass on to their offspring (see 'Cure', 610; and 'Evolution I and II', 711–712). This goes far beyond asexuality, androgyny, or ambiguous sexual identities.

But what about the Tok'ra? Biologically they are the same species, though they are depicted as the ideological opposite, the 'Other' of the Goa'uld. This opposition is indicated by something as simple as the choice of words: whereas the Tok'ra always speak of 'hosts', Apophis and his brethren sometimes use the word 'vessel' to emphasise the host's status as an object (e.g. 'The Children of the Gods', 101).

The depth of these differences, however, is called in question during the crisis in 'Death Knell' (716). A representative of the Tok'ra High Council doubts Selmak's loyalties by insinuating that he is unduly influenced by Jacob Carter. He says that humans from Earth do not make good hosts because 'their will has not been eroded by thousands of years of slavery', thus implying that their usual hosts are easier to dominate and effectively countermanding the idea of an equal sharing.[29] Tok'ra use Goa'uld techniques and strategies in their fight against them; they mimic their enemies like the human-form Replicators mimic those whom they aim to destroy. The more desperate they become, the more elements of Goa'uld behaviour they show towards their allies, humans and Jaffa alike. Still, by attempting to have a truly symbiotic relationship with their human hosts, the Tok'ra also try to rise above the limitations of their asexual origins. It is part of their efforts to create their own notion of 'self', even though they are in danger of relapsing into 'Otherness'.

* * *

Stargate SG-1 presents a whole range of group identities, on Earth as well as off-world, most of them with at least a hint of a hierarchical structure. It also confronts individuals adhering to or being at odds with one or the other group they belong to, be it by birth or by choice, thereby creating a multi-layered network of interactions and dependencies with the possibility to accept the 'Others' as they are and be accepted in return, a 'dialectics of acceptance'.[30] Acceptance, unfortunately, is nothing more than a 'possibility'. In the day-to-day interactions group dynamics often supersede individual tendencies. Samantha Carter is a human being with high moral standards, a member of SG-1, an officer of the US Air Force, a scientist, a woman, a friend – and more often than not these roles collide even inside the protected confines of the Cheyenne Mountain Complex.

The boundaries between 'self' and 'Other' have to be newly defined in an ongoing, never-ending process. There are only two species with whom these boundaries are non-negotiable, the Goa'uld and the Replicators. Their actions alone would speak for themselves but it is their lack of sexual differentiation that firmly and irrevocably establishes them as 'the enemy', thus superseding all other differences. Reduced to the lowest common denominator, 'self' thus would be defined as gender-differentiated and the 'Other' as non-differentiated, and the danger for the 'self' rises exponentially as soon as the 'Other' begins to take on the appearance of the 'self' by taking human hosts and human form – that is, by mimicking human behaviour. This way the 'Other' is less likely to be recognised and thus more likely to infiltrate and destroy the 'self'.

Sexual differentiations, however, are not to be treated as equivalent to gender differentiations; where one is a biological fact, the Other is a historically developed, sociocultural notion. In other words: that there are men and women is a given fact and cannot be challenged; what a society makes of this fact remains open to discussion.

Notes

1   Recommended introductory reading: R. J. Ackermann, *Heterogeneities. Race, Gender, Class, Nation, and State* (Amherst MA, 1996); Mikhail M.

Bakhtin, *The Dialogic Imagination* (Texas, 1981); Tzvetan Todorov, *The Conquest of America: The Question of the Other* (New York, 1992).

2   Homi K. Bhabha *The Location of Culture* (London, New York, 1994); Homi K. Bhabha, 'Cultural diversity and cultural differences', B. Ashcroft, G. Griffiths and H. Tiffin (eds), *The Post Colonial Studies Reader* (London, New York, 1995), pp.206–209

3   To the history and social construction of hierarchical gender roles, gender and sexual identities, see e.g.: Judith Butler, *Gender Trouble* (London, New York, 1990); Nancy Chodorow, 'Difference, relation, and gender in psychoanalytical perspective', *Socialist Review*, 9, 4 (1979), pp.51–70; G. Duby and M. Perrot (eds), *A History Of Women In The West* (5 vols – Cambridge MA, London, 1992–1994); Luce Irigaray, *Speculum of the Other Woman* (New York, 1985); Thomas Laqueur, *Making Sex* (Cambridge MA, 1990); Gerda Lerner, *The Creation Of Patriarchy* (Oxford, 1986) and *The Creation of Feminist Consciousness* (Oxford, 1993); Sigrid Weigel, 'Die nahe Fremde – das Territorium des 'Weiblichen'. Zum Verhältnis von Wilden und Frauen im Diskurs der Aufklärung', T. Koebner and G. Pickerodt (eds), *Die andere Welt. Studien zum Exotismus* (Frankfurt, 1987), pp.171–199.

4   All references to the episodes will be indicated parenthetically by episode number. See the Episode guide for further information.

5   It is only in the most dire, most emotional situations they refer to each other on a first-name basis – and even then Carter has to be prompted by O'Neill to do so; see among others 'Singularity' (114), 'Solitudes' (118), 'Metamorphosis' (616) and 'Threads' (818).

6   Wilhelm von Humboldt (1767–1835) was among the first philosophers who tried to undertake a complete, scientific overview of the differences between the two sexes. It's a synthesis of contemporary knowledge in fields such as biology, medicine and anthropology, combined with secularised notions stemming from philosophy and religious dogma. See among others Wilhelm von Humboldt, 'Über den Geschlechtsunterschied und dessen Einfluß auf die organische Natur', Wilhelm von Humboldt, *Studienausgabe in 3 Bänden*, vol. 1 (Frankfurt, 1970), pp.23–43.

7   Aside from Doctor Janet Fraiser, Carter can only count on three other women when she mounts the resistance against Hathor. Teal'c, also un-affected by Hathor's mind control, also helps ('Hathor', 113).

8   As a short conversation with Daniel Jackson in 'Singularity' (114) proves, showing deep feelings obviously goes against her self-perception as a member of the military: Carter: 'I know I'm supposed to be detached.' – Jackson: 'Who said that?' – Carter: 'Sometimes I forget you're not military.'

9   As a probably unintended side effect heteronormativity is potentially neutralised and a number of alternative possibilities are opened up. The

sheer number of fan fiction texts and websites dedicated to homosexual relationships among the members of the SGC speaks for itself. The most prominent pairings are Jack O'Neill and Daniel Jackson, and Samantha Carter and Janet Fraiser. See among others Area 52 (http://www.area52hkh.net/sitemap.php) and Abydos Gate (http://stargate-sg1.hu/fanfiction/index.php).

10 My understanding of 'personal identity' is mainly based on Erik H. Erikson's (1902–1994) still-valid theory of psychosocial development. It is a combination and synthesis of a person's sense of uniqueness and personal continuity with their sexual identity and their social identity, which in turn is derived from their roles in various groups (familial, ethnic, religious, occupational, etc.) See Erik H. Erikson, *Identity and the Life Cycle* (New York, 1959).

11 To quote O'Neill after he took on the knowledge of the Ancients for a second time in 'The Lost City I' (721): 'Carter, you're one of this country's natural resources, if not national treasures.'

12 For him it is simply inconceivable that one can have 'fun' in a laboratory. To give only one example: at the beginning of 'Nemesis' (322), O'Neill wants Carter to go fishing with him, but she prefers staying on-base to analyse her naqada reactor: O'Neill : 'What I'm describing here, Carter, involves a very special element.' – Carter: 'This is fun to me, sir.'

13 'Enemy Mine' (707), combined with 'The First Ones' (408), sheds an interesting light on how inter-mediality works in the series. The incident with the naqada mine is titled after the 1985 Wolfgang Peterson production *Enemy Mine*, while the plot of the film is alluded to in 'The First Ones' when Daniel Jackson is kidnapped by a young Unas and ends up making friends with him. Compared to this kind of sophistication the repeated citations and allusions to the *Wizard of Oz* (MGM, 1939 – director Victor Flemming), *The Simpsons* (since 1989), or *Alf* (1986–1990) are child's play – if one doesn't count the marked similarities between the asteroid threatening Earth in 'Fail Safe' (517) and the 1998 movie *Armageddon* (directed by Michael Bay, with Bruce Willis and Ben Affleck), including the problems with the timer of the bomb.

14 In 'Cor-ai' (115), Jackson tries to save Teal'c's life by gradually manipulating the rules of the local judicial system, while O'Neill is ready to free his friend by the use of brute force.

15 'Chain Reaction' (415). To get General Hammond reinstated O'Neill seeks the help of ex-NID agent Maybourne, whose contacts also help him to free Carter when she is kidnapped and almost killed by Adrian Conrad and his men ('Desperate Measures', 511). O'Neill also relies on Maybourne to get the information necessary to save Teal'c when he is stuck in the Stargate ('48 Hours', 514). From a certain perspective,

one could see Colonel Maybourne as the negative mirror image of O'Neill.

16 See notes 3 and 7.

17 For instance, the accidental death of O'Neill's son Charlie serves as the trigger mechanism of his recurrent self-sacrificing tendencies and his penchant to volunteer for potentially dangerous missions. To name only two examples: the first encounter with the Replicators on Thor's ship ('Nemesis', 322) and his premeditated taking on of the Ancient knowledge depository ('The Lost City', 721–722).

18 Only with the help of his wife, Sha're, does he stay grounded in the here and now and escape the temptations of power (see 'The Children of the Gods I', 101A).

19 It also is one of the rare occasions where especially O'Neill's attitude towards alien cultures is called into question, particularly his tendency to judge them according to his own set of values: Kytano: 'Yet again you remind me that our ways are different. We should abandon centuries of Jaffa tradition and follow the ways of the Tau'ri. Which of us is arrogant?' ('The Warrior', 518).

20 In Ishta's words: 'Then you doubt our abilities? Is that what this is about? You speak of progress and shedding of the old ways and yet you still think a woman needs your protection' ('Birthright', 710).

21 Their appearance is vaguely male or, to be more precise, neuter and they are living in a symbiotic relationship with the flora of their planet, without any kind of technology. All in all they are of little consequence for the main storyline.

22 For Cimmeria see 'Thor's Hammer' (109) and 'Thor's Chariot' (206); for Katal see 'Red Sky' (505); for Earth see 'Fair Game' (303) and 'Fail Safe' (517).

23 See 'Unnatural Selection' (612).

24 See Olaf's forced conversation with Heru'ur ('Thor's Chariot', 206). The Asgard monitor but do not influence the Cimmerians' natural intellectual development. For example, Thor's 'Hall of Might' was especially designed to test moral values, such as loyalty and team spirit, as well as intellectual qualities, in order to find out if the Cimmerians are advanced, enlightened enough to see their 'gods' in their natural form.

25 Thor, Freyr, Heimdall and Loki. Just for the record: in Nordic/German mythology Heimdall is the god of light and guardian of the gods. Born of nine virginal mothers he is seen as the father of the human race and antagonist of Loki, the one foretold to bring Ragnarok, the end of the world. In the show Heimdall is a geneticist trying by legitimate means to ensure the survival of the Asgard as a race, while Loki, the rogue Asgard scientist in 'Fragile Balance' (703), abducts humans for his pointless

experiments. See among others Wolfgang Golther, *Handbuch der germanischen Mythologie* (Wiesbaden, 2003 [first edition: Rostock, 1895]), pp.191–207, 337–355, 288–292 and 321–336.

26 The creative and special effects consultants of the show not only used her (distorted) voice but also patterned the movements of 'the Asgard puppet' after her.

27 The demonisation of women is at least as old as the hierarchical sex segregation and has influenced every major civilisation in history, especially the great monotheistic religions, fuelled by a psychologically founded fear of women and their reproductive powers. See among others Karen Horney, 'Die Angst vor der Frau. Über den spezifischen Unterschied in der männlichen und weiblichen Angst vor dem anderen Geschlecht', *Internationale Zeitschrift für Psychoanalyse* 18,1 (1932), pp.5–18.

28 'And Selmak is weak. She may not have the strength to heal him' ('The Tok'ra II, 212). And in contrast, in 'Allegiance' (609), Jacob talks about his symbiote: '[T]here's no way he [Selmak] could have hidden those feelings from me.' Once again, the example recalls a race directly out of Gene Rodenberry's *Star Trek* universe: the Trill, who live in a truly symbiotic relationship with their humanoid hosts. See especially Jadzia and Eszri Dax in *Star Trek: Deep Space Nine*.

29 In the same vein Kanan has no qualms using O'Neill against his will to try and free the Lo'tar of Ba'al ('Abyss', 604). 'Cure' (610) presents another example of Tok'ra double standards. As long as they do not know the identity of the symbiote queen the Pangarans use to create Tretonin they don't have any moral objections to her enslavement. This drastically changes as soon as they are told that the queen in question is Egeria and they insist that she is to be freed immediately.

30 That's one of the key principles of 'xenology', a concept in the political sciences aimed at getting different cultures and political systems to preserve their cultural identities and yet to work together for the benefit of both. The word itself is derived from Zeus Xenios, the god of hospitality and protector of strangers. See among others L. J. Bonny Duala-M'bedy, *Xenology. Die Wissenschaft vom Fremden und die Verdrängung der Humanität in der Anthropologie* (Freiburg, Munich, 1977) and W. Schmied-Kowarizik (ed.), *Verstehen und Verständigung. Ethnologie – Xenologie – Interkulturelle Philosophie* (Würzburg, 2002).

PART 2:
THE SYMBIOTE

8

STARGÅTE AS CANCULT?
IDEOLOGICAL CODING AS A
FUNCTION OF LOCATION

GAILE MCGREGOR

When a story is translated from one medium to another – novel to stage, film to television and so on – the first question people ask is how the copy differs from the original. The second is whether the differences are good or bad. And the third is what causes the divergence – differences in vision, differences in talent or technical differences relating to medium? In the case of the television and film versions of *Stargate*, I'm going to propose that the differences – and they are considerable – relate to the context of production. *Stargate*-the-movie[1] was produced in Hollywood; *Stargate*-the-series[2] is filmed in Vancouver, Canada. The goal of this project is to demonstrate how each of these texts may be read as an artefact of its place.[3]

On the surface, there is nothing revolutionary about this project. Others have looked at similar transplantations. Jeffrey Miller, for instance, detailed the changes made to British television comedies when they were transplanted to the USA, to bring them more in line with American tastes and values.[4] The problem in the present case is the view, which has become increasingly widespread since the eighties, that there is no real Canadian 'difference' to express. There are two versions of this thesis. One is the watershed model – Canada once had a distinct culture but it has been diluted by globalisation.[5] Another, more radical, holds that, apart from a few artificially nurtured elite forms, there never *has* been any authentic Canadian culture. Not, at least, in the world of media productions. 'Though Canada has a distinctive *anthropological* culture that differentiates it from its North American neighbour,' says Richard Collins, ' … Canada has no national *symbolic* culture.'[6] How do we respond to this?

The datum most frequently cited by the no-distinctiveness camp is the fact that, based on their consumption patterns, Canadians apparently *prefer* American culture, especially popular culture, to their own.[7] As Marjorie Ferguson points out, however, consumption per se proves nothing: '[A]ssumptions about an undifferentiated global culture as a consequence of consuming the same material and symbolic goods ... [ignore] the complexity of audience engagements and constructions cross-culturally.'[8] The only way to link use to homogenisation would be to show that the client countries replicate the imported patterns when they produce for themselves. In Canada's case, this is exactly what we don't find. Despite surface similarities, numerous observers have pointed out significant differences in what Canadians *do* with American models. Take television, for instance – supposedly the most thoroughly colonised of all popular media. As far back as the eighties, Mary Jane Miller documented the Canadian preference for ensemble formats, the eschewal of moral certainties and the prevalence of open endings.[9] More recently, Bodroghkozy has anatomised the way Canadian versions of American television genres use irony and double-coding to deconstruct the American Other.[10] I myself have looked at discrepancies in the treatment of heroes, as well as at different technical usages, from blocking to cinematography.[11] There are lots of differences if you look closely enough. In the end, though, what it boils down to is the fact that, as Geoff Pevere and Greig Dymond point out in their lighthearted *Mondo Canuck*, Canadian television just 'feels' different from American television:

> While the various gatekeepers of national identity would clasp hands and moan skyward over Canada's imminent cultural obliteration, we who watched too much TV knew better. We could spot 'Canadian' in an instance, simply with a flick of the channel, and we knew it was different. We knew *The Forest Rangers*, an 'adventure' show with a polite emphasis on collective problem-solving, was different from *Lost in Space*, and we knew that *Don Messer's Jubilee* would never be confused with *The Dean Martin Show*.[12]

Despite the recent blurring of the line between what is and is not home-made (multinational production partnerships use multinational crews to produce programming for multinational markets), I would maintain that the difference Pevere and Dymond talk about still persists. A generic pulp actioner made in Vancouver *feels* different from a generic pulp actioner made in San Diego. *Stargate*-the-series *feels* different from

Stargate-the-movie. What I want to do in this chapter is to try to pin down why.

The Hollywood variant

Stargate-the-movie opens in 1928 Egypt, with the discovery of a giant circular artefact near the great pyramid at Giza. Fast-forward to present-day America. The artefact has been identified (how, we are never told) as an off-world teleportation device. A young archaeologist named Daniel Jackson is enlisted to help government scientists decipher its hieroglyphic markings. Having cracked the code, and gotten the mechanism working, Daniel accompanies the military team sent on a reconnaissance mission under the leadership of Colonel Jack O'Neil. What the explorers find at the other end of the wormhole is a desert planet populated by descendants of ancient Egyptians kidnapped from Earth and enslaved by an alien intelligence named Ra. While Daniel himself is excited at the opportunity to study this displaced slice of history, O'Neil, we later learn, has secret orders to destroy the site in order to prevent any future threat to Earth. This scheme goes awry, however, when Ra turns up and captures part of the team. The primitives having been liberated from superstition and subservience by the revelation of their birthright of freedom, the movie ends with a series of suitably pyrotectic contretemps and rescues – Ra orders an attack on the native village; a gaggle of feisty adolescents rescues the Americans; Ra calls in his air force; O'Neil goes one on one with the leader of the alien warriors; and finally, in a set piece right out of a Cecil B. DeMille spectacle, the villagers en masse come charging over the dunes to turn the tide of battle. Abandoning his plan to blow up the gate, meanwhile, O'Neil teleports the bomb into Ra's fleeing ship, which disintegrates with a satisfyingly big bang.

As will be clear from this capsule summary, this film, at least on the surface, offers a classic example of American ideology, from its emphasis on self-help through its celebration of folk vitality to its demonstration of the liberationist potential of ideas (John Stuart Mill would be proud!). Floyd Cheung sees it as the ultimate neocolonial fantasy: the Third World client country rescued from its own benighted past by the grace and might of America – Iraq or Afghanistan with a less obstreperous (and more grateful) population.[13] While interesting for its analysis of how the USA camouflages its colonial adventures by posing as the archetypal *anti*colonial torchbearer, Cheung's reading elides a few inconsistencies. Coming hard on the heels of the First Gulf War, it is hard to imagine audiences not being struck by the familiarity of those images of high-tech alien aircraft mowing down unarmed primitives. And what are we to make of the fact that, in the end, it's the Americans who have to be rescued by their supposed rescuees?

What Cheung misses are the time-specific aspects of the subtext to this film. Its overarching elements notwithstanding, American ideology is not as monolithic as it may seem. Viewed historically, what may seem like a seamless construct actually breaks down into two distinct variants corresponding to the county's two founding myths: the Garden of Eden and the City of New Jerusalem. Unable to reconcile the conflicting values implicit in these image clusters, at least since the Revolution, American culture has tended to oscillate between two mindsets that I have elsewhere labelled Primitivism and Progressivism.[14] As one might guess from these referents, a key marker for change over the past two centuries has been the shifting of the sense of identity back and forth between nature and culture. It's important to realise, on the other hand, that this isn't just about attitudes towards the landscape. Some of the diverse ways in which these polarities express themselves are shown on the chart in Appendix 1. One interesting feature of the cycle is the shift back and forth between 'masculine' and 'feminine' modes of action. Another is the oscillation between history and myth. A third, particularly pertinent to the present subject, is the recoding of the pop culture hero.[15] Almost all American heroes have *some* traits in common – they are competent aggressors; they avoid commitment; they are 'good' (although not necessarily in a conventional or social sense); they are 'winners', sometimes just morally but most of the time literally; and they are characterised by a phenomenon that I call 'hulking' – what appears to be a meek and peaceable ordinary guy suddenly finds or reveals hidden powers. Beyond these commonalities, however, these figures vary significantly according to the climate. Progressive heroes have badges, uniforms, titles, high-tech weaponry and/or institutional affiliations. Primitive heroes have personal potency and inner moral certitude. Underlying this contrast are divergent attitudes towards the relationship between self and society. The most important item on the chart for our purposes, in fact, is the opposition between anti-authoritarianism and duty in the section entitled 'Socio-political Modes'.

Why important? Viewed in retrospect, it is clear that the early nineties marked a major paradigm shift. The key text was the film *Dances with Wolves*, where the centrepiece of the narrative is the trajectory of the hero from culture to nature, from the cavalry to the Indians. Proving that *Dances* wasn't an anomaly, however, the whole landscape of pop culture in the early nineties was suddenly littered with the signs and products of primitivism.[16] The mainstreaming of black music. The obsession with mammaries. The return of the gunfighter. The new working-class comedy. *Northern Exposure. The X-Files. The Simpsons. 90210.* Particularly notable for present purposes was the reappearance in popular film and TV of the 'bad' father and his nemesis, the rebel son. It was no coincidence that in 1995, the year after *Stargate* appeared, the Oscar for the best picture went to *Braveheart*, an archetypal rebel-son movie if there ever was one. Nine years earlier, the highest-grossing movie of the year – the second highest of the whole decade – was *Top Gun*, an almost-war story about a young maverick reconciling symbolically with his dead father, and in doing so becoming part of daddy's 'team'. By the time *Stargate* appears on the scene, though, Hollywood has switched to pushing filial discontent.

Like I said – a paradigm shift.

This single fact explains many of the peculiarities of *Stargate*, the elements that mark it not just as American but as American at a particular point in time.

It explains, first of all, why the villain of choice, the Goa'uld, is the ultimate bad father – an aeons-old, all-powerful entity who not only oppresses his 'children' but steals their bodies to keep himself alive.

It explains why the centre of consciousness for the film is not O'Neil, the good soldier, but Daniel, the soft, long-haired, vaguely effeminate intellectual. And I'm not just talking about the fact that it's Daniel's insight that opens the Stargate – Daniel brings us into the story; he leads us through the wormhole; he provides the link with the primitive Others, particularly the anima figure who leads him underground to discover the lost knowledge that will take his comrades home.

It explains the negative picture we get of the military. In marked contrast to the good fathers of *Top Gun* – not to mention Cheung's neocolonial rescue fantasy – the men who mounted *this* mission are professional paranoids whose first instinct, faced with the unknown, is to destroy. It is worth noting, in this respect, the covert link that is forged between the alien and the Americans in this film. The aforementioned image of fighter planes mowing down nomads is part of it. An even greater part is the common fixation on technology and control, as symbolised by the struggle for ownership of the bomb that O'Neil has brought through the Stargate.

Last, but certainly not least, it explains the denouement.

As in *Dances with Wolves*, the resolution in *Stargate* is signalled by the 'hero's' trajectory. Reluctantly but perceptibly over the course of the mission, O'Neil shifts his allegiance from culture to nature, from violence to sentiment, from his military masters to Daniel's noble savages – and, in doing so, is saved.

The Canadian spin-off

So, how does the Canadian version compare to this?

In tackling this question, I decided to limit myself to the first season. In part this was to avoid straying too far from the formative moment in time. In larger part it was an apples and oranges issue. As the series went on, as it developed an increasingly complex history and mythology, it was less and less recognisably an extension of its back-story. In the first season, however, we pick up what are ostensibly the same characters in the same place only a year after the film action ended. The texts are *supposed* to be contiguous, in other words. Despite this, it doesn't take long to realise that there are palpable differences.

The first difference that strikes us is the different 'look' of the television version. The action in the series is more closely linked to the subterranean headquarters than it was in the film. It's where most episodes start, where theories and fixes are developed, where the characters return to regroup. But, more than that, visually and psychologically the bunker defines the *zeitgeist* of the series. This makes it significant that the set as a whole is greyer, gloomier and altogether more claustrophobic than it was in the film. Although we're technically in the same place, the sense of enclosure which is the signature of the Canadian version is diluted in the film by the fact that the rooms and tunnels are suffused by an almost glowing light. The Canadian space, by contrast, feels like, well, an underground bunker.

The visual de-intensification is further emphasised by the more 'relaxed' camerawork. In contrast to the magisterial style of the movie, the cinematography in the television series is characterised by a greater depth of field and a more evenly distributed focus. We see more of the background, and it is more fully realised. Correspondingly, we see less of the personalities. Characters are shot at longer range, and with a less intimate, less confrontational lens. Adding to the defusing effect, there are fewer of the rapid-fire shot-reverse-shot sequences that epitomise American drama, more running and panning shots. We see an interesting demonstration of this difference in parallel feast scenes in the film and the pilot ('Children of the Gods', 101A & B). In the feast in the film, which takes place during a sandstorm shortly after the Americans have arrived at the native village, the camera cuts back and forth between focal characters, generally at semi-close to close range, with the additional people in each shot blurred out to make a backdrop for the speakers. It's as if each character has to have his/her uncontested turn in the spotlight. In the feast in the pilot, which also takes place during a sandstorm, this time in the Stargate temple, the camera still follows the dialogue, but this time the majority of shots are group shots showing the focal characters embedded in a crowd of equally well-detailed individuals. The effect of this usage is to play down the autonomy and singularity of the 'stars', and focus the audience's emotional identification on the entire group. These differences could seem coincidental, except for one thing: they are typical of Canadian television – and they have specific ideological concomitants. I'll come back to this later. For now, let me merely raise the possibility that it is this technical variance which, to a very large extent, accounts for the indefinable Canadianness that seems so tangible to Dymond and Pevere.

The second difference that strikes us about *Stargate SG-1* is the absence of the tension around authority. It may not mean much that the new Jack O'Neill (now spelled with two 'l's), in contrast to the spit-and-polish movie version, is irreverent, dishevelled and not very military. This is, after all, Jack-after-metamorphosis. What is even more striking, however, is the fact that the official father figure in the series, General Hammond, is not only not a martinet but a thoroughly decent guy. Patriarchy is no longer a problem, in other words.

Equally striking is the dehierarchalisation of the relationships *between* the personae. Apart from uniforms and a rather token insistence on titles, there is little parading of military-style protocols. Except in a few rare cases where it is necessary to establish a tension between 'Washington' and the project for plot purposes, with General Hammond caught in the middle (the two-part season finale is an example ['Within the Serpent's Grasp', 121; 'The Serpent's Lair', 201]), decisions are generally made and delivered on a cooperative basis. The SG-1 team is itself a microcosm of collegiality. Corresponding to the even focus of the camerawork, rank among members is more of a convention than a function. Labour – including the labour of leadership – is divided according to skill and opportunity, not according to status. The programme is also remarkably free of American-style social stereotypes. It is interesting to compare *SG-1* with, for instance, the ostensibly similar ensemble in *Star Trek: The Next Generation*. Even leaving aside TNG's insistence on hierarchy (as one might guess from this, the series was a creature of the *pre*-primitivistic eighties), the attributes of the members are clearly cued to their 'natures', from the cerebral European captain to the geeky adolescent ensign. The women are nurturers; the blacks provide instrumentality (martial arts, technological prowess); the 'American' (Will Ryker, first officer and good son, hails from Alaska, the last frontier) is the conventional hero. On the SG-1 team there is no such predictability. Daniel is the nurturer. Sam – Captain Samantha Carter – represents 'hard' science. Teal'c, the exotic Other, is notable not for his savagery but for the formality of his manners. More to the point, they don't play consistent roles in the narrative. Narratively, no character in *Stargate SG-1* is any more likely than any other to make decisions, take action, or bring about resolution. No, I'll modify that – of the four team members, it is actually O'Neill, the conventional choice for an effectuator, who, at least in the first season, is most likely to need rescuing and least likely to play hero.

This brings me to the third and most striking difference between the film and the television spin-off. Not only is there less violence in *Stargate SG-1* (this could be explained in terms of market and/or medium), but it is notably lacking in conventional heroics. There is no doubt that the denouement in the movie is brought about by martial action. The whole thing is framed as a giant battle between good and evil. The denouements in the first season television episodes, in contrast, are more likely to be worked out in shades of grey. In an episode called 'The Nox' (107), for instance, when SG-1 insists on using military methods to 'defend' a group of friendly, peaceable forest-dwellers from Goa'uld hunters, against the express wishes of their hosts, they not only lose the battle but are responsible for endangering the life of a native child. Later it turns out that that these primitives aren't really primitive at all – or helpless for that matter. They are members of an advanced species that abhors violence and uses non-lethal techniques such as teleportation and invisibility to avoid it.

Not all the episodes are as explicitly anti-aggression as this one, to be sure. Even when the 'frame' is more in line with genre norms, however, opportunities for straightforward action are oddly infrequent. In six episodes, resolution is achieved through cracking puzzles; in five through intervention or revelation by Others; and in one by sheer accident. In four episodes, including the three-episode season finale, no real resolution is achieved at all. This last cycle apart, if we had to generalise the 'feel' of this series, we could sum it up in exactly the same terms that Dymond and Pevere applied to *Forest Rangers*: 'an "adventure" show with a polite emphasis on collective problem-solving'.[17] Very unAmerican.

Northern exposure

If the series isn't conventionally American, that doesn't prove, of course, that it is 'Canadian'. The question we need to address is: how do we establish nationality in a media text? Miller, looking at British-to-American translations, assumes that ideological differences are both transparent and transparently expressed.[18] *All in the Family* softens the intra-familial nastiness of the British original. *Sanford and Son* mutes the class markers, displacing the conflict onto race. *Three's Company* makes the women dumber and more glamorous. If this is all there is to it, we can pin down *Stargate* just from what we have already seen. *Stargate*-the-series is nicer, politer and less aggressive than *Stargate*-the-movie, just as Canada (according to popular conception) is nicer, politer and less aggressive than the USA. The lack of intensity, the reduced violence, the self-deprecating characters, the collective decision-making, the uneasiness with moral absolutes – all standard textbook stuff. Or is it? 'S. M. Lipset ... points out that there is much less emphasis in Canada on equality than there is in the United States,' notes Robert Seilor, 'and that there is a greater acceptance of hierarchical, paternalistic patterns in Canada than there is in the United States.'[19] Oops. The Lipset formula works – it's true about the acceptance of 'hierarchical paternalistic patterns' – but only to a point. What about the visual equity and governance by committee that we see in the *Stargate* television series? Perhaps Lipset was over-influenced by one phase of the American cycle. (It is notable that he did his seminal work in the sixties, another primitivistic era.[20]) Or perhaps – and this is where I put *my* vote – the link between text and world is not as direct as Seilor's content-oriented approach suggests.

Let me explain what I mean by this. The problem with focusing on the story or the characters or the explicit 'messages' in texts is that, in the world of art – and I use the term very broadly – signs aren't identical to, and in some cases have little in common with, signifieds. This axiom generates three rules. First, don't confuse apples and pictures of apples. To pick out the indicators of Canadianness in a painting or a novel, it is less useful to measure the representation against the world it depicts than to measure it against other representations. Second, be careful not to take your findings too literally. The fact that Canadian filmmakers are obsessed with losers (as one popular theory would have it[21]) doesn't mean that Canadians are all incompetent, any more than the American obsession with superheroes means that Americans are all winners. The relationship isn't that simple. Third and most important, don't cherry-pick your examples. I have claimed elsewhere that culture is like a hologram – every little piece contains the whole picture in embryo.[22] The problem is interpreting the fragmented and vestigial data – like Lipset with his half a loaf. To get at the big picture – to grasp the kind of 'large cultural system' that Benedict Anderson sees as preceding and subtending specific ideology[23] – it is necessary to spread one's net widely, both in media and in time.

What does such an analysis tell us about Canada? Although this is not the place to go into details, to understand where *Stargate* is coming from it is necessary to at least note a few highlights.

The starting place for any discussion of the Canadian sense of self is the syndrome that Northrop Frye called the garrison mentality. More than merely a pioneer's trepidation about confronting new territory, the Canadian experience, according to Frye, was predisposed by the 'shape' of the initial encounter: 'The traveller from Europe edge[d] into [the St Lawrence] like a tiny Jonah entering an inconceivably large whale.'[24] And the further they penetrated, the worse it got. Rock scarps. Swamps. Impenetrable bush. Black flies. Unlike the lush countryside of the south, this was not a land that evoked comfort, moral lessons, or memories of home. 'One wonders,' Frye continues,

if any other national consciousness has had so large an amount of
the unknown, the unrealized, the humanly undigested, so built into
it. Rupert Brooke speaks of the 'unseizable virginity' of the Canadian
landscape. What is important here, for our purposes, is the position
of the frontier in the Canadian imagination. In the United States
one could choose to move out to the frontier or to retreat from it back
to the seaboard ... In the Canadas, even in the Maritimes, the
frontier was all around one, a part and condition of one's whole
imaginative being.[25]

What this experience produced, says Frye, was a sense of engulfment, of
the over-againstness and power of the Other, so intense and terrifying
that it imprinted itself on almost everything the newcomers said or made.

Without entering the debate about the psychological plausibility
of Frye's reconstruction,[26] the second part of his thesis – about the
impact – is unarguable. Early poetry is, indeed, marked by 'a tone of
deep terror in regard to nature' (p. 225). Early painting is full of
images of separateness, alienation and beleaguerment. As art forms
become more complex, the vision becomes more elaborate but retains
much of the same implication. Well into the twentieth century, the
most common Canadian novels are either cautionary tales about the

Stargate: Film, series – the Canadian difference. Photo by Lisa Dickson.

dangers of boundary violation (sex, heroism, art, power – anything that transcends the self is seen as hazardous to the health) or life lessons on how to survive poised on the edge of Otherness (keep your head down, be passive, play possum). This doesn't mean, on the other hand, that paranoia is the whole story. Isolation is, after all, the starting point for connection. I have said elsewhere that the real project of Canadian culture is 'boundary management'. Almost from the beginning, in fact, alongside the negative trend, we find a smaller but growing number of more positive fables centring around the notion of mediation. One might call this the 'reaching out' strain in Canadian thinking – the strain that produced Confederation and the railway and eventually, way down the line, the Canada Health Act. It's a strain that grows in both size and confidence as time goes on. By the thirties, maybe even by the twenties, connection is still scary, but with proper management it is at least thinkable.

Muddying the waters somewhat, in art and literature the first evidence of this development is an increase in ambivalence. The enclosure images which are everywhere in the corpus begin to shift from cage to cave, from claustrophobic to nurturing, and eventually even to masterful.[27] Containers turn into frames. Frames become a means of controlling Otherness. The idea of community is also ubiquitous. At first it is just shorthand for safety in numbers; later it assumes more complex and ambiguous guises. Community is the ultimate container.[28] It protects the good guys and constrains the bad ones. It bestows identity. Solves problems. Marks boundaries. Regulates interaction. Domesticates heroes. Provides protection against unpredictability and excessiveness. In short, community is the modern version of the original fort in the wilderness.

During earlier periods, the message is embodied mainly in the explicit content of the art. Fictional treatments are particularly unsubtle. The individualist self-destructs; cooperation saves the day. Shortly after World War II, however, something unexpected happens. Canadian creators begin experimenting with modes and vehicles that perform as well as merely talking about mediation.[29] The trend reaches a peak concomitant with the upsurge of cultural nationalism during the sixties and seventies. One notable development was the appearance of forms that literally crossed genres: prose poems; interactive theatre; quasi-, or semi-, or pseudo-documentary film. A second was a flirtation with indirect and aleatory narrative techniques that would later be identified as an early outlier of postmodernism. A third – particularly important in commercial media such as television – was an increasing facility with techniques of double-coding (i.e., saying something while appearing to say something else, or creating a text that says different things to different readers).

This brings us back to our main topic. I said earlier that many critics believe there is no real Canadian difference to express. As Bodroghkozy points out, however, there is one thing all Canadians share – ambivalence about the entity which, with the taming of nature, has become our most significant and problematic Other.[30] Uncle Sam. George Dubya. The USA. The whole project of Canadian culture, Bodroghkozy says, is working through this ambivalence. And television is the privileged site of struggle. Why? Because the closer the danger, the more defences it triggers. Like pop culture worldwide, Canadian television exists literally in the shadow of its American Big Brother. This explains the complexity of the sleights it employs. Long viewed as epitomising conventionality, Canadian television is actually one of the most profoundly subversive forms the country has ever produced. Serial drama provides particularly salient examples. What appear on the surface to be no more than clones of American heroic fictions – cop shows, lawyer shows, science fiction shows – not only tend to undermine the standard solutions at the level of narrative (heroism *creates* problems; collective action *fixes* them) but are counter-coded at the level of technical strategy. This is where that unAmerican cinematography comes in – the long shots, the panning shots, the emphasis on background. Rather than playing up the individuality of the actors, the camera is used in Canadian television to underline the extent to which people and events are 'contained' by an ongoing network of social relations.[31]

Meanwhile, back at the bunker

Reading *Stargate SG-1* against this back-story makes it easier to understand some of the patterns we have observed. The avoidance of confrontation, for instance. Because Canadians dissociate from power, we are uneasy about those who wield it, even when they are acting on our behalf.[32] We like our heroes domesticated, socially warranted (cops, soldiers) and preferably collective. Better yet, we prefer to avoid the necessity for heroism altogether. It is not coincidental that in Canadian fiction heroes are likely to cause more harm than they cure, including to themselves. Heroes, even reluctant heroes – even when they are pushed into their roles unwittingly and unwillingly, by events or necessity – go mad, or self-destruct, or precipitate catastrophe. Not only do we fear heroes, consequently; we fear even more *being* heroes. It's as if wielding power pushes us across some dangerous line. Hence the preference for 'polite collective problem-solving'. In this context, the pacifism of *Stargate SG-1* – the aversion to direct action that seems so oddly out of step with its military subject matter – is no more than predictable.

Or is it?

Despite what I just said, if one thinks about some of the other fantasy-cum-action shows produced in Canada for an international market over the last decade – *The Highlander*; *Forever Knight*; *Kung Fu: The Legend Continues* – the eschewal of violence in *Stargate SG-1*'s first season seems, at the very least, somewhat extreme. All these programmes 'qualify' their violent heroes in various ways – with rules, with ritual, with domestic or community ties – but, the fact is, they act when they have to. And they usually have to at least once every episode. *Stargate SG-1*'s first season seems deliberately designed to avoid the necessity for this. It's interesting in this respect to note the wording of the synopsis provided on the stargatesg1 website for an episode called 'The First Commandment' (105):

> Colonel Jack O'Neill and the SG-1 team are sent through the Stargate after SG-9 is declared missing in action. When SG-1 arrives on the planet, they learn that the primitive cave-dwelling inhabitants greeted SG-9 as gods ... The problem is that SG-9 leader Capt. Jonas Hanson has taken advantage of this opportunity for power. Hanson now rules the planet without mercy ... It is clear that Hanson must be stopped, but how do you stop a god? Dr Samantha Carter, who was once romantically involved with Hanson, thinks she can reach him. O'Neill is prepared to fight his way into Hanson's compound ... But, Daniel Jackson and Teal'c may have the best solution: with the help of Jamala, one of the planet's inhabitants, they set out to show the people of the planet that Hanson's power comes from technology, not divinity.[33]

Given three alternative ways to achieve resolution – emotion, force and reason – the writer chose the one which is arguably the least dramatic, certainly (in the annals of pop television) the least conventional. During its first season, *Stargate SG-1* repeatedly made this choice.

Why? Part of it no doubt had to do with the timing. One thing the foregoing overview skipped is Canada's reaction to the Primitivism/ Progressivism cycle. Given their consumption of American culture, it would be surprising if Canadians escaped unscathed from the American schizophrenia – and they don't. Where Americans oscillate between nature and culture, however, Canadians oscillate towards and away from Americanness. Not that this should surprise us, of course. While nervous about the larger manifestations of progressivism – militarism, big business, world domination – Canadians are clearly going to be more at home in a climate that emphasises social responsibility and civic duty. More to the point, they are clearly *not* likely to be comfortable with libidinal excess, rampant individualism and youth anarchy. The upshot of this antipathy is that, the moment the teen rebel starts breaking out of the closet, Canadians start dissociating from their erstwhile good buddies. It's no coincidence that contemporary Canadian culture was literally invented during the last two periods in which primitivism peaked in the USA, the twenties and the sixties. Nor is it a coincidence, I would suggest, that a film marked so heavily by primitivism, arriving on the cusp of a just-starting-to-be-felt paradigm shift, would trigger a greater than usual reactiveness in its Canadian adapters.

In the case of this particular film, on the other hand, timing was probably not the only thing that stirred the pot. One giveaway is the fact that many of the markers we have noted are characteristic of the earlier, more radical phase of Canadian introversion, before we figured out how to connect. Thinking about the iconography, it's not hard to see why. In terms just of basic ingredients, *Stargate* is a perfect text to trigger Canadian paranoia. A whole series built around a threshold to the unknown. It's notable that the first thing they did after the Stargate was moved to Canada, so to speak, was to install a titanium iris so they could control comings and goings. But it's clear from the episodes that followed that this precaution did not eliminate the uneasiness on the other side of the screen. Taken collectively, in fact, the whole season could be seen as a cautionary tale about crossing over. Certainly, it hammers us with the message that danger is 'out there'. The pilot begins with an incursion of death-dealing aliens. The second episode has the outsiders lobbing bombs at the gate ('The Enemy Within', 102). The three-episode finale begins with a visit to an alternative universe where the Earth is in the process of being destroyed by an alien invasion, and ends with the same invasion force heading for *our* Earth.

Other episodes reinforce the sense of beleaguerment more indirectly. It's not just a matter of enemies. Over and over, what the team finds on the other side of the gate are environments inimical to life – empty worlds, dead worlds, worlds denatured by plague, war, storms, volcanoes, radiation, eternal darkness, killer cold. In some episodes there is an implication that the life-threatening Otherness is literally contagious. In 'The Broca Divide' (104), for instance, the team brings back a disease that transforms people into brutal savages. In 'Brief Candle' (108), O'Neill is infected with nanocytes that cause him to age prematurely. In other cases it is the mind that is at risk. In 'First Commandment' (105), the episode discussed earlier, it is suggested that the would-be god has been driven mad by ambient radiation. In 'Fire and Water' (112), the team is implanted with false memories. In 'Hathor' (113), an alien who came to Earth aeons ago takes control of all the men on the base by dousing them with super-pheromones.

Not all the transformations are explicitly negative, to be sure. In 'Tin Man' (117) the members of the team have their cloned consciousnesses placed in artificial bodies which are invulnerable and immortal. In 'Cold Lazarus' (106), O'Neill is replicated by an empathic crystal life form which then helps him work through a painful personal history involving the death of his son. These replications are not as benign as they sound, however. It is notable that the doppelgänger is a common motif in Canadian literature, and that it is almost always associated with loss of the self.[34] The same holds true of the *Stargate SG-1* replication episodes. In 'Tin Man', the tragedy is that the copies, who feel exactly like the originals, can never go home. In 'Cold Lazarus', it is more a case of what the alter ego represents. Almost like a warped allegory of Canadian fears, the crystal consciousness – the potentially 'us' – is one of the last surviving members of a fragile, peaceable species which has been wiped out by exactly the kind of incursion that *Stargate SG-1* anticipates. But in some ways this is a red herring. Whatever the transformation is *into*, the real fear for Canadians is that crossing the line – to heroism, to Americanisation, to other worlds – will turn us into something alien.[35] The fact that it reiterates this fear is perhaps the most Canadian aspect of this series.

Whys and wherefores

Before closing, it seems useful to anticipate some of the objections that will almost certainly be raised against the claims I have made in this paper. Even apart from the sizeable contingent who have problems 'seeing' Canadianness, sticklers are going to want to know how, specifically, these markers got into the text, especially with a production team that includes both Canadians and Americans. Others are going to ask why, if the series really is as Canadian – and as *negatively* Canadian – as I claim, it achieved such worldwide popularity.

The first question is frankly not something I can answer – not, at least, to the satisfaction of the kind of person likely to ask it. To trace specific channels of influence would require detailed ethnographic and biographical research going far beyond the scope of this chapter. And, even then, it probably wouldn't be conclusive. The kind of imprinting I am positing is to a large extent unconscious and transpersonal. That doesn't mean I can't make a few guesses. The visual distinctiveness of the series, for instance, can probably be attributed simply to the fact that most of the crew would have been trained in Canada and indoctrinated with our distinctive way of seeing/constructing the world.[36] Plot peculiarities, similarly, can probably be attributed to the Canadianness (or not) of the writers. It doesn't seem coincidental in this respect that Brad Wright, co-creator of the series (with Jonathan Glassner) and consulting producer, who wrote many of the episodes, including the tone-setting pilot plus two others in the first season, has very deep roots in Canadian television.[37] It also doesn't seem coincidental that the least Canadian episodes in the sample were written by individuals with few or no previous Canadian writing credits. 'Emancipation' (103), by long-time American television writer Katharyn Powers,[38] is a prime example. This episode, in which the SG-1 team becomes embroiled with a fanatically patriarchal warrior race reminiscent of the ancient Mongols of Earth, offers not only an anomalously clear-cut moral message (oppressing women is wrong) but an anomalously conventional martial resolution (Sam whips the evil warlord in hand-to-hand combat). It is also one of the very few episodes I have seen where Sam appears in sexualised clothing. Is that enough to prove that the author was driven by some kind of American conditioning? No – but it *is* provocative, just as the counter-coding in the Canadian-written episodes is also provocative. Ultimately, pending more research, all

I can do is to fall back on the old adage that the proof is in the pudding.

The second question is equally elusive. For one thing, one would have to answer the more basic question of whether the series is popular because or in spite of its Canadianness. To do this to any degree of scientific certainty it would be necessary to correlate ratings in all the different markets – and probably, to be really thorough, in demographics within those markets[39] – with levels of Canadianness in different episodes and seasons. Again, this is a task which is beyond the scope of the present project. More importantly, it's beyond the inclinations of the author (though, if someone took it on, I would love to see the results). In the absence of 'hard' evidence, let me offer a few speculations.

First, I should point out that, although the characterisation and general modus have remained remarkably stable, including the penchant for puzzle-solving and the sharing of decision-making,[40] *Stargate SG-1* did become less aggression-averse in its later seasons. As the team gained more experience – as they acquired technology, knowledge and allies – they also became more competent and willing warriors. They won a number of important battles. Killed off some major bad guys. They even went on the offensive from time to time. Is that why the series became more popular? Perhaps it had something to do with it. But, before we jump to the conclusion that the secret to *Stargate SG-1*'s success was in shedding its wimpishness, let me just point out that not all the changes in this series were changes away from Canadianness.

I don't have the space to get into the later plot cycles, but there are a couple of general developments that seem particularly provocative. One interesting point to note, for instance, is the fact that Earth's most important allies in the war against the Goa'uld are, in a sense, related to their enemies. First Teal'c, First Prime of Apophis, is lured into abandoning his erstwhile masters. Then SG-1 forms an alliance with the Tok'ra, a race which is biologically identical to the Goa'uld except that the symbiotes and the human hosts share the same body voluntarily. There's an interesting kind of symbolism in this progression. I talked earlier about how Canadians use culture to work through their anxieties about Otherness. If you look at landscape painting from the early nineteenth through the early twentieth century, the phases in this process stand out very clearly.[41] At first what we see are various kinds of denial strategies: avoidance (bomb the gate!); conventionalisation (bring in the military, the protocols, the iris); domestication (Teal'c, perhaps?). Somewhere along the line, though, denial becomes appropriation. Old meanings are evacuated and new meanings imposed. Containers turn into frames. Landscapes, now safely distanced, become our warrants of patriotism (think about all those Group of Seven paintings on our classroom walls.). Americans become us. Well, maybe that's going too far. But certainly American culture, duly tweaked, becomes a tool for underlining our non-Americanness. That's perhaps what the Tok'ra represent. While depicted in the series as a race of dauntless fighters, relentless in the pursuit of their evil kin, their 'natures' tell a different story. What could be more Canadian than resolving the self/Other opposition through accommodation? Add to this the fact that, increasingly over recent seasons, SG-1 has taken on a more active role as a mediator between the various warring factions in the universe, and it seems plausible to suggest that what we have seen in the development of this series is not an escape from the Canadian syndrome but a completion of it.

So does that mean that the popularity of the show is because of, not despite, its Canadianness? Obviously, anything I say here is going to be a guess. It does seem to me, though, that, in an age of economic imperialism and global terror, a series that begins by expressing a sense of beleaguerment, that works through anxieties about violence and aggression, and that promotes solutions based on reason and co-operation could have considerable attractions.

Notes

1   *Stargate*, Dean Devlin and Roland Emmerich, Roland Emmerich (MGM, 1994)
2   *Stargate SG-1*, created by Brad Wright and Jonathan Glassner (MGM, 1997–present). All references to the episodes are indicated parenthetically by episode number. See the Episode Guide for further information.
3   For a historical overview of the features and evolution of the characterising Canadian modus, see Gaile McGregor, *The Wacousta Syndrome: Explorations in the Canadian Langscape* [sic] (Toronto, 1985). For an examination of the way these propensities are manifested in contemporary popular culture, see Gaile McGregor, 'A case study in the construction of place: Boundary management as theme and strategy in Canadian art and life', *Invisible Culture: An Electronic Journal for Visual Culture*, 5 (2003), special issue on national identity, http://www.rochester.edu/

in_visible_culture/Issue_5/McGregor/McGregor.html. All unreferenced generalisations about Canadian social psychology and cultural tendencies in this chapter draw on, and are more fully explicated in, these two sources.

4   Jeffrey S. Miller, *Something Completely Different: British Television and American Culture* (Minneapolis, 2000)

5   Bernard Ostry, 'American culture in a changing world', David H. Flaherty and Frank E. Manning (eds), *The Beaver Bites Back: American Popular Culture in Canada* (Montreal, Kingston, 1993). A variation on this is the political economy maxim that, in an increasingly globalised world, popular culture is 'nothing more than a manifestation of [international] monopoly capitalism'. Aniko Bodroghkozy, 'As Canadian as possible ...: Anglo-Canadian popular culture and the American Other', Henry Jenkins, Tara McPherson and Jane Shattuc (eds), *Hop on Pop: The Politics and Pleasures of Popular Culture* (Durham NC, 2002), p.567.

6   Richard Collins, *Culture, Communication & National Identity: The Case of Canadian Television* (Toronto, 1990), p.253. Collins is an Australian, but similar sentiments have been echoed by many of our home-grown communications scholars. A typical example is Rowland Lorimer's throwaway comment in 'Letter to the editor', *Australian–Canadian Studies*, 15, 2 & 16, 1 (1997–1978), p.201: '[W]hat we Canadians seem unable to do is build a coherent and integrative mythology that is present and current throughout the land.'

7   The reason for our unpatriotic consumption patterns, says Ted Magdar, is not some kind of illegitimate imposition but the fact that 'current cultural practices have been largely accepted and internalized by Canadians themselves'. He continues: '[T]here is little evidence that Canadian popular taste differs from American popular taste. The market, in fact, provides strong evidence that Canadian and American popular tastes are extremely similar.' *Canada's Hollywood: The Canadian State and Feature Films* (Toronto, 1993), p.17. For different perspectives on this situation, see Bruce Feldhusen, 'Awakening from the national broadcasting dream: Rethinking television regulation for national cultural goals', and Paul Rutherford, 'Made in America: The problem of mass culture in Canada', both in Flaherty and Manning, *The Beaver Bites Back*. For a discussion of the impact on Canadian cultural industries, see Kevin Mulcahy, 'Cultural imperialism and cultural sovereignty: US Canadian cultural relations', *The American Review of Canadian Studies*, 18 (2000).

8   Marjorie Ferguson, 'Invisible divides: Communication and identity in Canada and the US', *Journal of Communication* (Spring 1993), pp.44, 45. In developing her thesis Ferguson builds on Tamara Katz and Eli Liebes' seminal study, *The Export of Meaning: Cross-Cultural Readings of Dallas*

(New York, 1990). Differing from a number of his contributors, Frank Manning makes a very similar argument in his introduction to *The Beaver Bites Back*. Interestingly, Manning compares Canada's ostensible assimilation of Canadian culture to the 'cargo cults' that appeared in the South Pacific a century ago as a response to colonialism. 'On the surface the cults appeared to be an escapist attempt to mimic and achieve the "cargo" that the Europeans had introduced – money, goods, technology, modernity. But on a more significant level, the cargo cults were a subversive parody of the European lifestyle' (p.7).

9   Mary Jane Miller, *Turn Up the Contrast: CBC Television Drama Since 1952* (Vancouver, 1987), especially the concluding summary in chapter 12.

10 Bodroghkozy: 'As Canadian as possible ... '

11 See McGregor: 'A case study in the construction of place', especially the section on television.

12 Geoff Pevere and Greig Dymond, 'Introduction', *Mondo Canuck: A Canadian Pop Culture Odyssey* (Scarborough ON, 1996) np

13 Floyd Cheung, 'Imagining danger, imagining nation: Postcolonial discourse in *Rising Sun* and *Stargate*', *Jouvert: A Journal of Postcolonial Studies* 2, 2, http://social.chass.ncsu.edu/jouvert/v2i2/con22.htm

14 The birth and evolution of this phenomenon is traced in Gaile McGregor, *The Noble Savage in the New World Garden: Notes toward a Syntactics of Place* (Bowling Green OH, 1988). Discussions of various contemporary manifestations may be found in Gaile McGregor, 'Cultural studies and social change: The war film as "men's magic", and other fictions about fictions', *The Canadian Journal of Sociology*, 18, 3 (1993); 'Domestic blitz: A revisionist history of the fifties', *American Studies*, 34, 1 (1993); and 'Television for an age of transition: Closet monsters and other double codings', *Canadian Journal of American Studies*, 23, 2 (1993).

15 See, particularly, 'War films' and 'Television for an age of transition'. McGregor: 'Cultural studies and social change'

16 Ibid.

17 Pevere and Dymond: *Mondo Canuck*, p.ix

18 J. S. Miller: *Something Completely Different*, chapter 6.

19 Robert Seilor, 'Selling patriotism/selling beer: The case of the "I AM CANADIAN!" commercial', *American Review of Canadian Studies* (Spring 2002), p.54.

20 The key text, which Seilor cites, is 'Revolution and counterrevolution: The United States and Canada', Thomas Ford (ed.), *The Revolutionary Theme in Contemporary America* (Lexington, 1965).

21 See Robert Fothergill, 'Coward, bully or clown: The dream life of a younger brother', Seth Feldman and Joyce Nelson (eds), *Canadian Film Reader* (Toronto, 1977). For a somewhat different reading of the 'loser'

phenomenon, see Christine Ramsay, 'Canadian narrative cinema from the margins: "The Nation" and masculinity in *Goin' Down the Road*', *Canadian Journal of Film Studies*, 8, 1 (1999).

22   See Gaile McGregor, *EcCentric Visions: Re Constructing Australia* (Waterloo ON, 1994), especially the introduction and conclusion.

23   This concept, first set out in Anderson's *Imagined Communities* (New York, 1983), was borrowed and extended by Homi K. Bhabha in *Nation and Narration* (London, 1990), p.1.

24   Northrop Frye, 'Conclusion to a *Literary History of Canada*', rpt. in Frye's *The Bush Garden: Essays on The Canadian Imagination* (Toronto, 1971), p.217. For an elaboration and reinterpretation of Frye's thesis, see McGregor: *The Wacousta Syndrome*, chapters 1–3.

25   Frye: *The Bush Garden*, p.220

26   No-distinctiveness advocates insist that, even if one could talk about a common originary experience, which they tend to doubt, there is no mechanism by which the impact could be passed from generation to generation. For a rebuttal of this argument, see McGregor, 'A case study in the construction of place'. Details on the 'markers' cited in the remainder of this paragraph may be found in the same article.

27   See McGregor: *The Wacousta Syndrome*, chapter 5

28   Ibid., chapter 12

29   McGregor: 'A case study in the construction of place', *passim*.

30   Bodroghkozy: 'As Canadian as possible … ', p.572

31   McGregor: 'A case study in the construction of place', section on television

32   See my discussion of the magician figure in Canadian literature (and life) in McGregor: *The Wacousta Syndrome*, chapter 9.

33   Sci-Fi channel, *Stargate SG-1*, 'Episodes', online (accessed 16 August 2005, http://www.stargatesg1.com/stargatehb.html

34   McGregor: *The Wacousta Syndrome*, pp.242–245

35   Ibid., pp.250–261

36   For people who are accustomed to thinking that realistic art simply depicts what is, this is a hard notion to grasp. In fact, though, there is a good deal of arbitrariness in what we choose to look at, how we frame it, and what we convey about our felt relationship to it. One example should suffice. The so-called 'CPR painters' whom the railroad sent west in the 1880s as a publicity stunt to promote the mountains included both British–Canadians and Americans. Looking at this work in retrospect, one can actually detect the nationality of the painter in most cases by the fact that the Americans typically give us a panoramic view from a raised vantage point while the Canadians typically represent the mountains – which are, after all, nature at its most majestic – in a far humbler fashion from the bottom up.

37 Wright not only worked on a number of other Canadian–made American-style fantasy action series, such as *Highlander* and *Forever Knight*, but also wrote for such classic Canadian-style Canadian shows as *Madison, Mom P.I., The Black Stallion* and *Neon Rider*. For an analysis of some of these series, see McGregor: 'A case study in the construction of place', Appendix 2.

38 Prior to *Stargate SG-1*, Powers was best known for her work on such archetypally American shows as *The Dukes of Hazzard, Charlie's Angels* and *Falconcrest*.

39 Although, again, the topic is beyond the scope of this chapter, it is interesting to consider the anecdotal evidence that the core of the science fiction fan base is made up of the so-called 'geek' segment of male adolescents, a demographic which is arguably infected with the same sense of alienation, beleaguerment and powerlessness that characterises Canadians.

40 It is notable that, over the run of the series, all the characters except Teal'c (who is already enhanced) were given a turn to acquire superior wisdom, Sam by temporarily acquiring a symbiote, Daniel by temporarily ascending to a higher plane of existence, and O'Neill by absorbing the wisdom of the 'Ancients'.

41 McGregor: *The Wacousta Syndrome*, chapter 2

9

'IT'S A ZED PM': *STARGÅTE SG-1*, *STARGÅTE: ATLANTIS* AND CANADIAN PRODUCTION OF AMERICAN TELEVISION

STAN BEELER

American television occupies a special position in the world market; it is the product of a culture that paradigmatically denies the concept of cultural imperialism despite the fact that it is the source of most of the structural norms of television produced all over the world. Television that is created by the production system in the United States is almost never developed specifically for 'foreign' markets and makes no attempt to conceal its national origins. The American market is so large in comparison to the prospect of sales in other countries that it would be impractical for US firms to develop television strictly for sale outside their national boundaries. However, as Scott Robert Olson indicates in 'Hollywood planet', 'The international market is a huge share of American movie and television profits, and more emphasis is being put by Hollywood into developing foreign markets. In fact, entertainment is the second largest US net export, after aerospace.'[1] One might wonder if these two assertions are not inherently contradictory. It is clear that US television is a cultural juggernaut that rolls over the competition in smaller national markets; American television makes no attempt to disguise the fact that it is produced in and for the US market. Yet, Hollywood is attempting to develop foreign markets. How is this possible without modifying the product for the plethora of widely varied national markets? Olson argues that the products of American studios are generic enough that they can be appropriated by almost any 'alien' culture and made to represent local goals, desires and behaviours. His argument approximates the Jungian theory of archetypes, positing that American television provides a conveniently adaptable symbol set for the rest of the world. Although, to some extent, one can agree with this assertion, it is also possible to see that American television does make some attempt to reconfigure itself to local situations and to provide clues that regional audiences may recognise as their own. Although funded by an American corporation – MGM – and initially presented on several cable networks in the United States, the *Stargate SG-1* television series provides its Canadian audience with distinctive elements that allow us to embrace the show as, at least partially, Canadian. Of course, it is clear that *Stargate SG-1* is produced with an American audience in mind, but it is also apparent that the scenery, actors, writers and crew have added a definitely Canadian aspect to the series that is obvious to an audience aware of its origins.

Since its inception in 1997, *Stargate SG-1* has been produced in Vancouver, British Columbia, allowing the show to take advantage of significantly cheaper production costs in Canada. This practice is quite common and it has – if you will pardon the *Stargate*-inspired figure of speech – resulted in a somewhat parasitic film and television industry in Canada:

> In places like British Columbia, the hybrid motion picture industry is devoted *primarily* to foreign location production. Over time, local film workers have increasingly implicated themselves in the production of Hollywood films and television productions by assuming creative roles as performers, directors of photography, assistant directors and occasionally directors.[2]

In the case of *Stargate SG-1*, the use of local talent and scenery has resulted in a series that has many of the earmarks of Canadian television. Science fiction television, unless an outright parody, rarely draws attention to the limitations of scene and setting that are unavoidable when portraying adventures on other planets. In contrast, *Stargate SG-1* often uses the tree-covered environs of the British Columbia coast as a running gag. The attention of the audience is constantly drawn to the fact that almost all planets connected to the Stargate are covered in trees and inhabited by people who speak contemporary English. This sort of self-referential humour is not to be found in more established science fiction series such as the *Star Trek* franchise. In fact, like the writers and producers of the series, *Star Trek* fans are notorious for their lack of humour when dealing with their beloved 'Enterprise'. Canadian actor William Shatner, who starred in the original *Star Trek* series, has developed a comic monologue in which he laments the deadly serious attitudes of the series and its fans.

Despite the fact that *Stargate SG-1* is about travel through space and occasionally time, and the Earth terminus of this subway to the stars is located far beneath Cheyenne Mountain in Colorado, the perceptive audience member will notice that no matter how far the Stargate team travels, the new planets usually have that rainy, heavily forested look of coastal British Columbia. Sometimes the SG-1 team finds itself in a winter setting, be it on an ice-bound planet or the caves of Antarctica, which has – strangely enough – the snowy mountainous appearance characteristic of British Columbia's world-famous ski resorts. Location shooting has a number of functions in the production of film and television, but one that fits well with the desire for Hollywood to adapt itself for foreign markets is the frisson of pleasure that comes with recognising a bit of landscape as 'home'. Lance Strate succinctly sums up the pride of place that an audience feels in 'No(rth Jersey) Sense of Place: the cultural geography (and media ecology) of *The Sopranos*':

> While there is a certain pleasure to be found in knowing that people are filming in your hometown or region (even more if you can actually observe them), the greater gratification comes from viewing the finished product, knowing that millions of other people are watching it along with you.[3]

Strate believes the sense of local colour obtained by location shooting much of *The Sopranos* in New Jersey greatly enhances the series through audience recognition of familiar scenery. For *Stargate SG-1*, *vraisemblance* in location shots is not actually an issue. The Colorado shots are mostly framed in an underground bunker, and all underground bunkers look alike; thus residents of Colorado are unlikely to be offended. The off-world shots are also relatively immune to criticism by members of the viewing audience resident on Abydos.

Of course, the concept of location in television, or, for that matter, feature films, has often been considered – more or less – a part of the general illusion. Anchoring a series in a specific place is normally accomplished through the presentation of a few establishing shots with significant landmarks, be it the Empire State Building or the Tower of London, and then filming all interior shots in studio locations in California. *Stargate SG-1* is particularly guilty of this process with the oft-repeated shot of the tunnel-like entrance to the Cheyenne Mountain Complex in Colorado. This stock establishing shot has been repeated almost as often as the magnificent gate 'kawoosh' and serves to bring the action back from its science fiction travels to other worlds and anchor it firmly on planet Earth. Once the Cheyenne Mountain establishing shot runs, the audience is signalled that the series will now take on the characteristics of a military drama – at least for a while. One of the major reasons for the use of stock establishing shots is the reduction in cost that results from shooting the rest of the production at 'home base'. Because location shooting is relatively expensive, most productions tend to exploit the establishing shot technique. Strate comments that HBO is one of the few organisations that will undertake the expense of extensive location shooting even for series such as *The Sopranos*, which is heavily dependant upon New Jersey for its local colour. As mentioned above, *Stargate SG-1* has a slightly different problem with location shooting; its audiences tend to seek the unfamiliar. For this reason, in science fiction television the expense of location shooting is often replaced by the expense of elaborate computer graphics, and *Stargate SG-1* is no exception. The series combines a substantial number of 'location' shots in the forests, mountains and gravel pits in and around the city of Vancouver, with computer graphics of spaceships, floating cities and the Egyptian-inspired architecture of the Goa'uld. This is often accomplished with overlays, which place the fantastic computer-generated images on top of the natural beauty of the Canadian coastal mountain range, resulting in the happy combination of scenery recognisable by the regional audience and 'really neat alien stuff' that pleases the general science fiction fan.

Given that *Stargate SG-1* is so successful at visually presenting its Canadian elements in a science fiction framework, one may wonder why the Vancouver industry has not simply divorced itself from controlling interests in the United States. In *Hollywood North*, Mike Gasher argues that the development of indigenous film and television industries centred around location shooting for film companies from the US is a normal part of the globalisation process that has taken place in many industries:

> The perpetual flow of people, capital, goods, services, and images that characterize globalization carry significant implications for how we experience and imagine place, how we define community, and how we constitute identity. Globalization renders actual borders more porous and metaphorical boundaries passé.[4]

Stargate SG-1 is a perfect example of this kind of cultural globalisation that flies in the face of the accepted paradigms of a national film and television industry. On one level, the essentially Canadian nature of the production is effaced through the dramatic fictions of American and off-world locations. However, if one attempts to transcend this superficial level of perception, one quickly becomes aware that the product is essentially different from a series conceived and produced within the studio culture of Hollywood. This sense of the Canadian nature of the series is not only produced through the landscape of external shots, as the above quotation suggests, but is also a product of the character of writers, technicians, directors and actors. For example, one of the most distinctive components of television produced in a Canadian environment is the unique application of a self-deprecating sense of humour. This may be the product of a national identity influenced by a powerful, yet quite similar culture so nearby. Canadians often react to American dominance with a frank admission of the inequity of the situation and a wry smile combined with fierce pride in 'Otherness'. *Stargate SG-1*'s reliance on Canadian actors, writers, directors and production crews has resulted in a perceptible sense of ironic reflection on its status as a genre production – an admission that it stands low on the scale of cultural products and national pride. After all, would the Canada Council[5] fund a production that does not broadcast its Canadian nature from the masthead? This recognition of genre status often leads the writers to refer self-reflexively to other science fiction – both film and television – as well as to aspects of *mise-en-scène*, cast and plot that are directly related to the genre of science fiction.

Stargate SG-1's overt references to its status as a genre production are often combined with sly references to the specifically Canadian elements of the series, a technique that tends to break down the narrative illusion that the series is by, for and about Americans. For example, the Canadian actor Patrick McKenna, who initially appears in 'The Other Guys' (608)[6] as Dr Jay Felger, becomes a focus of Canadian-style humour. In his second appearance in the series in 'Avenger 2.0' (709), his character accidentally reveals that he has brought along a rucksack stocked with duct tape. A non-Canadian audience would not find this trivial incident significant, but to Canadians McKenna is famous as the co-host of the extremely popular *Red Green Show*.[7] This parody of the Canadian staples of masculinity, hunting, fishing and handyman television focuses on a character (Steve Smith as Red Green) who believes that all construction at his hunting lodge – perhaps even in the rest of the world – can be accomplished with the aid of a few rolls of duct tape. Shortly before 'The Other Guys' was aired, a feature-length film based on the characters of the *Red Green Show* entitled *Duct Tape Forever*[8] appeared in theatrical release. When McKenna drops a roll of duct tape into his pack before going off-world on a potentially dangerous mission there is a level of Canadian reference that breaks the boundaries of the narrative illusion – at least for the Canadian audience. Of the two credited writers of this episode, Paul Mullie and Joseph Mallozzi, only Mallozzi is Canadian by birth. However, the audio commentary by Amanda Tapping and director Martin Wood on the DVD edition makes it clear that this element is one of the many ad lib features of McKenna's performance. Tapping, in fact, makes a point of explaining the significance of this Canadian-specific reference to the American audience of the voice-over commentary.

There is some evidence to suggest that the series producers understand that the Canadian-specific elements of *Stargate SG-1* have become an integral component of its overall audience attraction. For example, Martin Wood mentions in his commentary that internet fans do not react positively to 'stand-alone episodes' like 'Avenger 2.0' because they take away from the central narrative of the series. Nevertheless, Wood and Tapping agree that the humour provided by McKenna and fellow Canadian David Hewlett, who plays Dr Rodney McKay in *Stargate: Atlantis*, is an important component of the series as a whole. In the commentary to 'Avenger 2.0' Wood states: 'Patrick McKenna, David Hewlett, these are characters that when they come in they inject something *Stargate* needs. *Stargate* needs that kind of character. David Hewlett does the same kind of thing.' However, he then goes on to say: 'You couldn't see a Felger character in every episode ... ' Tapping backs him up and they both agree that a comedic character of that sort would lose effect if overused. The irony of this is that Hewlett's character, although a comic staple, was reintroduced two years later as a much-beloved regular on the *Stargate SG-1* spin-off, *Stargate: Atlantis*. Apparently the humorous element was not too much when it was no longer in competition with Richard Dean Anderson's wry comic talent.

The use of Canadian-style humour in *Stargate SG-1* is particularly obvious in episodes featuring the comic talents of Patrick McKenna and David Hewlett, although it is not always directly a part of their dialogue. In 'The Other Guys' McKenna is introduced as a brilliant, but annoying scientist who goes along with SG-1 on a field trip off-world accompanied by his colleague Simon Coombs (John Billingsley).

Billingsley is immediately recognisable to fans of science fiction television as Dr Phlox on *Star Trek Enterprise* and the writers of 'The Other Guys' cannot resist inserting an overt reference to this role. When Felger urges Coombs to accompany him on an ill-conceived mission to rescue the SG-1 team from their imprisonment on an orbiting Goa'uld spacecraft, Coombs replies that '[W]e might as well be wearing red shirts … ' (608). Although Felger pretends to 'not get it', most science fiction fans will understand that this is a reference to a plot cliché of the original *Star Trek*[9] series. In the *Star Trek* 'universe' a red shirt was an indication of lesser rank, and whenever someone was killed on an 'away mission' it was one of the incidental characters wearing a red shirt. With this brief reference Billingsley has broken the narrative illusion of the episode, refers to his own status as a recurring character on the current incarnation of the *Star Trek* franchise, and points out the status of Felger and Coombs as potential cannon fodder.

In '48 Hours' (514) Dr Rodney McKay is introduced. Dr Rodney McKay is a brilliant, but quirky scientist who is called in to assist Samantha Carter with a problem with the Stargate. The title of the episode is derived from the 48-hour time limit that has been placed upon the technical mission to retrieve Teal'c from a malfunctioning Stargate.

Stargate comes to Canada. Photo by Lisa Dickson.

The technical problem serves only to reintroduce the fifth-season plot thread focusing on the conflict between the Air Force administration of the Stargate programme and the fictional Black-Ops organisation designated NID. One of the less endearing qualities of *Stargate SG-1* is the desire to introduce an element of political intrigue into the ongoing story arcs. Although there is a science fiction element underlying the plot of '48 Hours', the primary focus is on the conflict with outside forces seeking control of the gate programme. Rodney McKay serves as representative of these outside forces, and Samantha Carter represents the familiar group of heroes. The conflict also extends to sexism as McKay is contemptuous of Carter's intellectual abilities. In this initial appearance there is no hint of McKay's Canadian origins. This rather dark episode serves to introduce Hewlett's character in an extremely negative fashion.

The next time that McKay appears is in the first episode of season six, 'Redemption Part 1' (601). McKay returns to Stargate Command in order to assist Carter in defending against a Goa'uld attempt to sabotage the Earth Stargate. Naturally, his assistance is not particularly welcome. The voice-over commentary points out that, although everyone in the audience hates the character McKay, the entire cast loves the actor David Hewlett. He returns in 'Redemption, Part 2' (602) and the character starts to develop some positive aspects through revelations concerning McKay's childhood and his admission of admiration for Carter's scientific abilities. This slow progression from a negative character to a figure of comic relief occurs over the course of seasons five through eight and culminates in a reformed McKay who is a suitable primary character in the spin-off, *Stargate: Atlantis*. In season eight of *Stargate SG-1* McKay appears in the final two episodes of the series, 'Moebius Part 1' (819) and 'Moebius Part 2' (820), as the lead scientist for the Stargate project in an alternate reality created by a time travel error on the part of SG-1. In these two episodes he reprises his initial representation as arrogant and sexist, but the impact of this negative representation is lessened by the fact that McKay is actually a much more sympathetic regular in *Stargate: Atlantis*, which was running in parallel with *Stargate SG-1*'s season eight. Both Carter and Daniel Jackson are presented as ineffectual nerds in the alternate reality of the two 'Moebius' episodes. It is interesting to note that McKay is never revealed as a Canadian in his role in the original *Stargate SG-1* series. He is generally presented with no overt national identity and therefore is subsumed under the general American identity of the cast of the series. This changes significantly in *Stargate: Atlantis*.

McKay, in his more sympathetic role as chief scientist in *Stargate: Atlantis*, more or less takes over the function Carter fulfils in the first eight seasons of *Stargate SG-1*. McKay's transition to *Stargate: Atlantis* also entails his 'outing' as a Canadian. In the series pilot 'Rising 1' (101) McKay is asked to explain to Jack O'Neill his theory of powering the Stargate with a device called a Zero Point Module (ZPM). McKay refers to this device as a Zed P M, which confuses O'Neill until he is told by Daniel Jackson that McKay is Canadian. (One of the differences between Canadian English and American English is that Canadians refer to the last letter of the alphabet as 'zed' while Americans pronounce it as 'zee'.) O'Neill murmurs a sympathetic 'I'm sorry' in the tone of one who has heard that a colleague suffers from an unfortunate infirmity. A Canadian audience will recognise this as a cliché of American response to Canadian identity.

'Rising 1' elaborates upon the plot structures representing political struggles for control of the gate technology in a way that allows for a more Canadian approach to a project. One of the more common representations of Canadian national identity is that Canada is a mosaic made up of many founding nationalities. This is presented in contrast to the American image of a melting pot which overrides the immigrant's original nationality with a new, better, nationality. Unlike the simple black and white representation of *Stargate SG-1* in which the evil NID struggles to wrest control from the heroic Air Force, *Stargate: Atlantis* has a more diverse presentation of the administration of a complex enterprise. The expedition to the Pegasus Galaxy is under the command of a civilian diplomat, Dr Weir (Tori Higginson), and is comprised of a multinational force, all of whom wear their nation's flags prominently displayed as arm patches on their uniforms. One might consider this to be an example of Hollywood striving for an international audience in a relatively subtle fashion or as an example of a Canadian paradigm in action. Naturally, the expedition leader and the chief military figures are represented as Americans, but many of the more important figures are from other countries. McKay's role develops as a rather overcautious, self-aggrandising figure of humour who is, nevertheless, a decent human being underneath it all. His comic talents are best displayed in dialogue with John Sheppard (Joe Flanigan) and Dr Carson Beckett (Paul McGillion), a Scot, who is, ostensibly, a neutral third party, neither

American nor Canadian. The international face of *Stargate: Atlantis* can be perceived in more than one way. It certainly allows for the series to relate to a more diverse, worldwide market. However, it might also be a way in which the Canadian members of the production crew can assert their political notions of internationalism.

In 'Hide and Seek' (*Atlantis* 103) there is another subtle reference to Canadian culture and American reactions to it. John Sheppard is recounting the plot of the horror film *Friday the 13th* to a group of alien children. When he says that the terrifying murderer is wearing a hockey mask, the children stop him and ask what that might be:

> Sheppard: Hockey's a game. The guys
> skate around the ice and try to put a puck
> in the net. The goalies wear masks! It's
> really [pause] scary.
>
> Children: Tell us more of this game. Can
> we play it?
>
> Sheppard: Actually, I don't really see the
> attraction. Now football. Ha ha. Football's
> a real man's sport.
>
> ...
>
> Sheppard: Listen, Teyla. Don't tell McKay
> what I said about the hockey not being a real
> man's sport. It's a Canadian thing. They're
> a little touchy about it.

Later, McKay, Sheppard, Teyla and Ford are watching a recording of a classic football game in which Doug Flutie[10] is instrumental in leading his team to victory. When Ford indicates that he won the Heisman Trophy that year, McKay comments, 'And then went to play in Canada.' Teyla responds with a question: 'He played hockey too?'

To an American audience this probably does not indicate much more than a simple preference for one sport over another; to a Canadian, Sheppard's football-over-hockey stance is an instance of an American dismissing a central facet of Canadian culture. *Stargate: Atlantis* has affirmed its Canadian identity in an oblique fashion as subtle as the pronunciation of a single letter of the alphabet. The recording of a football game that Sheppard chooses to bring with him,[11] which is, as Dr Weir points out, his only item of personal baggage, is significant in a metaphorical sense on more than one level of interpretation. Sheppard believes that the game is a parallel to the Atlantis Expedition in that it represents a desperate, yet ultimately successful effort on the part of one team: '[A]gainst all odds ... It's the biggest Hail Mary in human history!' (*Atlantis* 103). A Hail Mary pass is a long forward pass in which the football is thrown as far as possible into the opposing team's territory. It is usually performed in desperation when other, less risky, strategies are not possible. The parallels with the Atlantis Expedition are obvious. On the other hand, McKay's short comment about Doug Flutie's career is less transparent. Flutie was born in the United States and, although at first successful in his homeland, did not truly come to his full potential until he was forced to move to Canada after a series of problems with American teams that led to a sharp decline in his career prospects.[12] He is something of a hero to Canadian football fans and is the subject of a song by the Canadian rock band Moxy Früvous.[13]

For this reason McKay's comment about Doug Flutie may be interpreted as something of a metaphor for the American television industry: successful in its own country and then moved to Canada for economic reasons.

It is clear that subtle aspects of national identity and sense of place for *Stargate SG-1* and *Stargate: Atlantis* are strongly influenced by the series' Canadian location and staffing. It is also obvious that the highly visible superficial layer of nationality of these shows is eminently American; the heroes are from the United States and the Earth-based locations are clearly labelled American. The economic and social impact of this hybrid nature is difficult to determine. *Stargate SG-1* has never achieved the runaway economic success of Chris Carter's *The X-Files*,[14] another US production initially filmed in Canada. Yet, like *The X-Files*, it has maintained a steady audience for nine years. Moreover, its spin-off, *Stargate: Atlantis*, appears to have 'legs' and is going into its second broadcast season with a considerable measure of success. A Canadian nationalist might point to the common element of Canadian location as the source of the long-term success of both series; after all, it was not long after the *X-Files* moved to Los Angeles that it was cancelled. Personally, I will reserve my judgement until a few more seasons have appeared.

Notes

1 Scott Robert Olson, 'Hollywood planet', Robert C. Allen and Annette Hill (eds), *The Television Studies Reader* (New York, 2004), p.115

2 Mike Gasher, *Hollywood North: The Feature Film Industry in British Columbia* (Vancouver, 2002), p.9

3 Lance Strate, 'No(rth Jersey) Sense of Place: The cultural geography (and media ecology) of *The Sopranos*', David Lavery (ed.), *This Thing of Ours: Investigating the Sopranos* (London, New York, 2002), p.180

4 Gasher: *Hollywood North*, p.14

5 'The Canada Council for the Arts, reporting to Parliament through the Minister of Canadian Heritage, is a national arm's-length agency which fosters the development of the arts in Canada through grants, services and awards to professional Canadian artists and arts organisations, as well as administering scholarly awards, and having under its aegis the Public Lending Right Commission and the Canadian Commission for UNESCO' (http://www.canadacouncil.ca/aboutus/)

6 All references to the episodes will be indicated parenthetically by episode number. See the Episode guide for more information.

7 *The Red Green Show*, executive producers Dave Smith, David C. Smith, producers Steve Smith, Max Smith (DVD Acorn Media 2003, 1991–)

8 *Duct Tape Forever*, directed by Eric Till, written by Steve Smith (DVD Video Service Corp. 2003, theatrical release 2002)

9 *Star Trek*, executive producer Gene Roddenberry (Desilu/Paramount, 1966–1969)

10 'Doug Flutie, born October 23, 1962 is a fan-favorite quarterback who has played professionally for 19 years, appearing in the United States Football League, the National Football League, and the Canadian football league. He is the older brother of the CFL's all-time reception leader Darren Flutie. He has an autistic son, Doug Flutie Jr. in whose name a foundation dedicated to autism research has been established.' online. (accessed 30 July 2005, http://www.dougflutie7.com/index.php).

11 This game took place in 1984 between Flutie's team, Boston College, and the University of Miami. Because it was broadcast nationally on the day after American Thanksgiving, it received a lot of public attention and greatly raised Doug Flutie's profile. online (accessed 30 July 2005, http://www.dougflutie7.com/index.php).

12 'Following his college career, Flutie was projected to be selected in the top three rounds, but signed with the New Jersey Generals of the USFL for a record 6 year, $8.3 million contract. At the time, it was the richest rookie contract in any sports league. Flutie played one season in the USFL before the league folded in 1986.

With his USFL experience under his belt, Doug signed on with the 1986 Defending Super Bowl Champion Chicago Bears and played sparingly before playing for the New England Patriots from 1987–1989. Unfortunately, Doug was never truly given the chance to showcase his talents, despite accumulating a winning record as a starting quarterback at the time.

In 1990, with his professional football career in jeopardy, Flutie travelled north to play for the CFL's BC Lions. He performed very well for the Lions in 16 games that season. During his second season at the helm of the Lions, Flutie began re-writing the CFL record book, compiling of the most prolific seasons in professional football history and setting the following CFL records: 730 pass attempts, 466 completions and 6,619 yards. He also earned his first of six Most Outstanding Player Awards following the 1991 season.' online. (accessed 12 August 2005, http://www.cfl.ca/index.php?module=ContentExpress&func=display&ceid=598).

13   'Doug Flutie Song' by Moxy Früvous. online. (accessed 12 August 2005, http://www.fruvous.com/lyr-set2.html#doug).

14   *The X-Files*, executive producer Chris Carter (20th Century Fox Television, 1993–2002)

10

SELLING THE STARGÅTE: THE ECONOMICS OF A POP CULTURE PHENOMENON

JUDITH TABRON

As fans we have an odd relationship to capitalism. The books, movies and television shows that inspire us develop their fandoms because they tell stories that extend beyond their own boundaries. But the stories exist first as products, mass-produced, broadcast or distributed in order to make money for their producers. As fans we tend to be uncomfortable about our alter egos as customers. But we might as well give it up. We wouldn't have the tales we love if they didn't make someone money.

In fact, we owe the continued existence of our stories to their continued ability to make money. Even a fantastic television show, such as Joss Whedon's *Firefly*, can be cancelled almost immediately after its debut. Shows that have survived for several years, with contracts for production, such as Rockne O'Bannon's *Farscape*, can be cancelled. There is no point in its life cycle where a television show is 'safe', although arguments can be made that, when a show enters contention for the longest-running show in its format, it has earned a little stability.

But how does a show such as *Stargate SG-1* arrive at the point where it is contending with *The X-Files* for longest-running American sci-fi show of all time? *Stargate SG-1* has never had a gay episode; it has never had an abortion episode. In fact, it has never had any politically controversial episodes at all. It has no overarching storyline, little sex, and the babies born on it have all been to minor characters. It just had its first wedding, in its eighth season, and it was not the sort of wedding with any product tie-ins or media blitz. In short, the show has never generated any of the sort of water-cooler buzz that traditionally accompanies hit television shows.

Until recently. And now, the water-cooler buzz is about *Stargate*'s longevity. It is succeeding through success. Because what it *does* have is a very solid position in both basic cable and syndication, eight years (soon to be nine) of episodes in the can, and an enviable franchise market position. Buzz is building on this television show because after eight years it's still on the air, still delivering respectable ratings, and now with its spin-off, *Stargate: Atlantis*, it's delivering the kind of franchise success that ought to have the *Star Trek* folks taking notice.

Fans tend to point to the interesting combination of history and fantasy at the core of the show's fictional universe. Or the excellent writing and direction by some of the show's notable creators (Peter DeLuise, Robert Cooper, Jonathan Glassner and Brad Wright are among my favourites). The special effects are often excellent, on a par with those of major motion pictures. And primary stars Richard Dean Anderson, Michael Shanks, Amanda Tapping and Chris Judge are clearly fine actors as well as some of the hottest people on television.

And yet, these characteristics don't really distinguish the show from other genre shows such as *Farscape*, *Babylon 5*, *Buffy the Vampire Slayer*, or the *Star Trek* shows – none of which has lasted nine seasons. It may also be worth noting that *The X-Files*, which holds the record for longevity in this category, featured some great writing and excellent actors but was never known for the coherence of its central mythology and hardly depended on special effects. *The X-Files* did create a lot of water-cooler buzz – the sort *Stargate SG-1* has never created.

The qualities fans tend to appreciate in their television shows aren't necessarily what make those shows financially successful. Obviously, there's no formula to financial success for a television show. But there are some rules of thumb that it helps to follow, and *Stargate SG-1* has followed them in some interesting ways. At the same time the show has managed to benefit from the vertical market amalgamation and corporate globalisation that have dominated the television industry over the last decade.

While there is not space in this chapter to examine these developments in the television industry completely, it may be observed that, during the decade or so that *Stargate SG-1* has been in production, the cable television industry has been a collection of fast-moving pieces in the game of global communication markets. Deregulation in the United States has led giant corporations such as Sony and Viacom to buy as many channels of distribution as possible. Since it makes no competitive sense to buy multiple distributors in the same channel, the corporations build 'vertical' organisations with means of distribution in most major media modes. One corporation will own a television and movie production studio (these already tended to be related companies, for historical reasons)[1] as well as a set of cable television channels and other means of distribution for associated materials such as music, games and DVDs.

At the same time, some US regulations on international corporations have relaxed, and some media conglomerates are finding ways around them. Sony, for instance, has long been prevented from buying television networks in the US, but in 2004 finally acquired MGM, *Stargate SG-1*'s distributor. At the same time, developing countries all over the world are building their own telecommunications infrastructures, and they are interested in acquiring content to broadcast, as it is often cheaper to buy content than to produce it.

This has resulted in a global media structure that values some specific qualities in television shows. They should translate culturally, so that they can be sold overseas. At the same time, television shows can't be too time- or location-specific. Shows might be sold to multiple markets immediately, or over years; it may be tougher to sell material that looks 'dated'. They should be able to be sold piecemeal. If selling the show requires that it be bought in its entirety, that may result in lower profits than if its owner can sell it in usable pieces over time. Ideally, for a media reseller, the episodes of a television show should be able to be seen in any order, over and over, infinitely into the future.

Purposefully or accidentally, *Stargate SG-1* has several features that makes it perfect for this new media market. It is an action show, and action travels well internationally. Because its primary action, travelling to new worlds through the Stargate, is operated by a military organisation, most of the characters are military, and much of the military setting, including props and costumes, therefore both translate cross-culturally and do not become dated. In addition, various directing techniques, such as the establishing shot, also add to the timeless quality of the show, helping it to translate internationally and age well. And perhaps most importantly, the show has primarily had a series rather than a serial format, which is to say that, for the most part, each episode is a stand-alone story, easily viewed out of order, and wrapped up within the hour.

A brief examination of each of these elements will demonstrate how each contributes to *Stargate SG-1*'s financial success.

To producers, a well-made action show – with lots of guns and explosions – is money in the bank. In his 1999 Foreword to *Consuming Environments: Television and Commercial Culture*, George Gerbner quoted one television producer on international sales:

> Syndicators demand 'action' (the code word for violence) because it 'travels well around the world,' said the producer of *Die Hard 2*. 'Everyone understands an action movie. If I tell a joke, you may not get it but if a bullet goes through the window, we all know how to hit the floor, no matter the language.[2]

Gerbner goes on to point out that the largest portion of the US export in television programming is made up of its most violent programming. As the editors of the book go on to demonstrate, shows that feature violence actually get lower ratings in the US than other types of shows, '[y]et producers continue to manufacture them for first run on the domestic market because, with their generic plots, they sell better overseas than situation comedy or drama, and export revenues more than supplant revenue loss caused by lower ratings in the United States'.[3] In other words, the shows' global marketability is more valuable than its advertising revenues in the United States alone.

Stargate SG-1 is certainly an action show and features the requisite number of guns and explosions. And yet, because of its fantasy setting, the guns are often the alien equivalent of ray guns, and the violence looks like what one might see in an action show from the eighties such as *The A-Team* or *MacGyver* rather than the realistic violence of one of today's shows such as *The Shield*. The cartoony, fantasy quality of the violence on *Stargate SG-1* may owe something to Richard Dean Anderson, the show's star and one of its executive producers, who also starred in *MacGyver*, which was known for its anti-gun stance as well as its exciting action sequences and which is also very popular in syndication and international sales.[4]

The particular quality of the violence is only one of the show's narrative elements that is open to widely different interpretations. *Stargate*'s violence could be considered either realistic or fantastic, depending on the point of view from which one examines it. As a narrative element there is a great deal of play in the way the show presents it. It is fantastic in the sense that major characters often survive mortal wounds, yet realistic in the sense that the American airmen carry P90s. The audience's probable familiarity with the show's commonest narrative elements, such as soldiers, rebel fighters, galactic overlords and ray guns, and the audience's opportunity to value such narrative elements in their own way may well give *Stargate SG-1* what media studies researcher Scott Robert Olson calls 'transparency'. Transparency, says Olson, is 'the capability of certain texts to seem familiar regardless of their origin, to seem a part of one's own culture, even though they have been crafted elsewhere'.[5] What makes a text internationally popular, according to this line of research, may be its ability to allow local values and local archetypes to be imprinted upon it. While the show is clearly an American show of the late twentieth century, there seems to be narrative space for non-American audiences to watch the show differently. Their (many) tale(s) of soldiers and ray guns may not be the same as the American tale of soldiers and ray guns, but all the tales are embodied in the same product, a television show which can be marketed to all audiences and interpreted in various ways. What looks to American audiences like eighties fantasy violence may be more culturally transparent to other audiences than something more modern and more culturally specific.

Also a hold-over from the eighties is the show's use of establishing shots, a visual storytelling marker that is probably very familiar to international audiences of those older shows. Establishing shots are a visual shorthand that most current television viewers understand instinctively. If a stationary camera shows us the entrance to the Stargate Command (an unprepossessing hole in a mountain, guarded, with chicken wire, and military vehicles both going in and out), we automatically know where in the story's world we are.

Viewers might not even realise how old-fashioned this visual shorthand is. They recognise it; they're comfortable with it. They don't equate it to their experiences seeing similar scenes in action adventure shows of the seventies or sitcoms of the nineties. But the establishing shot convention does add to the timeless quality of the show. It is used so often that it might seem excessive to modern American audiences. In reruns, a modern viewer may react negatively to the many, many uses of establishing shots in an eighties action show such as *Scarecrow and Mrs King*,[6] where they provide establishing shots at almost every scene change – sometimes, a cynical viewer might say, in lieu of a plot that might indicate more clearly where the viewer was and what was going on. Modern viewers' awareness of the establishing shot is only foregrounded when a show foregrounds it, which is almost never. A recent episode of the sitcom *Scrubs*, 'My Life in Four Cameras',[7] was about the contrast between the life of the doctors in *Scrubs* and the easier, more upbeat lives of people in more traditional sitcoms; an external establishing shot of the Sacred Heart hospital on that show actually jolts the viewer out of his or her complicity with the convention and makes the convention look old-fashioned for the purposes of contrast to the camera conventions of the current show.

But while it tends to be used more sparingly these days, the establishing shot is still used, and often to provide an emotional punctuation to a scene as well as just a visual setting shorthand. *Babylon 5*[8] uses the convention to indicate scene changes as its galactic story bounces from the Babylon 5 space station to Earth to Mars to alien planets. *Angel*[9] uses establishing shots not just to identify that a scene has changed to Wolfram & Hart's law offices, but also to say that those law offices are fundamentally evil; the evil is visually indicated by the dark, brooding corporate appearance of the building. *Stargate SG-1* uses the establishing shot of the Cheyenne Mountain base far more than a modern viewer would expect and more than it probably needs to if its sole goal is to remind us where we are in the story. On *Stargate SG-1*, this repetitious establishing shot reminds us that this is a story set in a military world, but it also reminds us that this is an old-fashioned television series, one whose conventions we can understand – a soothing feature in a sometimes complicated sci-fi story.

And – this is particularly important in international markets – it is *because* the establishing shot device is so old-fashioned that it can be marketed almost anywhere and understood. Non-US markets that have bought television programmes from the US for the last 30 years have educated their viewers in this convention. It translates cross-culturally without language barriers, just like the military uniforms and the violence. Without jarring their awareness of the show, the convention draws the viewers in and locates them, a very useful technique on a sci-fi show that might otherwise seem too bizarre, particularly for viewers who don't usually watch sci-fi shows.

And because the device is a little old-fashioned, it adds to the timeless quality of the show. One of the things that makes a show popular can be the way it taps into current trends in fashion, politics, or pop culture; but shows that depend heavily on being up to the minute with fashion, politics or pop culture age badly. In addition to the timelessness of the military clothing and the sets, the establishing shot could be a from a show produced any time in the last thirty years – or the next 30. Because it is not cutting-edge, it does not age.

Stargate SG-1's establishing shots have a very useful narrative purpose on a show where the characters might travel between several locations on Earth and several locations off Earth all in the same 45 minutes. In an episode where the action flips back and forth between Earth and space, the establishing shot might be used sparingly or not at all ('Tangent', 412),[10] whereas if action is flipping back and forth between the SGC and, say, Russia the establishing shot helpfully indicates which Earth-bound location we're in ('48 Hours', 514). The familiarity of the establishing shot can even help to create tension: when it's obvious that what's at stake is the safety of the SGC itself ('Foothold', 314; 'A Matter of Time', 215), the establishing shot reminds us of that stake and heightens our awareness that it is in danger.

And yet – and this is not an inconsiderable point – the establishing shot costs nothing. It is canned, reused over and over again – indeed, it would have to be in order to be, by definition, an establishing shot. If it looked different each time it appeared, it would not have the same visual shorthand effect. While a very long establishing shot would be too noticeable, it can vary in length, and it adds nothing to the cost of the episode. It calls upon viewers' already established familiarity with television conventions to convey information to them seamlessly, cross-culturally. And it does it for free.

The show's careful use of the establishing shot is only one of a number of aspects that keep the show visually consistent and relatively timeless. As previously mentioned, the military uniforms are immediately visually identifiable anywhere in the world and also do not age. On a show like *Buffy the Vampire Slayer*[11] fashion is of paramount importance: no one is more fashion-conscious than the American teenager. On *Stargate SG-1* fashion is of no importance whatsoever. Characters appear in the Air-Force-issued clothing that is appropriate to their situation, or they appear in civilian clothing that is very plain and classic in itself. Occasionally there is a reason for the show to make an effort to present clothing that is 'futuristic', such as the episode '2010' (416) set in that year; however, in that arena the costume designer has as much leeway as for episodes set in the distant past such as '1969' (221). And in fact the designs are generally kept very simple and plain. On those rare occasions when an article of clothing that reflects actual current US trends appears in the show, such as Sam Carter's pink bouclé jacket in the 2004 episode 'Affinity' (807), it's actually rather jarring, appearing out of place in the otherwise fashion-neutral show.

This is not to suggest that the show is always and in all ways fashion-neutral. Sam's hairstyles, for instance, reflect changing trends in women's short hairstyles in the US over the time period of the production of the show, just as, to a lesser extent, Jack O'Neill's and Daniel Jackson's hairstyles change as appropriate for men. However, for the most part it would be bizarre for these characters to be fashion icons: we would not expect an alien Jaffa such as Teal'c to sport dreadlocks just because they are a fashionable hairstyle, and it would just be wrong for an American Air Force general such as Gen. George Hammond to shave his head.

The visual timelessness of the show would mean nothing in the current television market, however, if it were not a series rather than a serial. In *Television Culture* Jonathan Fiske defines the difference between serials and series this way:

> A series has the same lead characters in each episode, but each episode has a different story which is concluded. There is 'dead time' between the episodes, with no memory from one to the other, and episodes can be screened or repeated in any order. The lead characters appear to have a life only in each episode, not between them, and do not grow or change as episode follows episode. Serials, on the other hand, have the same characters, but have continuous storylines, normally more than one, that continue from episode to episode. Their characters appear to live continuously between episodes, they grow and change with time, and have active 'memories' of previous events.[12]

In recent seasons, particularly in recent episodes, *Stargate SG-1* has developed something of a serial character, but for most of its run it has very definitely been a series. The primary value of this for syndication is that, as Fiske points out, episodes can be screened or repeated in any order. Channels can feel free to buy them and show them however they like; viewers can join the series at any time and not feel confused.

Two interesting points about this: first, it is in direct contrast to another popular show broadcast on the Sci Fi channel, *Farscape*,[13] which was cancelled around the same time that the channel picked up first-run broadcasts of new *Stargate SG-1* episodes from the Showtime channel. Bonnie Hammer, president of the Sci Fi channel, said that *Farscape* had got too tough to watch; you had to know what was going on to follow it. In an interview with *TVGuide Online*, Hammer said that *Farscape* had got too 'in' and was 'too much work'.[14] *TV Guide* reviewer Matt Rousch said in his 11 August 2003 column in *TV Guide* that Hammer had probably taken some heat for saying that '[s]ometimes shows are too smart for the audience. *Stargate* is smart, but it doesn't make people do homework.'[15]

It is conventional wisdom in TV land that series are easier to sell than serials; advertisers want the occasional viewer to drop in and see their ads. *Stargate SG-1* clearly built its audience as a series, and most of the episodes of its first eight years can be viewed as entirely stand-alone stories.

But, again, this is not a hard and fast rule. Recent viewers might have a tough time making sense of events unless they had some familiarity with the show. But even early on there were episodes that contributed to the overall fictional world the show created, and their aftermath persisted. It isn't necessary to have seen 'The Tok'ra, Part 1' (211) and 'The Tok'ra, Part 2' (212) in the second season to be able to watch later episodes in which the character of Jacob appears and within which it is clear that he is both a Tok'ra and Sam's dad. The fallout from 'In the Line of Duty' (202) has reappeared throughout the show, as it explains the presence in Sam's blood of naqada, which has many plot implications. And important villains and allies, such as Apophis, Anubis, the Tollan, the Nox and Master Bra'tac, blur the line between recurring characters on serials and occasional guest actors on series. *Stargate SG-1* seems to have a policy that it is a series, while enjoying some of the hallmarks of a serial that reward loyal fans and add to the richness of the show's storytelling.

This balancing act is important to marketing in another way. The division between series and serials is also a gendered one. As Fiske describes, generally serials are sold to women viewers, while series are sold to men. Hammer was widely quoted at the time of *Farscape*'s cancellation as saying that it did not fit in with the channel's goals of increasing its viewership among women. Unless Hammer was simply lying, that would mean that *Farscape*, though a serial, was bringing in fewer women viewers than *Stargate SG-1*, a series. It could be that the key to success with both male and female audiences is the right balance between series and serial.

Second, it's impossible to leave the topic of *Stargate SG-1*'s serial qualities without noting that the show does have one fan-related minor media frenzy to its credit, and that this was caused in 2002 when Michael Shanks decided to leave the show. Shanks' departure prompted many fans to launch campaigns to 'Save Daniel Jackson' (Shanks' character on the show). It could be argued that, of the few serial elements of the show, most of them pertained primarily to the Daniel Jackson character. The series began with Jackson's loss of his wife, and he joined the team primarily to find and save her. That recurring storyline gave *Stargate SG-1* most of the few serial episodes of its first five seasons, which may well have given its female viewership a slim thread of continuous character growth to which they could cling. In other words, its most serial-like feature – the storyline of the Dr Daniel Jackson character – provided *Stargate SG-1* with its biggest media blitz, and yet is supposedly at odds with its generally stand-alone, and more saleable, nature as a series.

In fact, *Stargate SG-1* has performed this balancing act all along. It balances its nature as an action show with its gentler fantasy elements; it balances its series and serial elements; and it adheres most strongly to a visual timelessness that need not detract from a show with a military atmosphere that is immediately identifiable and understandable to international audiences. How has it paid off?

Like the parent movie from which it spun off, the show has, as they say in show business, legs.

A convention dealers' room. Photo by Lisa Dickson, 2005.

Stargate SG-1 was, of course, originally based on the movie *Stargate*.[16] The first surprising thing about the television show was that it was made at all. When the movie was released it did not look like the sort of money-making machines that produce television series spin-offs. A 1994 *Variety* reviewer said, 'Commercial prospects for this curiously unabsorbing yarn border on the dire.'[17]

While *Stargate*-the-movie's revenues weren't that dire, they weren't fantastic either. It remained in theatres for five months and generated more than $71 million in box office.[18] On a movie with a $55 million budget, those revenues were not stellar. However, its box-office revenue was nothing compared to its global video growth. By the year 2000 it had grossed $700 million in combined business worldwide.[19] As a sleeper the movie generated a steady stream of income for MGM, its distributor. It's possible that the debut of the television show fed back into video earnings, causing a positive and profitable feedback loop in marketing. But clearly the movie was generating enough ongoing revenue after its 1994 release that, by 1996, as Cynthia Littleton reported for *Broadcasting & Cable*, MGM was leaning towards making a syndicated television series from the movie.[20] While some reports indicate that its original creators would have preferred to produce movie sequel(s), MGM, the owner of the property, obviously thought that a syndicated television show would be more profitable.

And the television show was.

Removed from its original creators Dean Devlin and Roland Emmerich, the premise was handed over to producers Brad Wright and Jonathan Glassner. As the show was revamped from the original movie centred around two characters to a show centred on four, Richard Dean Anderson and his long-time producing partner Michael Greenberg were brought aboard as executive producers as well.

Eleven years after the money-making prospects of *Stargate*-the-movie looked 'dire', its television offspring would be referred to as one of the 'three strongest Sci Fi shows that have ever been brought into syndication', along with *Star Trek* and *Andromeda*, the Gene Roddenberry sci-fi show that the same article describes as the 'No. 1 action hour on television in 92 countries around the world'.[21] That's heady company for *Stargate SG-1*. In December 2001, in *SG-1*'s fifth season, *Broadcasting & Cable* noted that '*Hercules* and *Xena* may have garnered the majority of headlines over the past several years, but *Stargate SG-1* has quietly become a force in the action-hour genre'.

Stargate SG-1 is a player in both cable and syndication. It is currently in its fifth season on Showtime, which gets the original episodes first; local stations get each season a year after they air on the cable network. MGM executives say the sixth season, which will be on Sci Fi Channel next fall instead of Showtime, will be its last.[22]

But it wasn't, and now there is a ninth season. In other words, falling far from the tree of its parent movie, *SG-1* survived switches from its original network (Showtime) to its current network (the Sci Fi Channel) and was successful on both. At the same time, original episodes aired in syndication – and did quite well there too. Since that 2001 article the series has put another three seasons of episodes in the can and the producers are making a ninth, albeit with significant changes. Also, the show has given birth to a spin-off, the *Atlantis* show Schlosser speculates about in 2001, and its offspring is beating it in the ratings.

Xena and *Hercules* get the *TV Guide* covers and the viewing parties in bars, and *Andromeda* outsells it internationally. It debuted as part of a dramatic, fantastic line-up on Showtime produced by MGM that included *The Outer Limits* and *Poltergeist: The Legacy*. *Stargate SG-1* has outlasted all those shows. And *Atlantis* may well be the kind of money-making spin-off for *Stargate SG-1* that *Xena* was for *Hercules*.

Such attention to the bottom line seems callous, corporate, even abominable to fans of a television show such as *Stargate*. Academia tends to analyse pop culture products as interesting texts, if it analyses them at all, not as business products. The enduring value of a show such as *Stargate SG-1* must lie in its content, not its marketing. Does it really matter how much money the show generates? Past a certain tipping point of survival versus cancellation, does it really matter how much money a show makes?

For the makers of the show, of course, the answer is 'yes'. For the companies that produce these products, that's all that matters. While television and movie producers might make some products in order to get the chance to make other more personally meaningful projects, at the corporate decision-making level the bottom line is the profit line. It surely can't be overly cynical to say that, when it's true. And, if it's true, then surely there's some value in analysing the fiscal as well as creative success of a long-running show such as *Stargate SG-1*. It is the product of the entertainment business, and the 'business' part of that description can't be ignored, not in the modern media world. To global media companies, *Stargate SG-1* is what they want every television show to be: a cost-effective show that can feed into the syndication pipeline and generate more of those profits.

And those profits are pretty big from any business' perspective. In 1998, Robert McChesney reported that Universal, the parent company that at the time owned the Sci Fi Channel, which has become *Stargate*'s primary first-run broadcaster, earned over half of its $7 *billion* revenue from its production of television and film.[23] In this era of media conglomeration, the numbers associated with media markets have not gone down. A 2003 article in *Variety* indicated that News Corp., the parent company of the Fox conglomerate, posted a $275 million *profit* on third quarter revenues of $4.4 billion. Of that number, $207 million were profits on the $1.13 billion in revenue generated by the unit's broadcast network and television stations.[24] The American entertainment and media market is one of the largest industries in the world – PricewaterhouseCoopers estimated a value for it in 2003 of around $479 billion.[25] In the new pie of media amalgamation – News Corp. also makes money on film, books, magazines and newspapers – television clearly seems to be the most profitable slice.

Just as a film's revenue in DVD sales is now one of its primary indicators of fiscal success, a television show's second life in syndication is now a major moneymaker – and the goals of the executives reflect this. News Corp.'s chief operating officer, Peter Chernin, says in the same article that, just as the film unit intends to release movies that generate steady returns in the DVD arena, the goal for the television unit is to 'create cost-effective new shows ... and add one or two new shows a year to the syndication pipeline'.[26]

Stargate SG-1 is one of those money chutes into the syndication pipeline. Its distributor, MGM, sells first-run rights not only to the Sci Fi Channel (a daughter corporation of USA Networks, recently of Vivendi Universal, now part of NBC Universal) but to local channels all over the world. It gets the best of both deals. The Sci Fi Channel is currently received in 84 million homes in the US ('SCI FI Channel Brief'). This puts it in the ranks of top cable networks although it is not in the top ten.[27] The channel's favourite show may change: the mini-series *Taken* gets mentioned in many promotional materials including bios of Bonnie Hammer, the channel's president, and currently *Battlestar Galactica*, the new series, is generating attention. Nevertheless, in any given week, *Stargate* shows are at least 11 hours of the Sci Fi Channel's programming and the success of the spin-off is reflecting well on the channel.

At the same time MGM sells first-run rights to local channels in syndication, which show a year after Sci Fi airs them. Episodes don't look visually dated and can be watched out of order, so no broadcast detracts from a viewer's willingness to watch shows aired on other networks, and all broadcasters' advertising becomes advertising for the show itself. A viewer who catches an episode on a local independent channel can see the week's new episode on Friday night on the Sci Fi Channel, or a six o'clock rerun any day of the week on the same channel, and suffer from no cognitive dissonance. All the episodes run everywhere can serve to increase rather than decrease viewership for episodes shown everywhere else. Even where the show's omnipresence does not feed into this advertising synergy (a viewer who simply never watches his or her local station may not ever know that the show is broadcast there as well as on Sci Fi), it does reach markets beyond those of the Sci Fi Channel, a basic cable broadcast network that does not reach every home. *Battlestar Galactica* simply can't say the same.

MGM's website for *Stargate*, which is different from the Sci Fi Channel's, reports that the show can be seen not only on the Sci Fi Channel and in syndication in the US, but on the WIC network in Canada, on both Channel 4 and SkyOne in the UK, and on Channel 7 in Australia.[28] Sci Fi also has distribution deals throughout Europe, Latin America and South Africa. The show is a globally marketed product.

In the fall of 2004 the Sony Corporation agreed to buy Metro-Goldwyn-Mayer (MGM), *Stargate*'s distributor, for about $5 billion. In their press release they specifically stated that it was one of their goals to establish cable channels featuring Sony and MGM content.[29] That's not just the catalogue of MGM movies; that includes television products such as the *Stargate* shows, television products that are reliable revenue generators.

Like News Corp., MGM brings in serious revenues – the 10-Q form it filed on 28 October 2004 with the Securities Exchange Commission of the US government indicates that it has yearly revenues of about $1.6 billion. It continues to post net losses but its losses for 2004 were significantly less than its losses for 2003 – thus a company ripe for a buyout, and Sony agreed to shoulder its debt in the purchase agreement. In the 10-Q, MGM said of its improved losses,

> The improvement of $54.8 million reflected increased profit margins, as the 2004 Period included higher television licensing revenues which carry lower distribution costs, as well as decreased theatrical

print and advertising costs, which were $98.7 million lower than in the 2003 Period as the film slate in the 2004 Period had lower releasing costs. Other benefits included the performance of *Stargate SG-1* in worldwide home video markets, as well as the collection of an insurance recovery of $6.1 million in the 2004 Period.[30]

In other words, MGM's improving losses directly reflected more revenue on television licensing, which was cheaper for them to distribute than film products. It specifically mentions the revenue generated by *Stargate SG-1*'s home video sales. While it does not provide information on that revenue, the paragraph implies that it is probably on the order of the other revenues the form mentions – somewhere between the $6.1 million the company received in insurance and the $98.7 million it saved on theatrical distribution costs.[31]

That's a decent amount of dough.

And it's implied that this was a windfall that helped generate this particular improvement. The regular revenues generated by *SG-1* through sales to Sci Fi and the syndication channels aren't indicated, and there are good corporate reasons not to spell them out. Exact costs of advertising minutes in particular time slots on particular channels are not public knowledge. Presumably, if the Sci Fi Channel, as well as those syndicated stations, couldn't make money selling advertising time during their showings of *Stargate SG-1*, they wouldn't buy the show. And they do buy the show, contributing to MGM's earnings. Although fans tend to heap scorn or praise on the Sci Fi Channel (depending on what's happening there this week), it's actually the distributor, MGM, that funds most of the production of the show and gains most of the profits from its distribution. And if, as MultichannelNews reported in 2004, the costs of producing an episode of *Stargate SG-1* are about $1.7 million per episode, we have to assume it makes MORE than the roughly $36 million it costs to make per year – a lot more, if MGM's SEC filing is anything to go by.[32]

Stargate SG-1 has taken years to achieve the sort of notice that flashier hit shows generate. Smartly sold as a two-year investment to the Showtime channel, it had its first two years to build up its viewership, to get on its feet, and develop a rich universe all its own. Since then it has continued to be a model of marketing savvy as well as an enjoyable show. May all genre producers everywhere learn from its lessons, because the outcome of its marketing savvy has been not just profits for its producers, but more great entertainment for us.

Notes

1 For more on the historical relationship between television and movie studios, see the brief history of television in J. Michael Straczynski, *The Complete Book of Scriptwriting* (Cincinnati, 1996).

2 George Gerbner, 'Foreword', Mike Budd, Steve Craig and Clay Steinman (eds), *Consuming Environments: Television and Commercial Culture* (New Brunswick NJ, 1999), p.xvi

3 Ibid., p.15

4 *MacGyver*, executive producers Jerry Ludwig, John Rich and Henry Winkler (ABC, 1985–1992), is shown on both the Spike and TVLand cable channels in the US several times a day. These basic cable channels broadcast primarily rerun material aimed at specific demographics (Spike markets itself as 'The First Network for Men' whereas TVLand markets itself primarily as an outlet for television nostalgia. *MacGyver*'s first season was also released on DVD in January 2005.

5 Scott Robert Olson, 'Hollywood planet: global media and the competitive advantage of narrative transparency', Robert C. Allen and Annette Hill (eds), *The Television Studies Reader* (London, New York, 2004), p.120

6 *Scarecrow and Mrs King*, created by Brad Buckner and Eugenie Ross-Leming (CBS, 1983–1987)

7 *Scrubs*, 'My Life in Four Cameras', written by Deb Fordham, directed by Adam Bernstein (NBC, 2001–present)

8 *Babylon 5*, executive producers Douglas Netter, J. Michael Straczynski (Warner Brothers/Babylonian Productions, 1993–1998)

9 *Angel*, executive producer Joss Whedon (20th Century Fox Television/Mutant Enemy, 1999–2004)

10 All references to the episodes will be indicated parenthetically by episode number. See the Episode guide for additional information.

11 *Buffy the Vampire Slayer*, executive producer Joss Whedon (Warner Brothers/UPN, 1997–2003)

12 Jonathan Fiske, *Television Culture* (New York, 1987), p.150

13 *Farscape*, created by Rockne S. O'Bannon (Sci Fi, 1999–2003)

14 Michael Ausiello, 'Far out', *TV Guide Online*, 7 January 2003

15 Matt Rousch, 'Ask Matt', *TV Guide*, 11 August 2003

16 *Stargate*, written by Dean Devlin and Roland Emmerich, directed by Roland Emmerich (MGM, 1994)

17 Leonard Klady, '"Stargate"', *Variety*, 24 October 1994

18 Andrew Hindes, '"Fifth" goes first; no pop "in Fathers"', Variety.com, http://www.variety.com/index.asp?layout=print_vpage&articleid=VR1116680579&categoryid=38, 12 May 1997

19 'mediaconnect', *MediaWeek*, 10, 33, 21 August 2000, p.40

20 Cynthia Littleton, 'MGM eyes syndication for "Stargate": show debuts on Showtime, is candidate for fall 1998 broadcast play', *Broadcasting & Cable*, 126, 48, 18 November 1996, p.39.

21 Debra Kaufman, '"Andromeda" 100th Episode', *Hollywood Reporter*, 18 January 2005

22 Joe Schlosser, 'The quiet force in action', *Broadcasting & Cable*, 3 December 2001, p.25

23 Robert W. McChesney, 'The global media giants', Robin Andersen and Lance Strate (eds),*Critical Studies in Media Commercialism* (Oxford, 2000)

24 Jill Goldsmith, 'News Corp. reports $275 mil profit', *Variety* (Gotham edition), 13 May 2003

25 This figure, from PricewaterhouseCoopers' 11 June 2003 'Global entertainment and media outlook: 2003–2007', was widely reported; see 'Media industry to grow modestly for 5 years: PwC' and 'Canada world's fastest growing entertainment and media market in 2002; Canadian industry of US$21.7 billion in 2002 expected to reach US$31.0 billion in 2007'.

26 Goldsmith: 'News corp'.

27 Statistics on top cable networks from NCTA, the National Cable & Telecommunications Association, from www.ncta.com list of top cable networks, at http://www.ncta.com/Docs/PageContent.cfm?pageID=281. Discovery is number 1 with 89.5 million viewers and the Cartoon Network is number 2 with 87.1 million, so the Sci Fi Channel is clearly in the same ballpark with these networks and competition at the top is fierce.

28 'MGM: Stargate SG-1', online (accessed 18 August 2005, http://www.stargatesg1.com/stargatehb.html)

29 'Consortium … ' press release, Sony Corporation, online (accessed 13 September 2004, http://www.sony.com/SCA/press/040914.shtml)

30 'Form 10-Q for the quarterly period ending 30 September 2004, Metro-Goldwyn-Mayer Inc.', Securities and Exchange Commission, Washington, DC, online (accessed 17 August 2005, http://www.sec.gov/Archives/edgar/data/1026816/000119312504180458/d10q.htm)

31 The statement also says that '[w]orldwide syndicated television revenues increased by $8.6 million, or 26 percent, in the 2004 Quarter as we realized higher basic cable sales due to the delivery of our new series *Stargate: Atlantis*'.

32 Mary McNamara, '"Stargate": rise of a fertile franchise', *MultichannelNews* (Multichannel.com: Reed Business Information), 3 May 2004

11

READING *STARGÅTE*/PLAYING *STARGÅTE*: ROLE-PLAYING GAMES AND THE *STARGÅTE* FRANCHISE

MELANIE MANZER KYER AND JEFFREY A. KYER

In 2003, Alderac Entertainment Group (AEG), a leading publisher of role-playing games (RPGs), introduced *Stargate SG-1: The Roleplaying Game*. Since the instructions and background information necessary for playing role-playing games are published in book form, they combine the act of passively experiencing a set story with the open-ended and creative experience of playing a game. As such, role-playing books based on *Stargate* provide interesting tangible cultural artefacts to those interested in the franchise and its fan base. Furthermore, the *Stargate* franchise holds a unique place in the world of role-playing games because of its early introduction to and adoption by fans. The AEG book based on *Stargate SG-1* appeared in print only six years after the premiere of the television series. It allows fans of the series to participate in a shared game creating new stories and adventures. At the time of printing, five books (supplements) for this game have been published, all of which make extensive use of photographs, quotations, and background from the series itself. These books range from season episode guides to the *Unknown Worlds* (official worlds which are set in the *Stargate* universe, but which the SGC will never visit). The books themselves are chronicles of the *Stargate* universe with extrapolated details of the how and why behind the science and the stories. More than simply an outlet for fan fiction, the *Stargate SG-1* RPG is itself a part of the officially sanctioned franchise, yet is unique in providing a personalised vehicle for exploring *Stargate*. The benefits are tangible on three levels: in addition to the entertainment experienced by role-players themselves, and the monetary advantage that a built-in audience of established series fans provides to the publisher, the series itself experiences increased fan loyalty as the role-playing game fosters in players a sense of ownership in the franchise. This article will discuss the participatory experience provided by the *Stargate* RPG and those aspects of the world that have made the game a success.

Role-playing games: an overview of types, audiences and academic literature

While the RPG has become a relatively common concept, it will be helpful to give a brief description of the various types and how the *Stargate SG-1 RPG* fits into the RPG spectrum. RPGs fall into two main categories: socially interactive games and computer-based games. Although both are extremely popular, this article will focus primarily on the socially interactive RPG, which can be broken down still further into play-by-post (email- or bulletin-board-based games), LARP (live action role-playing with simplified rules, costuming, and improvised acting) and classic or 'table-top' RPGs. The latter is the most commonly known variety, so-called because it often takes place around a table top, with a map illustrating character placement and a small cardboard screen separating the notes and materials of the narrator or game-master (GM, also called a dungeon master or DM in *Dungeons and Dragons*) from the players. In classic gaming, players assume roles in the collective storytelling as the group explores the world the GM presents – their characters acting and reacting to the imaginary people and places they encounter.

The RPG is an excellent simulation tool for conflict resolution as one can clearly see the consequences of one's actions. From killing monsters and looting dungeons to negotiating treaties with foreign powers to courtly intrigue and romance, a good GM presents his players with a series of challenges based on the players' own actions and responses. Characters interacting with these challenges are central to all RPGs. Thus, a successful RPG is based not only on marketing, writing and genre, but also on the quality of the players and the GM. The art of good game-mastering can be distilled down to the following essential, as described by Robin Laws, game designer and author of *Robin's Laws to Good Gamemastering*: 'What would be the most entertaining thing that could possibly happen right now? The rest is mere detail.'[1]

Though the creativity of the GM and the quality of the world may be the most salient aspects of a given game, these 'mere details' – the mechanics behind game play – are also crucial to game success. There are currently several popular game systems on the market (also known as game engines), but the most popular remain the various permutations of *Dungeons and Dragons*.[2] Games based on other genres and mechanics such as White Wolf's *World of Darkness* games (including *Vampire: The Masquerade*) are almost as popular. More recently, the introduction of the *d20 System*[3] – a series of games from the *Dungeons and Dragons v3.5* rule set – has allowed many game publishers to present their own games as compatible variations on a single system. The *Stargate SG-1 RPG* put out by AEG uses this game engine.

Several varieties of game systems exist based around types of dice used, contest resolution and game focus. Some systems are considered 'rules-light', where there is a minimum number of simple rules applied with varying levels of realism. Other, 'rules-heavy' systems have detailed resolutions for many kinds of contests, while the extensive sets of rules and examples provide a high level of what is called 'reality modelling'. In this, the rules are designed to closely mirror as realistically as possible every conceivable circumstance the players might encounter, often at the expense of narrative enjoyment and ease of play. Indeed, the sheer amount of detail in such an approach can bog the gaming down considerably. Noted game designer Ron Edwards divides RPGs into three 'game styles': gamism, simulationism and narrativism.[4] Gamism, he writes, is characterised by a sense of competition between the participants themselves as opposed to their characters, while simulation-ism is concerned with the internal logic of the game and focuses on exploration as a priority of play. The third game type, narrativism, focuses, as the term implies, on the storyline and its group creation via role-playing. Its characters are protagonists in the literary sense rather than competitors. All the above qualities easily apply to games set in *Stargate SG-1* as players may choose to focus on competitive problem-solving (will Carter find the solution before Teal'c?), the exploration of a new technology (how does that Asgard weapon work anyway?) or simply the telling of a compelling story (every *SG-1* episode).

Stargate SG-1 as an RPG represents an example of the genre of science fiction. Three other important basic genres in the RPG hobby include fantasy, superheroes and horror. Of course, there are hundreds of published variations on these, let alone the myriad 'home-brew' games produced by gamers for their own groups. Some of the most popular game worlds are those based on various literary or licensed works such as Chaosium's *Call of Cthulhu* – a horror game based on the work of H. P. Lovecraft – or the various licensed *Star Wars* and *Star Trek* RPGs published by several companies. Other game worlds are unique, created by gamers and writers for the express purpose of role-playing. For example, *Forgotten Realms*, from Wizards of the Coast, is a fantasy world in the classic sense while AEG's *Legend of the Five Rings* is set in the Asian-flavoured 'Empire of Rokugan', where samurai and courtiers exist in a mythical world loosely based on a variety of Asian myths.

So, who is it that is doing the gaming these days? While role-playing has been stereotyped as a pursuit dominated by reclusive male college students with a less than ideal grasp on reality and personal hygiene, this is not an accurate picture of the contemporary role-playing scene. Although the hobby was almost exclusively male in the early days (Gary Alan Fine, writing in 1979, cites that fewer than 5 per cent of the hard-core gaming population was female,)[5] women today make up about 30 per cent of the gaming base. Females are also seen in higher numbers at LARP events, which focus more on acting and costuming for game effects than on exhaustive rules. There are still far more male players, but women have found their niche in the world of gaming, particularly as the gaming population ages and marries.

The issue of ageing is crucial to the gamer demographic. Many gamers who were around when the hobby began in the late 1970s are now married with children of their own and are initiating them into the hobby. The authors know of children as young as seven who are successful role-players. However, college seems to have remained a key recruiting ground for gamers as well as a highly desirable marketing demographic. It is less common to see gamers beyond the age of 65 or so, but that will likely change as the population continues to age. Gamers can be found in nearly all economic classes, since the expense for the hobby is relatively small. (Although the books can be expensive, the core book is a one-time expense and even that is not strictly required for game play if someone in the group has a copy.) Minorities and all sexual orientations are strongly represented in RPG groups, and conventions sometimes host panel discussions to address issues of special populations within gaming.[6]

The attendance at game conventions in general is a staggering testament to the growth of the hobby. The largest and oldest hobby-game convention in the country, GenCon, was first held in 1968 as purely a wargames convention with 168 attendees. In 1978, one year after the debut of *Dungeons and Dragons*, the convention had over 1000 participants.[7] In 2004, that number had topped 30,000 and moved from Milwaukee to Indianapolis because of the need for more convention space. A similar convention, Origins, held annually in Columbus, Ohio, boasts over 13,000 players. Why is the hobby so popular? There are almost as many reasons for the appeal of role-playing as there are role-players themselves, but three main reasons for the popularity of the hobby include its ability to provide outlets for socialisation, empowerment and creativity.

Socialisation is one of the most important aspects of the conventional RPG. Regular meetings of a social group of individuals who share a hobby are particularly reassuring when that hobby is as obscure as gaming. Although the dynamic is similar to getting together once a week to play cards, or watch the Sunday game, the bonding is even more crucial to the social development of those involved. At least hobbies such as sports and card-playing are regularly affirmed by the media and mainstream popular culture, as opposed to role-playing games, which even today are sometimes criticised by conservative Christian groups as pagan or satanic.

Another reason for the popularity of the modern RPG is empowerment. RPGs provide a safe outlet for imaginary violence which can allow players to let off stress from their daily lives. Since so little is under one's personal control in the modern world, RPGs allow one to carve out a character's destiny – to take the opportunity to be a hero or a villain and achieve (albeit vicariously) fame and fortune.

RPGs offer far more than the release of violent impulses, however. One of most important facets of gaming is its unique outlet for creativity and fantasy – building and exploring a mutable, shared fantasy world. Some players can take this to extremes, establishing radically different characters and revelling in their character and the setting's facets. Others are concerned with the shared storyline, enjoying their contribution to an ongoing narrative and relishing the plot twists along the way.

An initial search for academic research on the topic of role-playing games as a hobby provides limited results at best, revealing instead a plethora of articles in the fields of sociology and psychology on the broader concept of role-playing in general. Still, two works are worth mentioning as key texts for those interested in the history and demographics of the hobby. The first, *Shared Fantasy: Role-playing Games as Social Worlds*, was written by Gary Alan Fine in 1983 and based on research conducted with a variety of gaming groups from 1977–1979. As the first major work to seriously discuss the phenomenon of the role-playing game hobby, Fine's work remains an excellent introduction to the basic history of and philosophy behind table-top RPGs. Fine, a sociologist, discusses the early demographics of gaming, the aspects of collective fantasy and, in particular, 'small group cultures, particularly the techniques by which gaming groups develop small-scale culture, the content of this culture, and how the gaming culture relates to private friendship cultures of individuals'.[8] Daniel Mackay's work, *A New Performance Art: The Fantasy Role-Playing Game*, was published in 2001, nearly 20 years after *Shared Fantasy*. Much of the information on the basics and history of RPGs is similar, though more thorough in keeping with the changes in the hobby over the past two decades. However, since Mackay's area of expertise is performance studies, he takes a different approach to the topic of RPGs and examines the cultural structure, formal structure, social structure and aesthetic structure of role-playing as both a hobby and an art form. As this chapter will focus on the relationship of the role-playing game hobby to a single specific setting, we will undertake to be more descriptive than sociological or aesthetic, instead referring interested readers to the works of Fine or Mackay if desired.

Since the genre of science fiction is so large and varied, a discussion of the state of academic research in this field might take us on a tangent from which we could not easily return.[9] Contemporary academic research on science fiction literature and media covers topics from feminism to Marxism to rock 'n' roll. However, one text is worth noting as we discuss the intersection between television, fans and participatory culture: *Textual Poachers: Television Fans and Participatory Culture* by Henry Jenkins.[10] In this classic work, Jenkins discusses *Star Trek* fans and lends legitimacy to the subculture of fandom by invoking the critical paradigm of 'poaching'. Through the appropriation of television worlds in fan fiction, Jenkins argues, fans are able to control their subculture rather than be manipulated by it. Critic Ilsa Bick disputes this control as an illusion in her article 'Boys in space: Star Trek, latency, and the neverending story'.[11] While it is true that fans do not truly control their subject, neither do they seem to mind this lack of control so long as the end result is more of the desired product. In this respect, fan fiction and role-playing share the desire to produce 'more of the story'. Although both fan fiction and the RPG involve the appropriation of a previously existing genre, there is a significant difference in the case of the RPG, which is an officially sanctioned property. *The Stargate SG-1 Roleplaying Game* is licensed through Sony/ MGM and thus an extension of the intellectual property (IP) itself.

The *Stargate SG-1* RPG: adapting the series to game play

Until recently, the existing licensed RPG for *Stargate SG-1* was the one published by AEG using their *Powered by Spycraft* game system – a derivative of the *d20 System* mentioned above. While the game does require the use of the *Dungeons and Dragons Player's Handbook v3.0* to play, it is otherwise a stand-alone game system. One advantage to this system it that it makes the game very accessible to those already playing RPGs. D&D in one form or another is familiar to the majority of players. On the other hand, the *d20 System* is a classic 'rules-heavy' approach to RPGs that can be very daunting to anyone not already familiar with RPGs. This can discourage fans who are seeking to make *Stargate SG-1* their first RPG experience.

While the *Stargate SG-1* television series chronicles the exploits of the SG-1 team, and there are options available for playing members of SG-1, the series mentions (at last count) the existence of over 20 other SG teams with a variety of functions ranging from marine assault teams to diplomatic envoys. The *Stargate SG-1 RPG* provides a framework for additional adventures without upsetting series continuity, since players usually create their own characters who then participate in missions created by the GM. Collectively these constitute a campaign and feature the ongoing story of the player's own SGC team.

Characters are created using a series of statistics (usually generated randomly) that range from three (terrible) to 18 or more (great). These 'stats' (strength, constitution, dexterity, intelligence, wisdom and charisma) reflect the character's strengths and weaknesses. Once created, the character then becomes a member of a character class – these range from soldiers like Jack O'Neill, scientists such as Daniel Jackson, or even Jaffa Guardians like Teal'c. Some characters, such as Samantha Carter, have more than one class (and are referred to as 'multi-classed' – she is a Pointman/Scientist, which gives strength in scientific abilities and in assisting or leading others). Classes provide the characters with specific arrays of skills and special abilities which the players can customise to make their character unique. As they participate in various missions, characters grow in experience and capabilities.

Typical adventures can follow the whole gamut of missions experienced by the stalwart SG-1. These can range from simple exploration of newly discovered worlds to dealing with twisted

A fan in SG-12 regalia. Photo by Lisa Dickson, 2005.

machinations of the Trust back on Earth. Since much of the main *Stargate SG-1 RPG* rulebook is background material, it is possible for the characters to follow up on previously televised *SG-1* episodes or even take the place of SG-1 or other existing SG teams in one of the shows. In time, such a campaign may very well diverge from the series canon, as the players' characters' actions influence their own version of the *Stargate* universe, making different decisions and gaining the Tau'ri different enemies and allies. As such, although it is generally accepted that player actions will affect canon to some degree, such changes do not generally affect the basic premises of the franchise. Large-scale elements such as the Goa'uld's inherently evil nature, the Asgard's status as beneficent, cryptic allies, and the growing Jaffa rebellion are difficult to affect. Other plot elements, such as the relationship with the Tok'ra or the covert struggle with the NID, are more subject to the player's efforts and may change radically from canon as a campaign progresses. However, if a game master wishes to change some of these basic elements to suit his play group, the *Stargate SG-1 RPG* has several suggestions for making alternative realities for play – something that the series has touched upon as well in several episodes.[12]

An example of a typical adventure is taken from the work of Paul Rocchi,[13] detailed here. In it, the player's SG team visits a world called Thalasa – whose inhabitants are descended from Classical Greeks. The 'Tribute to Crete' motif from the ancient Greek myths of King Minos works well with the parasitical aspects of Goa'uld society. Odiweikos, the local king, wishes the SG team to stop the annual tribute of seven maidens and youths to a minor System Lord named Minos, for this year his daughter is among them. Over the course of the story-arc, players find their SG team collectively taking the role of Theseus against Minos' Minotaur as the characters try to overthrow the Goa'uld and gain new allies for the Tau'ri. However, there are plot twists – Minos is the Judge of Hell, after all!

In order to play the game, one must first purchase (or borrow) some start-up material. At a minimum, one would generally purchase *Stargate SG-1 Roleplaying Game*, the 'core rulebook'. However, AEG has currently produced five books in the *Stargate SG-1 RPG* line. The main rulebook covers character generation, world creation, mission profiles, aliens such as the Goa'uld or the Asgard, and background information on episodes, gadgets and gear, System Lords, and write-ups of characters from the series. *Fantastic Frontiers* and *Friends and Foes*, the first and second season episode guides, have detailed descriptions of the episodes, background on the worlds visited, rules for new technologies and aliens met, and new character classes. These allow GMs to run 'follow-up' missions based on these episodes, as much of the material in the book is additional information, extrapolated beyond what is seen on television.

Living Gods, the System Lord supplement, contains detailed descriptions of every System Lord seen in the series during the first seven seasons – living or dead. This allows for GMs to use 'presumed dead' Goa'uld to change their campaign from the canonical version or to use these powerful enemies in their own stories before they perish at the hands of the Tau'ri or other Goa'uld. In addition to some of the most powerful villains in the *Stargate* universe, the book contains a vast supporting cast of lesser Goa'uld, Jaffa, allies, and enemies along with dozens of Goa'uld-controlled worlds for the players to explore. Rounding out the book is a chapter that assists GMs to create their own System Lords complete with minions, subject worlds, and their place in the Goa'uld pecking order.

First Steps is an 'Unknown Worlds' book. In it are detailed ten worlds that will never be visited by the SGC – allowing narrators complete latitude in how they can be integrated into their campaign. Some of these worlds are previously unknown Goa'uld holdings while others are independent of the System Lords. One world even deals with the aftermath of the Nazis' possession of Earth's Stargate during the 1930s and 1940s. Also provided are extensive sections for adventures in space, particularly rules for vehicle chases and spacecraft – areas that were previously neglected in the game system prior to this book.

While these books aid the role-player, they also have other uses. For those who want further material on *Stargate SG-1*, these books are loaded with background information on the episodes and the series in general. One fascinating and rewarding aspect of the RPG is that the writers of this additional material have been told that the television writers of *Stargate SG-1* were using these works as reference material. Indeed, there has been some recursiveness, in which written material from the RPG inspires the writers and is discussed in future shows.[14]

Other role-players are less than happy with using the existing system for their *Stargate* role-playing. As noted above, the *d20 System* is rules-heavy and many players feel it is less conducive to role-playing than it is to 'rules playing'. Whether or not this is the case, many design their own 'home-brew' *Stargate* games, using their favourite gaming system and adapting it to the *Stargate* universe. Many of these unofficial and non-sanctioned RPGs can be found on the internet and use an incredible array of systems.

The licensing of *Stargate SG-1* as an RPG is not without some controversy. As of February 2005, AEG is no longer publishing the *Stargate SG-1 RPG* and several other publishers are negotiating for the licence, a tribute to the popularity of the property. One of these will likely publish their own version of the game. It is likely that this new version will not be compatible with the existing one but rather based on the new licensee's proprietary system.

Why the *Stargate* property works as an RPG

As we have seen in the previous section, RPGs fulfil a variety of needs for those who play them, including socialisation, empowerment and creativity. Naturally, different game worlds and engines are variously suited to these needs. The *Stargate SG-1* property works so well as a game for many of the same reasons it is a successful television programme. Of course, the television show's success is certainly a contributing factor to the game's initial popularity, but such a positive initial boost does not always equate to game success. Media franchises such as *Buck Rogers* and *Indiana Jones* both started out with an extremely high recognition value, but for a variety of reasons neither property succeeded as a licensed RPG. *Stargate SG-1* lends itself well to an RPG setting for many reasons including genre, timing, character development and premise.

The premise of *Stargate SG-1* is a particularly important factor in its adaptability to RPG design. The Stargate itself represents a magical door to adventure through which any imaginable scenario may be found. It is this lure of the unknown, lying just beyond the portal's watery surface, which keeps fans of the series tuning in to see what world will be explored next, and this same concept makes the premise extremely attractive to both potential GMs and players alike. A gaming group can choose to visit a different planet and culture each week (an episodic model), or to revisit favourite worlds and to establish relationships (a story-arc model), all with the built-in stability of a home base on Earth.

Another advantage to the 'magical door' premise is the availability of cultural interaction provided by the Stargate, and the focus on the importance of sociological and anthropological knowledge. Of the six specialities (or roles) listed in the game rules (team commander, heavy weapons expert, intelligence/communications officer, lingual/cultural expert, mission specialist and medical specialist), the lingual/cultural expert is the only one required on all SG exploration teams aside from the team commander. Even though the language used in the television series is exclusively English, ancient Egyptian, Goa'uld and other languages are frequently mentioned, and cultural negotiations are of prime importance to nearly every episode. While the GM may choose to de-emphasise this focus on culture, most appreciate the opportunity to incorporate information from various cultures (or even other RPG worlds). In this way, the Stargate serves a similar function to another science fiction plot device, the time machine, except, in this case, the technology is decidedly less messy, with no dangerous space–time continuum to worry about.[15]

Character development is another reason *Stargate SG-1* lends itself so well to the RPG sphere. With appeal to both sexes, *Stargate* allows women to be every bit as heroic as men and to choose any character speciality available. In contrast, although Greg Stafford's world of Glorantha is extremely popular, its supporters must constantly explain and justify the somewhat rigid, if not entirely traditional, sex roles the game prescribes.[16] While it would be stereotypical to assert that the military and strategic aspects of *Stargate* appeal only to males and the character development or diplomatic aspects are purely a female forum, the variety of roles available make the game accessible to all sexes, orientations and interests. However, it should be noted here that most RPGs including *HeroQuest* (the game system used in the world of Glorantha) use the aspects of race, sex and character class to create a character, and in this respect *Stargate SG-1* is less flexible. Nearly all *Stargate SG-1: The Roleplaying Game* character classes are by nature military-based, but, as Jack O'Neill's character can bear witness, not every participant in the SGC is entirely orthodox in his or her execution of military protocol.

As a television series airing on the Sci-Fi network, *Stargate SG-1* is usually characterised as simply 'science fiction'. However, the science fiction genre is highly nuanced, and can be divided at the very least into high/hard science fiction (where scientific terms and explanations of technology are required) and low science fiction (where the technology is taken for granted and no attempt is made at explanation).

Other genre subtleties include retro science fiction, planetary romance, military science fiction, and even space opera. *Stargate SG-1* lies somewhere between high and low science fiction, as the main characters begin the series with little more 'advanced' knowledge than early twenty-first-century humans, but are introduced to successively more complex alien technologies. The series lacks much of the bombastic nature of such other futuristic worlds as *Star Trek* and *Star Wars* and as such has a quality of magical realism that gives it wider audience appeal. In fact, the show often draws more from conventions of the traditional action/adventure genre than from science fiction. A strong tie to Earth makes it easy for the average person to experience the wonder of the main characters as they learn about new worlds and technologies for the first time – regardless of whether or not he or she is actually a fan of science fiction. Although some characters on the show or in the RPG may know the scientific details behind the functioning of alien technologies, to other characters they remain simply 'magic', much as would happen in a standard fantasy RPG.

One of the most compelling reasons for the success of the *Stargate SG-1 RPG* is the timeliness with which it has hit the market. The first episodes of the *Stargate SG-1* television series aired in 1997, and the first book of the RPG appeared a mere six years later. In comparison, it took ten years for the first *Star Wars* RPG to appear, and more than 16 years for the first RPG based on *Star Trek*. True, *Star Trek* premiered in 1966, more than ten years before the first RPG was even invented, but the principle remains that timing is important to the success of an RPG property. In this case, *Stargate* is fortunate on two fronts: it was introduced after the series had already established itself as a success, yet while the show was still in production. Based on a current television show, *Stargate SG-1 RPG* is able to tap into mainstream popular culture and name recognition: nearly everyone with a television is at least aware of the show's existence. This familiarity makes it much simpler to introduce new RPG players to the game than in cases where the world requires extensive explanation.

An additional advantage to a game world that is freely available for weekly television watching is the 'ownership' players feel for the television show and its characters. If their previous gaming session was spent fighting Replicators on a distant planet, players will readily identify with Samantha Carter and Daniel Jackson as they try to thwart the Replicators in this week's episode. The game-playing audience is encouraged to keep watching, and those who do not yet watch may be inspired to do so by the close ties between their table-top adventures and the on-screen ones. Although it is possible that actions the player-characters undertake in their missions may (will!) cause a divergent continuity between the group's campaign and the television series, the players should regard the rules and information from the published *Stargate SG-1 RPG* books as canon. In other words, while diverging from the books or the series is possible and probable, it should involve a conscious choice on the part of the players and their game-master. The books are the written counterpoint to the series and their content is just as valid.

As much as playing the *Stargate SG-1 RPG* may encourage fan loyalty, the mere existence of a written RPG serves another function for the *Stargate* fan base. RPG reference books and adventure modules serve as a complement to the series world, explaining cultures, technologies and character motivations for all those interested in the minutiae of this fictitious world. As *The Simpsons* and *Saturday Night Live* have both illustrated in parodies of *Star Trek* and *Star Wars* conventions, devoted fans pay attention to every aspect of a series and are likely to be curious about far more intimate details than writers have time or interest in explaining during an episode. Even the FAQ on the *Stargate SG-1* website contains detailed information on the brands of watch and sunglasses worn by each cast member.[17] Since the *Stargate SG-1 RPG* books contain exhaustive descriptions of the cultures encountered in each episode as well as the science or mechanics behind new technologies, the books are a helpful reference whether or not a fan is interested in role-playing. Likewise, the fan who does role-play may appreciate the opportunity to manipulate and interact with a particular culture or technology which they find fascinating.

Conclusion: beyond *Stargate SG-1*

With the recent change in licensing, it is difficult to foresee the future of the *Stargate SG-1 RPG*. Yet, the potential for continued success is very good. Demos at gaming conventions have been consistently well attended. Paul Rocchi, a professional game instructor with AEG, noted that, at GenCon 2004, his first *Stargate SG-1 RPG* adventure was a 'huge hit'. But, he continues, 'What AEG and I hadn't counted on was that some fans at the con were, well, fanatic. They didn't sign up for one SG-1 demo session – they signed up for several – and AEG had only one scenario prepared. I was faced later in the con with a pair of players who'd both done the AEG provided scenario and my scenario – and wanted more *Stargate*.'[18] This incident illustrates the intense dedication of the fans of *Stargate SG-1*, both the series and the RPG. Using MGM-sanctioned tools, players and GMs alike are encouraged to develop original storylines and worlds featuring heroes and villains of their own. In this way, the *Stargate* franchise creates a triangle of communication between the series, the published role-playing guides, and the fan's unique imagination and interests. Playing *Stargate* allows for players of virtually every interest and background to interact with the *SG-1* franchise and 'save the world(s)'.

Notes

1   Robin Laws, *Robin's Laws to Good Gamemastering* (Austin TX, 2002)

2   The current edition, *Dungeons and Dragons v 3.5*, is published by Wizards of the Coast.

3   *d20 System* and the Open Gaming License are owned by Wizards of the Coast and licensed to other companies for use in their games free of charge in a fashion similar to LINUX.

4   For a full discussion of Ron Edwards' game types, see 'GNS and other matters of role-playing theory', by Ron Edwards (http://www.indie-rpgs.com/articles/).

5   Gary Alan Fine, *Shared Fantasy: Role-playing Games as Social Worlds* (Chicago, 1983), pp.62–71

6   For example, the online events listing for the 2005 Origins game convention (http://www.originsgames.com) lists seminars on gender in gaming, the Islamic religion as related to gaming, as well as the issue of homosexual gamers.

7   For more information on the history of GenCon, see official GenCon historian Randy Porter's online article, 'A little history', http://php.iupui.edu/~wrporter/Genconhistory.html.

8   Fine: *Shared Fantasy*, p.123

9   It will suffice to give two recent examples for future reading. First, editor Maureen Barr's *Envisioning the Future: Science Fiction and the Next Millennium* (Middleton CT, 2003), which contains essays on subjects of feminism in science fiction, tales of apocalypse, and the academic field of science fiction studies. The second volume, *Edging into the Future*

(Philadelphia, 2002), edited by Veronica Hollinger and Joan Gordon, likewise addresses issues of postmodernism, utopia and sexuality in science fiction.

10 Henry Jenkins, *Textual Poachers: Television Fans and Participatory Culture* (New York, 1992)

11 Ilsa J. Bick, 'Boys in space: Star Trek, latency, and the neverending story', *Cinema Journal*, 35, 2 (1996), pp.43–60

12 c.f. 'There but for the Grace of God' (119)

13 Paul Rocchi is a seasoned GM who runs *Stargate SG-1 RPG* sessions in an official capacity for AEG at both GenCon, Origins and elsewhere. His missions are considered good examples of play by AEG.

14 For example, the season two episode guide that 'explained' the technology required for the virtual reality pods in the 'Gamekeeper' episode. During the seventh season, Jeffrey Kyer, who wrote the episode guide for 'Gamekeeper', noticed that a new episode which revisited the concept of the virtual reality pods fitted precisely with the description he had provided. Personal correspondence with Rob Vaux, *Stargate SG-1 RPG* line developer for AEG.

15 It is worth noting that the Stargate indeed can function as a time machine under certain circumstances.

16 Greg Stafford and Robin D. Laws, *HeroQuest: Roleplaying in Glorantha* (Concord CA, 2003). Note, for example, p.49, where deities are listed with the gender of those who may worship them.

17 Available online at http://www.stargatesg1.com.

18 Paul Rocchi, personal correspondence with the author.

1 2

SAM I AM: FEMALE FANS' INTERACTION WITH SAMANTHA CARTER THROUGH FAN FICTION AND ONLINE DISCUSSION

RACHEL MCGRATH-KERR

Samantha Carter in *Stargate SG-1* has engaged fans from the series' beginning in 1997. As the series has progressed, the character has received promotions (she is now a lieutenant colonel in the USAF), has earned increased responsibilities, and has increased her (already astounding) knowledge. Samantha Carter may be used as an example of what can be achieved by today's woman when she utilises her brains, even in a traditionally male-dominated career path of the hard sciences in the US Air Force. What might be seen as character development has not been received in flattering terms by certain groups of online fans, who openly declare that they hate 'Super Sam'. This discontent with the series' principal female character has interesting implications in the fans' treatment of the *Stargate SG-1* universe in fan fiction. Certain examples of fan fiction (or fanfic) have been used to redress the imbalance that fans see in the series: for example, Carter is 'put in her place', realises how she has shut out people, or makes errors that have a significant impact upon the rest of the SG-1 team and/or Stargate Command. Through the interviews with fanfic writers, the motivations and thoughts of fan fiction writers about Samantha Carter are examined in this chapter, and gender and feminist issues inherent in the series' and fans' treatment of the character are analysed.

Samantha Carter (Amanda Tapping) is both a scientist and a soldier. With a Ph.D. in astrophysics as well as years of experience in the USAF, she is committed to both serving her country and extending scientific knowledge. With these attributes, Sam Carter appears to be the epitome of female achievement – a proud exemplar of successful second wave feminism. She has succeeded in the 'hard' sciences and the 'hard' military, both of which are overwhelmingly dominated by men. Even though a sexual division of labour along gender lines still exists in the military (for example, there are more male pilots than females, and more female nurses than males), Sam Carter has managed to succeed in spite of it. She does not ask for special or preferential treatment as a woman serving in the USAF: she carries her own pack, can fight with the best of them, and shows that she is both daring and courageous – attributes that have propelled her rise through the ranks during the series from captain to lieutenant colonel.

In some science fiction series in the past, the female characters have been marginalised in order to emphasise storylines concerning the principal male characters, or they have been placed in occupations that are seen as typically female. Lieutenant Uhura, the female communication officer in *Star Trek* in the 1960s, played a smaller and less active role over the series than male officers did, and in *Star Trek: The Next Generation* (1987–1994)[1] the two principal continuing female roles were in stereotypically female occupations: Chief Medical Officer Beverley Crusher and Counsellor Deanna Troi. Unlike these earlier series, *Stargate SG-1* has been consistent in featuring Sam Carter in a prominent position throughout its eight seasons. Moreover, she is featured in a variety of contexts: her expertise has been a key factor in solving many scientific problems; she goes on away missions through the Stargate with the other members of SG-1; and even her family and home life have been featured, including, in later series, her love interests. For many female viewers, Sam Carter is a role model.

However, the positioning of Sam Carter as an exemplar of equality in the workplace is seen by some female viewers as problematic. In an era of 'postfeminism', the goalposts of acceptable female behaviour have moved, and, while the inclusion of a bright, committed officer of the USAF is seen as providing a point of interest for female and male viewers and an aspirational role for many, the character of Sam Carter generates quite conflictual emotions in some fans. Years after second wave feminists fought for revolution and reform in equity and rep-resentation in the 1960s and 1970s, Sam Carter is living in a postfeminist world, and like female viewers of the series she must traverse the inherent contradictions of what an ideal modern woman is expected to be. While Sam seems to be showing what a woman can now achieve thanks to the earlier efforts of feminism, there is also an unease that some women feel about Sam's emotions, her behaviour and her goals as shown in the series. The unease between the second wave feminist movement and the current postfeminist movement is shown by second wave commentators such as Susan Faludi, who notes that the media 'declared that feminism was the flavour of the seventies and that "postfeminism" was the new story – complete with a younger generation who supposedly reviled the women's movement'.[2] Nowadays, rather than overarching feminist philosophies, there seems to be a 'generational shift' in which younger women 'assume their rights to opportunities [gained by second wave feminists] yet they regard feminism as a prescriptive way of thinking that discourages exploration on an individual level'.[3] Older feminists see a relaxation of ideals as problematic, potentially 'giving in' to demands that women revoke their hard-won gains, and younger 'postfeminists' see new areas in which parity and equity are still to be achieved without renouncing individuality.

'"Postfeminism" has new currency, which is often hostile and directed towards feminists in particular',[4] creating a discourse in which 'women, and young women in particular – declare that there is no more need for feminism because they believe equality (equal rights) has been achieved'.[5] Thus, differing attitudes towards feminist issues could be reflected in fans' views of Sam Carter. Given that contemporary young postfeminists might dislike any overt referencing to second wave activities such as pressuring patriarchies for equality (for example, the episode 'Emancipation'[6] [103]), it is equally likely that those who are influenced more strongly by the philosophies of second wave revolutionary or reformist feminists might recoil at exposés of Sam's emotional attachments (for example, her emotional attachment to Jack O'Neill). Thus, debates within the feminist movement over the feminist credentials of postfeminism[7] are played out in female fans' attitudes to 'Super Sam'.

Sam Carter is a character regularly featured in specialist cult and television magazines and regularly features on lists of favourite female characters in science fiction.[8] Interviews in these magazines with Amanda Tapping are respectful not only towards the actress but also to the character she plays, with very few, if any, unpleasant or difficult questions. The chosen discourse in such magazines is one of admiration, sharing of the fans' and the actress' opinions, and participation. However, different discourses can emerge from different contexts of appreciation. As Cassandra Amesley writes of group television watching: 'A new discourse emerges *from the viewers* which exists as counterpart to the original text' (emphasis added) and, given the number of fans who are interacting and creating a discourse with the text, it is to be expected that 'different readings can emerge all the time, as different questions raised outside a particular reading can be developed in different forms during it'.[9] Furthermore, with the advent of online fan communities, fans need not be in the same physical location to create a discourse. *Stargate SG-1* has been screened at a time when internet usage has increased exponentially in the developed world, specialised cable channels have promoted science fiction and cult television and movies, and worldwide syndication has increased. For many, fan interaction occurs principally through the medium of the internet, whether it be through specialised sites with bulletin boards for fans (e.g. GateWorld,)[10] or newsgroups (moving from the original Usenet groups to groups hosted by Yahoo!). In some forums, fans also share fan fiction created by group members.[11] Appreciation of Sam Carter is not confined to websites that look specifically at that character – her popularity is such that she is also celebrated on bulletin boards at *Stargate-SG-1*-specific websites as well as multi-show websites, not to mention the many sites and portals dedicated specifically to Sam, her place within SG-1 (for example 'Smarter than you: The Major Carter fanlisting').[12]

Given the ordinarily positive discourse about Sam Carter and the exemplary female professional character that she is consistently shown as, it is interesting to find out the reasons why some female fans do not like her. During the transmission of season eight, I put up posts on online *Stargate SG-1* fan fiction forums and emailed fans seeking women's responses to an open-ended qualitative survey about the character of Sam Carter. I wished to find out what fans thought of her: her best and worst qualities, and whether or not she was a role model. I also sought out what they thought of her development during the course of the series. Responses were anonymous and identified numerically. The 34 female respondents ranged in age from 18 to over 55 years. The majority (73 per cent[13]) were aged between 36 and 55 years. All read fan fiction, and 74 per cent of the respondents were also writers.

From survey responses, it appears that fans' readings of the *Stargate SG-1* metatext do not always accord with the dominant interpretation shown in public discourse in magazines, publicity and the series' episodes themselves. Rather than accepting Sam Carter as the epitome of modern womanhood in every aspect, viewers bring to their assessment of Sam's character the requirement that she exemplify aspects of femininity in some areas, while avoiding hyper-feminisation in others. Some fans disapprove of Sam's perceived arrogance and of the occasions when she has not acknowledged the contributions of others: it is more important that she be fair rather than be a 'glory hound'. While the inclusion of the romantic element wherein Sam has romantic feelings for her commanding officer (CO) Jack O'Neill may endear an otherwise 'strictly professional' woman to viewers who are interested in romance, such an element strikes a number of viewers as a jarring note in her subjectivity. These fans draw the line at Sam demonstrating weakness in relation to her sexual desires. This weakness is seen to demean her character (both professionally and in relation to her commitment to her team), which suggests that some fans are strongly attached to the second wave notion that female success can be jeopardised by strong emotional attachment.

Respondents remarked upon a number of Sam's positive qualities, describing a confident, capable and intelligent woman. Most respondents considered her best qualities to be her intelligence and scientific curiosity (71 per cent) followed by compassion (29 per cent), referring most frequently to her concern for the young orphan Cassandra. Sam's military leadership and commitment to teamwork (23 per cent) were exemplified by comments noting that not only does Sam have 'the respect of those around her' (Respondent 27), she also 'works well with the men of Stargate [Command] (not just SG-1)' (Respondent 29). Sam's self-assuredness and belief in herself and her loyalty and her duty were nominated by 23 per cent of respondents.[14] Sam's strength, moral values and bravery were also considered to be among her best qualities, although these qualities were cited by twice as many respondents aged 36 and above than by those aged between 18 and 35. One respondent explained why Sam's moral values and the conflicts that can arise when they are challenged are a positive attribute for a television character:

> 'Scorched Earth' (409) ... showed [Sam] in a serious conflict of ethics versus duty and showed her weighing duty more highly: that's not necessarily good or admirable as it leads to wartime horrors, but it is REAL and added to her depth and believability and told us she's capable of mistakes of good conscience. (Respondent 34)

A consistent theme through the responses was that most enjoyed and respected the character as she was shown in seasons one to three, but became less happy with her in later seasons. The comment that '[t]he early seasons (one through three) were the best for Sam' (Respondent 27) is indicative. One respondent expanded by saying: 'She seemed to be able to balance being the military professional and scientific professional with being a woman in a man's world, but I don't believe that's true any longer [with the emphasis upon her crush on Jack O'Neill].' When respondents nominated episodes that showed Sam's best qualities, the majority were in early seasons. These frequently demand a combination of Sam's emotional strength, courage, military professionalism and intelligence. Thirty-one per cent of all respondents nominated 'Singularity' (114) as an episode showing Sam's best qualities and all, with one exception, were aged 36 years and older. A key theme of this episode is Sam's affection towards the young girl, Cassandra and her subsequent determination to risk her own life to save her. Sam later offers to foster Cassandra but must reluctantly admit that her job is not ideal for child-rearing. This episode is appreciated even by a respondent who did not consider that Sam had any good qualities: 'It at least proved she was normal and had feelings' (Respondent 07). Respondent 10 remarked: '[In] "Singularity", it shows that Sam isn't just a military machine but a caring human being.'

Other episodes showing Sam at her best according to respondents were 'Foothold' (314) and 'Jolinar's Memories' (312). Twelve per cent nominated 'Children of the Gods' (101), 'Hathor' (113) 'Solitudes' (118) and 'The Devil You Know' (313). The most favoured group of episodes are those featuring the Jolinar and Tok'ra storyline ('In the Line of Duty', 202; 'Jolinar's Memories', 312; 'The Tok'ra Parts 1 and 2', 211 and 212; and 'The Devil You Know', 313), all of which are in seasons two and three. Respondent 15 commented that '[m]y favourite Sam eps [episodes] are those that require a lot of emotional strength from her and shape her character ... Coincidentally, these are all Jolinar related, but I think that's because Jolinar [the Tok'ra] was one of the strongest influences on her character and let her grow a lot.' It appears that these fans appreciate Sam's physical and emotional strength when it does not detract from her military ability but rather enhances it.

Among Sam's worst qualities, respondents included arrogance, unrealistic scientific ability (the 'Super Sam' phenomenon) and lack of mature emotional control, but the most prevalent response related to her emotional attachment to Jack O'Neill, cited by 47 per cent of respondents. Postfeminist views suggest that emotionality is compatible with feminist aims, but the fans who engage critically with the character of Sam Carter seem to differ from this perspective. They admire her intelligence, loyalty and bravery, all of which are fine qualities for a USAF officer, but have increasingly expressed dislike at the series writers' attempts to accentuate Sam's emotional vulnerability,[15] a state which comes from strong attachment. In some cases, respondents

More magnets. The team and their fans: complex dynamics. Photo by Lisa Dickson, 2005.

mentioned that they dislike the attention being taken away from Sam's professionalism and teamwork in order to focus on her romantic relationships: 'When it comes to her friends or her hormones, her hormones seem to win out at all times. No one pretends that romantic love is always edifying but did the writers really have to make Sam quite so small a person once her feelings for O'Neill kick in?' (Respondent 35). Although emotional dilemmas and choices were watched with interest in the earlier episodes such as 'Jolinar's Memories' (312), it would seem that excessive emotionalism is not seen as an asset. Sam's sexual and romantic attachment with her CO interferes with her ability to do her job and shows women to be weak and inferior in contrast to male officers. Furthermore, emotionalism that detracts from her strength and her image as an officer are rejected by a number of fans. Thirty-eight per cent cited Sam's emotional immaturity (including weepiness, needing someone's shoulder to cry on, or being envious or jealous of others) as one of her worst qualities, and that that quality affected her professional demeanour and leadership position. To quote one typical response:

> She can be self-centred, insubordinate, and unprofessional ... 'Heroes', while otherwise an excellent and emotive story, showed the depths to which the character had fallen, particularly in the way she callously dismissed Cassie's pain and grief ... by shrugging, 'She's tough. She'll survive.' She then sobs until Jack is forced, but with obvious reluctance, to hug her. Sam gets the comfort but young Cassie is given none. (Respondent 17)

It would seem that, in this and similar cases, Sam is showing an in-compatibility with second wave feminist aims through her excessive emotionalism, which interferes with her maturity and her profession.

Twenty-six per cent said that the Super Sam phenomenon (wherein Sam is an expert of not only theoretical astrophysics but any other branch of science imaginable) stretched the bounds of credibility, showing a lack of inspiration on the part of the series writers. Although the respondents were pleased to see a woman in the 'hard' sciences as an example of the increased number of areas in which women can now work, they saw the later exaggeration of her abilities as mocking and undermining both Sam and scientific professions. Furthermore, the perfection that comes from inflated scientific abilities and her infallibility is alienating to the respondents. Using the character of Super Sam is 'sloppy story-telling that gets propagated by fanfic writers who show the same laziness' (Respondent 34). Respondent 15 considers that the Super Sam quality 'makes [Sam's] character all-round perfect in every way, and perfect characters are boring. Characters need to have flaws to be interesting.' Twenty-nine per cent see her single-mindedness, inflexibility and inability to 'look outside the square' as some of her worst qualities. For example, '[i]n "A Matter of Time" (215) she's so wrapped up in the science she forgets the people involved' (Respondent 27). One of the fan fiction writers surveyed later expounded this further: 'Being a genius astrophysicist is extraordinary, her knowledge of geology, medicine, engineering, etc. – how do you write that effectively? She's like the catchall drawer in the kitchen but with ovaries' (Writer T). Twenty-nine per cent of readers mention Sam's arrogance and inability or unwillingness to acknowledge others' inputs and assistance as her worst qualities (although few specific instances were cited). 'She takes credit for things others have done' (Respondent 11) was an indicative response. Although the inclusion of a bright female scientist who can extrapolate and learn quickly appears to be a positive item that confirms second wave feminist assertions that women can succeed in any professional arena without being constrained by their gender, this exaggeration of the acquisition of skills ends up as a type of parody of second wave feminism.

However, it is not only the exaggerated depiction of second wave feminist aims in the area of intelligence that is rejected by some respondents. The majority of respondents showed that they also reject aspects of postfeminism in the area of the acceptability of emotionalism, particularly that which could compromise good character by leading to poor decisions. The high incidence of respondents commenting negatively on Sam's attachment to Jack O'Neill and its effects upon her professional behaviour was reflected in the later-season episodes that respondents identified as showing Sam's worst qualities, in particular 'Heroes Part 1 and 2' (717 and 718). The season seven two-parter finished with the death of Dr Janet Fraiser in combat, felled by a blast from a Jaffa weapon. Although seen as 'understandable under combat conditions' by some fans, others said Sam showed 'dereliction of duty' or 'poor judgment' when she abandoned her post to check on Jack O'Neill when he was felled by enemy fire, thus opening up a gap in their defences which allowed a Jaffa warrior to get through the lines and kill Dr Fraiser. Eighteen per cent considered 'Grace' (713) to show her badly. 'Grace' showed Sam marooned aboard an underpowered spaceship, and, in sequences that could be hallucinations, dreams or the urgings of a mysterious entity, Sam encounters not only her teammates but also a young girl called Grace. Amanda Tapping explained: 'Some people think [Grace is] Sam's inner child. Others feel she's Sam's child if she had chosen family over career. That's the one I'm going with.'[16] At this point, Sam appeared to make a choice to stop any pining for her commanding officer, Jack O'Neill, and to deliberately move on with her life. Fans disliked the episode because of the emphasis on her love life when they would rather see her being the bright, warm professional woman they know and admire. They were also ambivalent about a received subtext that children make a woman complete. One respondent remarked that she used to think that Sam was a feminist but changed her mind after seeing 'Grace'. Similarly, 'Divide and Conquer' (405) and 'The Lost City' (721 and 722) were all nominated by 11 per cent as showing Sam's negative qualities, particularly Sam's feelings towards her CO and the potential for those feelings to create inattention towards duty.

Two episodes, 'Avenger 2.0' (709) and 'Scorched Earth' (409), were cited as examples of Sam's lack of leadership, her poor decision-making and her scientific arrogance. In 'Avenger 2.0', Sam supports the ideas of a junior scientist, which unfortunately has far-reaching effects when the Stargate system is infected with a computer virus. In 'Scorched Earth', SG-1 is divided on the best way to assist a newly settled civilisation when the surface of their new planet was being razed by a terraforming spaceship belonging to another, long-journeying civilisation. Although Sam has some reservations, she continues to carry out orders that contradict those received at Stargate Command on Earth. Fabrisse's comments in her essay 'Scorched earth', are echoed by other fans:

> Impaired judgment by a commanding officer should not lead to impaired judgment in those under his command. There may be those who think that I'm stating my case too strongly. Or that 'since it's only a television show, why does it matter?' The answer is that fiction reflects life, and good drama reflects our difficult moral choices.[17]

I wished to find out whether female fans saw Sam Carter as explicitly feminist and whether they thought she was a role model. Two respondents saw Sam as a suitable role model for their own young daughters. In the words of one of those respondents:

She absolutely is a role model. My daughter wants to be just like her when she grows up, to the point of planning on going to the Air Force Academy and then to a career with the Air Force. (Respondent 12)

Other respondents either stated that they wouldn't see Sam as a role model for themselves, or that Sam was a role model only in early seasons when her professionalism was not problematised by a growing emphasis upon her 'perfection' and her emotions. Respondent 30 remarked, 'I think it's wonderful that the producers want to show a female character as a warrior, as a potential leader, as a role model, but they don't seem capable of actually realizing that desire,' citing Sam's flawlessness and her relationship with Jack as impediments to that realisation.

Opinion is divided on whether or not Sam Carter can be seen as a feminist. Her opening remarks in 'Children of the Gods' (101) and her behaviour in 'Emancipation' (103) were seen by some as forced, whereas others found the fact that Sam disagreed with women being treated as second-class citizens an admirable quality. Sam refuses to be treated any differently from men, and actively fights against limitations that may be placed upon her by others, for example in '48 Hours' (514), where Sam 'reacts sharply against being denigrated and limited to her gender', (Respondent 22). However, what a number of respondents consider to be an unprofessional crush on her CO is also seen to negate her ability to be considered a feminist. One respondent remarked that 'it's the person's ability to do the job that should count, not their gender', but the revelation of Sam and Jack's feelings for each other in 'Divide and Conquer' (405) problematised Sam's appearance as a feminist (Respondent 28). Her apparent neediness and emotional immaturity, seeking outside validation from men (particularly her CO, with attendant anti-fraternisation problems), shows a lack of self-respect, seen as an integral part of being secure in oneself as a woman: 'What woman these days would still have respect, admiration and ... love for a man who talks to and treats [her] the way Jack does?' (Respondent 19) Another respondent describes Sam as 'the very worst antithesis of a feminist ... [She is a] woman who plays lip service to being a feminist then plays the fainting heroine when it means she can manipulate others.' (Respondent 32) The respondents who viewed feminism as out of date, irrelevant or a sign of misandry were in the 18 to 25 years age bracket, with one exception.

Anti-fraternisation in the chain of command has not been seen as similarly problematic in earlier science fiction series. In *Star Trek*, Lieutenant Uhura was not pitched to the viewer as the love interest of Captain Kirk. The one moment that posited any physical affection between the two characters was in 'Plato's Stepchildren',[18] in which the characters were under alien mind control and thus the attraction was involuntary. The attraction between Captain Jean-Luc Picard and Doctor Beverley Crusher in the television series *Star Trek: The Next Generation* was not thoroughly developed on-screen during the series. Perhaps the reason why some viewers see the romantic relationship between Sam Carter and Jack O'Neill as being particularly problematic is that the series, although in the science fiction genre, is set in the present day and deals with a real institution – the USAF.[19] Much has been made of the series' connections with and support from the USAF and viewers expect that the producers will take care with details such as military hierarchy, choice of weapons, uniforms and behaviour. There is no comforting distance of time and geography as can be seen in future-based series with a military hierarchy, such as series in the *Star Trek* franchise.

Nonetheless, opinion remains divided upon the merits of Sam and Jack acting upon their UST (unresolved sexual tension). At the time of data collection, the season eight episode 'Threads' (818), which was suggested to tie up a number of threads concerning SG-1 team members' futures, had not been aired. Writers of fan fiction have been able to work out their own preferred storylines with the characters' relationships through their own not-for-profit stories,[20] shared with other fans nowadays principally through the medium of the internet. There are many fans who are in favour of a happy resolution to the UST and who support this through their online activities: for example, there are 3402 fan fiction stories archived or linked at 'Sam/Jack directory',[21] 441 fans who are members of the 'Sam/Jack relationship fanlisting',[22] and hundreds of members in Yahoo! groups.

From the initial 38 responses, I asked a further 13 female fans more questions concerning their thoughts about Sam on-screen and how they have responded to and worked with the character in their own writing. The respondents were fan fiction writers[23] who had expressed concerns about Sam's character development. In particular, I wished to find out whether or not the writers felt obliged to write the character of

Sam similarly to her portrayal in the television series, or if they consciously change it. The potential fluidity of characterisation in both the series and fan fiction is well known among fans:

> [Sam], along with all characters, is at the hands of the writers and their perceptions … She will always be written in a variety of ways, some close to canon, others far removed from it. That's the joy of fanfic. (LAW)[24]

The majority of writers surveyed choose to write the character selectively, either adapting the character to avoid traits that they dislike, or to avoid the character altogether. Ximeria chooses to 'write her the way we saw her in the early episodes – a far more well-rounded character'. Alphekka writes that she wishes to write Sam as 'honourable, dedicated [and] professional', rather than the 'hypocritical' and 'unprofessional' person she considers that Sam has become. Writer 1, who has lived in military accommodation, finds Sam 'demeaning, shallow and false': any officer in real life who had acted the way that Sam has (such as having a crush on her CO, committing gross errors and showing poor judgement) would have been transferred from the SGC or court-martialled by now. Consequently, Writer 1 now has no desire to write about Sam in her fiction.[25]

The reconciliation of fans' perceptions of Sam, their wishes for her character, and the way she is actually portrayed on television may be played out in two main ways in fan fiction: to ignore Sam completely (for example, sending her on another mission while concentrating on characters such as Jack O'Neill or Daniel Jackson,)[26] or to 'set things right' (for example, Sam is given a salutary lesson or two, or alternatively written as the woman and officer that fans have hoped to see on-screen). '[T]he active and productive part played by female audiences in constructing textual meanings and pleasures'[27] should not be underestimated. Women as media consumers are not 'cultural dupes', nor are they 'victims of inexorably sexist media';[28] however, along with the creativity and criticism with which women interact with a televisual text, there is rarely uncritical gratitude towards the (often) male media producers who cast (or deign to add?) a strong, professional female character into one of the lead roles. Rather, the addition of multi-talented female characters to a contemporary-based series seems to raise the bar even higher. While a certain level of fallibility and occasional cracks in the heroine's facade bring further dimensions to the character, viewers are well aware that this is fiction. One writer adds:

> The main modifications I make are when I am aware that reality would create a difference ... I let Sam be a little more free in her language and I let her NOT know stuff and I restrict her area of expertise to what seems reasonable in light of the astrophysicists I know ... then I add a little for extra brilliance. I see that as respecting the character and liking her, as opposed to using her as a cut out for a fantasy. (Livengoo)

Fanfic authors actively humanise Sam, breaking the sometimes impenetrable shell of self-confidence and self-assuredness seen on-screen. It should be noted that the stories do not overwhelmingly make Sam more 'feminised', or detract from her intelligence and skills. Rather, the emphasis is upon adding to her emotional repertoire to develop her character beyond that seen on-screen. Devra writes: 'My Sam character actually is written with personality traits and caring from the first three seasons,' and Babs comments that she hates it when Sam is not allowed 'to be human and fallible'. In Babs' and Devra's collaborative stories 'Amusement park' and 'Guardians of the heart' Sam examines her feelings of guilt and sorrow, shows concern for her friends when they are ill and is an integral and cooperative part of the larger SGC team.[29] This ambiguity towards excessive and/or appropriate emotionalism is, in some ways, typical of the debate about Sam. Sam is condemned for being overly emotional and playing up emotionality as a point of strength that can help her gain what she wants. However, if she is shown as being too clinical and detached from what may be considered as 'emotional' situations, she is then condemned as a cold-hearted bitch. It appears that writers and readers of fan fiction are treading a fine line in discovering and determining what is appropriate, praiseworthy and blameworthy in Sam's character and that the boundaries may move depending upon time and circumstance as well as the participants in the debate at the time.

The process of adding what fanfic writers consider to be 'appropriate' emotionalism or a 'deeper dimension' is also shown in stories by authors who were not surveyed. For example, in Rowan Darkstar's 'Ice for melting', a fanfic set immediately after 'Lost City, Part 2' (722), Sam is overcome with despair at leaving Jack O'Neill behind in Antarctica and breaks down in tears in private.[30] In 'Cold comfort' by Denise (set after the season three episode 'A Hundred Days', 317)

Sam realises that the refugees from Edora were not unanimously grateful for her help, and she was hurt by Jack's flat affect when he was rescued from the planet.[31] Once again, although Sam has shown that she feels deeply about her predicament, she is shown to be acting initially with selfish purposes and thus receives her due.

By not being constrained by official story-arcs, fanfic authors can tackle issues that have not been addressed in the series, such as the opinions of people who work with Sam, or potential ramifications of her actions. Fabrisse, another writer who admired Sam as the 'occasionally flawed but striving officer' of the early seasons, examines Sam's behaviour when encountering the command split after Jack O'Neill was promoted to brigadier general.[32] In the same story, Jack notes negative points about his and Sam's behaviour: 'Not only had he endangered the team by allowing himself to bask in the glow of attraction, he'd hurt Carter's career.'[33] In 'Realizations' by Debi C., what Sam overhears at Stargate Command makes her realise that she is self-centred and hasn't acknowledged the help of her team-mates.[34]

It would appear to be nigh on impossible to create a female character in a science fiction series who will meet with universal approval. If she is too perfect, with professional acclaim and emotional satisfaction coming easily to her, she will alienate women who are all too aware of the difficulties of being in the workforce and the effort required to keep relationships working. If the character is emotionless or dispassionate, relating mostly to machines or the ideals of theoretical science, the character will appear to be either masculinised or robotic, either of which is, again, an alienating trait when displayed in a female character. However, should she show emotional or moral weaknesses, such as jealousy, disloyalty or heartlessness, she is likely to be criticised for that as well. Some fans see that the television series is not privileging and prizing Sam Carter's emotional stability and adult relationships and, instead, the series is now infantilising Sam's character traits to the point that her emotional responses are those of a teenager while her intellectual gifts are those of an adult. Through the agency of fan fiction, writers can reconcile Sam to what they think a professional woman should be, not only according to the writers' own lives, but with additional aspirations given Sam's extraordinary genius and ability. It might be assumed that some fans are responding from the perspective of their own experiences of trying to live out second wave feminist goals in the context of strong feelings of attachment and emotionality. Fan reaction is always a meeting point between audience aspirations and experiences and the range of meanings ascribed in texts. Fan reactions to Sam Carter attest to the difficulty of negotiating between the range of discourses on femininity, feminism and what it means to be a woman in today's world. In particular, they suggest that the possession of true strength and equality is more achievable where emotions of attachment are downplayed. This emotional disengagement is privileged in the text by the military context. This belief that excessive emotion is incompatible with strength and equality in itself brings into question central tenets within postfeminism, and could suggest that, although Sam Carter has been displayed as an icon for equality and achievement in a postfeminist world, she is not a feminist.

Notes

1   *Star Trek: The Next Generation*, executive producers Gene Roddenberry, Rick Berman, Michael Piller, Jeri Taylor (Paramount, 1987–1994)

2   Susan Faludi, *Backlash* (New York, 1992), p.14

3   Kathy Bail, 'Introduction', K. Bail, *DIY Feminism* (Australia, 1996), pp.3, 5

4   Lynne Alice, 'What is Postfeminism? Or, having it both ways', L. Alice (ed.), *Feminism, Postmodernism, Postfeminism: Conference Proceedings* (New Zealand, 1995), p.7

5   L. S Kim, 'The F word on television', *Television & New Media*, 2, 4, November 2001, p.321

6   All references to the episodes are indicated parenthetically by episode number. See the Episode guide for further information.

7   Ann Brooks, *Postfeminisms: Feminism, Cultural Theory and Cultural Forms* (New York, 1997)

8   For example, Sharon Gosling, 'Ten women who shook Sci-Fi', *Dreamwatch*, 119, July 2004, p.45. Sam Carter was also ranked fourth in the list of the Top Ten Feisty Females in *Cult Times Special*, 30 (2004).

9   Cassandra Amesley, 'How to watch *Star Trek*', *Cultural Studies*, 3, 3 (1989) p.337

10 GateWorld, 'Gateworld: your complete guide to Stargate', online (accessed 1 July 2005, http://www.gateworld.net)

11 Only one respondent commented that her responses may have been influenced by other fans with whom she interacts online.

12 'Smarter than you: The Major Carter fanlisting', online (accessed 1 July 2005, http://carter.sholvah.org/index2.php)

13   A content analysis was performed upon responses to the questions asking what the viewer saw as Sam Carter's best and worst qualities. Respondents were able to nominate as many or as few qualities as they liked, and responses were grouped according to similar themes.

14   It should be noted that not every respondent saw good qualities in the character: 'She doesn't really have any' (Respondent 07); 'None – she's just a secondary character' (Respondent 22); 'She has good qualities??' (Respondent 32).

15   C.f. 'Sherrie A. Inness, 'Boxing gloves and bustiers', *Action Chicks* (New York, 2004), p.14

16   Steven Eramo, 'Major player: Interview with Amanda Tapping', *TV Zone*, 172 (2004), p.15

17   Fabrisse, 'Scorched earth' (unpublished, 2004)

18   *Star Trek*, 'Plato's Stepchildren', written by Meyer Dolinsky, directed by David Alexander (Desilu/Paramount, 1966–1969)

19   For example, Richard Dean Anderson, star of *Stargate SG-1* and the series' executive producer, was given a rare award by the Air Force Association on 14 September 2004 for the series' positive depiction of the USAF.

20   This is discussed in Henry Jenkins, 'Fan critics', chapter 3 in *Textual Poachers: Television Fans and Participatory Culture* (New York, 1992).

21   'Sam/Jack directory', online (accessed 1 July 2005, http://samandjack.net/directory/main.html.

22   'The Sam/Jack relationship fanlisting', online (accessed 1 July 2005, http://samjack.sholvah.org/)

23   These writers are identified (with their permission) only by their chosen pseudonyms or preferred identifiers.

24   This echoes Henry Jenkins' observation of 'fans' powerlessness over the narrative's development' and 'of the degree to which the fan's own pleasures are often at the mercy of producers ...' (*Textual Poachers*, p.118).

25   Writer 1 explained that she now doesn't wish to see Sam on *Stargate SG-1* DVDs or videotapes, to the point of editing media formats to remove the character.

26   This is most often seen in the subgenre of slash fiction, in which a homoerotic relationship between two persons of the same sex is posited, for example, between Jack O'Neill and Daniel Jackson.

27   Ien Ang, *Living Room Wars: Rethinking Media Audiences for a Postmodern World* (New York, 1996), p.114

28   Ibid.

29   Babs and Devra, 'Amusement park', online (accessed 1 July 2005, http://www.thealphagate.com/stories/AmusementParkAGoodbyetoDreams*MissingScene*.asp), and 'Guardians of the Heart', online (accessed 1 July 2005, http://www.thealphagate.com/stories/GuardiansoftheHeart.asp)

30 Rowan Darkstar, 'Ice for melting', online (accessed 1 July 2005, http//rowan_d.tripod.com/ice.html).

31 Denise, 'Cold comfort', online (accessed 1 July 2005, http://www.geocities.com/sky_diver119/missing/season3/cold.htm).

32 Fabrisse, 'Points of departure', online (accessed 1 July 2005, http://www.thealphagate.com/stories/PointsofDeparture.asp).

33 In one story, Jacob Carter, who is a retired general, bluntly tells Sam about her relationship with Jack: 'You're 12 years younger, 10 times brighter, have absolutely nothing in common and you could both go to Leavenworth over this.' Jobeth, 'A long day's journey into Minnesota', online (accessed 1 July 2005, http://www.thealphagate.com/stories/ALongDaysJourneyIntoMinnesota.asp).

34 Debi C., 'Realizations', online, accessed 1 July 2005, http://www.thealphagate.com/stories/Realizations.asp)

APPENDIX:
AMERICAN MODES[1]

GAILE MCGREGOR

Primitivism		Progressivism
1880s, 1920s, 1960s		1900s, 1940s, 1980s

transformers[2]

I-site[3]

Nature (Garden of Eden)		*Culture (City of New Jerusalem)*
wilderness	small town, inner-city slum	city
(alt. garden, countryside)		(civilisation)
margins, hinterlands	frontier (escapism vs conquest)	the centre

Psychosexual Orientation

The Feminine (anima)	phallic potency	The Masculine (patriarchy)

General Adjuncts

space	time
myth	history
dream	logic
magic	science and technology

spirituality	religion
chivalry	militarism
'innocence'	'experience'
(intuition, heuristics, bricolage)	(education, theory, tradition)
body, senses, emotion	mind, intellect, logic
carnival, desire, libidinality	asceticism, self-discipline
primary process thinking	concern with structure, boundaries
promiscuous/ polymorphous sexuality	marriage, family
personal morality	ethics, aesthetics

Socio-political Modes

horizontal relations	vertical relations
democracy	hierarchy
(emphasis on autonomy)	(emphasis on gender, generation, class)
anti-authoritarianism	civic duty, leadership
rebellion to radicalism	reform to repression
libertarianism/anarchy	social regulation
will	law
achieved status	ascribed status
communalism/ primitive capitalism	welfare liberalism/ corporate capitalism

Cultural Markers

popular/folk culture	avant garde (transgressive vs elitist)	'fine' arts
intellectual iconoclasm		hermeticism, academisation
collectivity, amateurism spontaneity, sincerity, authenticity		specialisation technique, artifice, decoration

performance (individual expression)		spectacle
fantasy, naturalism		realism, abstraction
parataxis, montage		narrative

heroes:

outsiders (gunslinger, gangster)	anti-hero (anti-social vs non-heroic)	social champions (cop, soldier)

traits:

natural instrumentality	technological instrumentality
(personal powers, animal/ magical helpers)	(weapons, hardware, cybernetics)
self-elected, self-validated	state-authorised (uniforms, credentials)

villains/sources of threat:

society, agents of the father	outsiders, agents of disorder, libidinal excess

images of women:

natural (tomboy vs sex kitten)	social (good mother vs femme fatale)

icons:

noble savage types (exotics, peasants, madmen, fool-saints)	children, working class	social elite (the rich, the royal, the famous)

Notes

1   ©Gaile McGregor. This schema is extrapolated from previous work and was prepared for purposes other than the present. It is included here only to give the reader a sense of the 'flavour' of the two opposing paradigms. For further explanations and applications, see the publications listed in note 14 in McGregor's article.

2   During transition periods we see a proliferation of characters and symbolic motifs that are double-coded such that they can be 'read' as either primitive or progressive or both simultaneously. This facilitates a shift of meaning while allowing for denial. The examples shown here are far from exhausting the possibilities.

3   The term designates both normative setting and symbolic location for the self.

STARGÅTE SG-1 EPISODE GUIDE

MARTHA TAYLOR

Stargate (1994 movie)

Writers: Dean Devlin and Roland Emmerich; Director: Roland Emmerich

Ostracised from the academic community for his unorthodox opinions about the true architects of the Great Pyramids, Daniel Jackson discovers aliens really did build the pyramids when he translates the markings on a cover stone laid over a mysterious artefact found on the Giza Plateau. Colonel Jack O'Neil (he gains a second 'l' in the television show) leads a team on a suicide mission through the Stargate to find a colony transplanted from Earth 5000 years ago and still in thrall to their tyrannical but extremely beautiful god king, Ra.

Season One: 1997–1998

101A. Children of the Gods 1

Writers: Jonathan Glassner and Brad Wright; Director: Mario Azzopardi

Jack is called out of retirement; Daniel uncovers the Abydos Stargate and loses his wife and brother-in-law to Apophis.

101B. Children of the Gods 2

Writers: Jonathan Glassner and Brad Wright; Director: Mario Azzopardi

Jack fails to rescue Sha're and Skaara, but does gain the loyalty of Apophis' First Prime, Teal'c.

102. The Enemy Within

Writer: Brad Wright; Director: Dennis Berry

Major Kawalsky returns from Chulak infected by a Goa'uld, and Jack allows him to die when medical intervention fails.

103. Emancipation

Writer: Katharyn Powers; Director: Jeff Woolnough

Sam's demands for the equal treatment of women in a transplanted Mongol society go unheard until she saves the lives of a local Romeo and Juliet by prevailing in mortal combat.

104. The Broca Divide
Writer: Jonathan Glassner; Director: William Gereghty
On a planet which apparently doesn't rotate upon its axis, SG-1 contracts a disease which causes its victims to devolve into their prehuman predecessors.

105. The First Commandment
Writer: Robert C. Cooper; Director: William Berry
Sent to study a human colony living in wretched conditions, SG team commander Jonas Hanson instead declares himself a god. His and Sam's past engagement does not simplify the situation.

106. Cold Lazarus
Writer: Jeff F. King; Director: Kenneth J. Girotti
A blue crystalline entity accidentally wounds Jack, and, in an attempt to heal him, assumes his form and returns to Earth to find Jack's dead son, Charlie.

107. The Nox
Writer: Hart Hanson; Director: Charles Correll
In what proves a familiar pattern in first contact situations, SG-1 drastically misjudges the Nox, mistaking the near-omnipotent beings for helpless innocents.

108. Brief Candle
Story: Steven Barnes; Writer: Katharyn Powers; Director: Mario Azzopardi
Jack contracts sexually transmitted nanocytes engineered as part of a millennia-old Goa'uld experiment, and begins to age decades by the day.

109. Thor's Hammer
Writer: Katharyn Powers; Director: Brad Turner
Daniel's theory that the Goa'uld may not have been the only alien species to have visited Earth is borne out on Cimmeria, where SG-1 finds a colony of Vikings brought from Earth by their god, Thor.

110. The Torment of Tantalus
Writer: Robert C. Cooper; Director: Jonathan Glassner
Fifty years after Catherine Langford's financé disappeared through the Stargate, SG-1 finds him in Heliopolis, once the meeting place of four ancient alien species.

111. Bloodlines
Writer: Jeff F. King; Director: Mario Azzopardi
Returning to Chulak hoping to prevent his son from being implanted with a Goa'uld, Teal'c instead finds Rya'c so ill that only the healing properties of a larval Goa'uld can save him.

112. Fire and Water
Story: Brad Wright and Katharyn Powers; Teleplay: Katharyn Powers; Director: Allan Eastman

The roster of alien visitors to Earth continues to lengthen when Nem kidnaps Daniel to question him about the fate of his mate Omaroca, killed while fighting the Goa'uld on Earth 4000 years before. The rest of SG-1 mourns Daniel's apparent demise.

113. Hathor
Story: David Bennett Carron and J. Larry Carrol; Teleplay: Jonathan Glassner; Director: Brad Turner

Freed after a 2000 year imprisonment in a Mayan pyramid, Hathor arrives at the SGC intending to rebuild her Jaffa army and breed new Goa'uld larvae.

114. Singularity
Writer: Robert C. Cooper; Director: Mario Azzopardi

SG-1 brings the sole survivor of Goa'uld-engineered plague back to Earth. It's all a trap: Nirrti has implanted a naqada bomb in Cassandra's heart.

115. Cor-ai
Writer: Tom J. Astle; Director: Mario Azzopardi

Teal'c is put on trial for a murder he committed as Apophis' First Prime. He refuses to consider escape, telling Jack that he deserves to be punished for his crimes.

116. Enigma
Writer: Katharyn Powers; Director: William Gereghty

SG-1 rescues the Tollans first from their dying world, then from the NID. Narim falls in love with Sam, who reciprocates by giving him a cat.

117. Tin Man
Writer: Jeff King; Director: Jimmy Kaufman

As if the Goa'uld hadn't already complicated mind/body issues for our heroes, a lonely scientist on a mechanical world copies SG-1's consciousnesses into androids.

118. Solitudes
Writer: Brad Wright; Director: Martin Wood

A gate malfunction sends Jack and Sam through a hitherto unsuspected second Earth Stargate, this one buried in an Antarctic glacial crevasse.

119. There but for the Grace of God
Story: David Kemper; Teleplay: Robert C. Cooper; Director: David Warry-Smith

Daniel touches the quantum mirror and winds up in a universe where Apophis' apocalyptic assault on Earth is already under way.

120. Politics
Writer: Brad Wright; Director: Martin Wood

Senator Kinsey ends funding for the Stargate programme. Jack suggests a bake sale.

121. Within the Serpent's Grasp

Story: James Crocker; Teleplay: Jonathan Glassner; Director: David Warry-Smith

SG-1 tries to thwart the attack on Earth Daniel foresaw in 'There but for the Grace of God'.

Season Two: 1998–1999

201. The Serpent's Lair

Writer: Brad Wright; Director: Jonathan Glassner

SG-1 destroys Apophis' fleet, gets rescued by the space shuttle, and even Daniel, left for dead, manages to gate his way home.

202. In the Line of Duty

Writer: Robert C. Cooper; Director: Martin Wood

The Goa'uld Jolinar, a member of the Tok'ra resistance force, takes Sam as an unwilling host, but later saves her life after an attack by a Goa'uld assassin.

203. Prisoners

Writer: Terry Curtis Fox; Director: David Warry-Smith

SG-1 breaks out of the alien prison planet Hadante, unfortunately releasing a mass murderer known as the Destroyer of Worlds in the process.

204. The Gamekeeper

Story: Jonathan Glassner and Brad Wright; Teleplay: Jonathan Glassner; Director: Martin Wood

Imprisoned in an arboretum, Jack's and Daniel's memories are mined to entertain a bored civilisation who are waiting out an environmental catastrophe in suspended animation.

205. Need

Story: Robert C. Cooper and Damian Kindler; Teleplay: Robert C. Cooper; Director: David Warry-Smith

Daniel goes darkside – Jack's succinct analysis – when he becomes addicted to cycles in the sarcophagus.

206. Thor's Chariot

Writer: Katharyn Powers; Director: William Gereghty

Destroying Thor's hammer has left Cimmeria vulnerable to Goa'uld attack. SG-1 summons the Asgard, who turn out to be the greys of UFO folklore, to save the planet.

207. Message in a Bottle

Story: Michael Greenburg and Jarrad Paul; Teleplay: Brad Wright; Director: David Warry-Smith

An orb found on an airless moon skewers Jack to a gateroom wall to prevent SG-1 from sending the orb back.

208. Family

Writer: Katharyn Powers; Director: William Gereghty

Teal'c's wife has remarried and his son has been kidnapped and brainwashed by Apophis, but well-timed zat blasts solve both problems.

209. Secrets

Writer: Terry Curtis Smith; Director: Duane Clark

Sha're gives birth to Apophis' son, a journalist investigating the Stargate is killed in a suspicious hit-and-run accident in front of Jack, and Sam's father is dying of cancer. Nobody's happy.

210. Bane

Writer: Robert C. Cooper; Director: David Warry-Smith

Teal'c begins mutating after being stung by a big alien bug.

The Tok'ra

211. Part 1

212. Part 2

Writer: Jonathan Glassner; Director: Brad Turner

Sam's memories of Jolinar lead SG-1 to the Tok'ra base; Sam's father, Jacob, becomes host to the Tok'ra Selmak in order to save both their lives.

213. Spirits

Writer: Tor Alexander Valenza; Director: Martin Wood

The Pentagon turns a deaf ear to the Salish people's refusal to allow strip mining on their adopted planet. Jack manages to convince the aliens who have been posing as the Salish spirits not to blow up the SGC in retaliation.

214. Touchstone

Writer: Sam Egan; Director: Brad Turner

Forget diplomacy – the NID is sending its own teams through the second Stargate to steal alien technology.

215. A Matter of Time

Story: Misha Rasovich; Teleplay: Brad Smith; Director: Martin Wood

Jack can't save an off-world SG team being sucked into a black hole, but does save Earth from the same fate. Sam demonstrates Einsteinian physics with a glazed doughnut.

216. The Fifth Race

Writer: Robert C. Cooper; Director: David Warry-Smith

After the knowledge of the Ancients is accidentally uploaded into his head, Jack modifies the Stargate and travels to the Asgard homeworld. Gently admonished for mankind's precociousness, Jack replies that his is a very curious race.

217. Serpent's Song

Writer: Katharyn Powers; Director: Peter DeLuise

Mortally wounded in battle with Sokar, Apophis seeks sanctuary at the SGC.

218. Holiday

Writer: Tor Alexander Valenza; Director: David Warry-Smith

Ma'chello lost everything in his lifelong fight against the Goa'uld and appropriates Daniel's body in recompense.

219. One False Step

Story: Michael Kaplan; Writer: John Sanborn; Director: William Corcoran

SG-1 brings plague to a civilisation of naked mimes. Jack and Daniel air their differences.

220. Show and Tell

Writer: Jonathan Glassner; Director: Peter DeLuise

'Mother' of the Reetu, a race of giant invisible insects, engineers a human boy to warn Earth of the danger posed by rebel factions of her own kind.

221. 1969

Writer: Brad Wright; Director: Charles Correll

Sent back in time by a solar flare, SG-1 roadtrips across 1969 America to find the mothballed Stargate and gate themselves home.

222. Out of Mind

Story: Jonathan Glassner and Brad Wright; Teleplay: Jonathan Glassner; Director: Martin Wood

Hathor abducts SG-1 and tells them they've been in cryogenic sleep for the past 79 years.

Season Three: 1999–2000

301. Into the Fire

Writer: Brad Wright; Director: Martin Wood

Continued from 'Out of Mind', it's Teal'c, Master Bra'tac and General Hammond to the rescue.

302. Seth

Writer: Jonathan Glassner; Director: William Corcoran

Daniel Googles the name 'Seth' to find Goa'uld still alive and well on Earth. Teal'c memorably demonstrates Jaffa humour.

303. Fair Game
Writer: Robert C. Cooper; Director: William Corcoran
At Thor's behest, Jack represents Earth during treaty negotiations with the Goa'uld System Lords.

304. Legacy
Writer: Tor Alexander Valenza; Director: Peter DeLuise
Twice burned by Ma'chello, this time Daniel winds up in a padded cell after being infected by one of Ma'chello's Goa'uld-killing inventions.

305. Learning Curve
Writer: Heather E. Ash; Director: Martin Wood
Jack kidnaps an 11-year-old girl from a civilisation which uses their children as organic accumulators of knowledge.

306. Point of View
Story: Jonathan Glassner, Brad Wright, Robert C. Cooper and Tor Alexander Valenza; Teleplay: Jonathan Glassner and Brad Wright; Director: Peter DeLuise
Major Kawalsky, still alive, and a long-haired, understandably rather weepy Sam escape from their own Goa'uld-infested universe through the quantum mirror.

307. Deadman Switch
Writer: Robert C. Cooper; Director: Martin Wood
SG-1 convinces Aris Boch, a bounty hunter with a heart of gold, to rescue a Tok'ra spy rather than turning him over to Sokar.

308. Demons
Writer: Carl Binder; Director: Peter DeLuise
A village transplanted from medieval England suffers the predation of an Unas in the employ of Sokar. Teal'c summarily dismisses the idea of a Goa'uld assuming the role of the Judeo-Christian god.

309. Rules of Engagement
Writer: Terry Curtis Fox; Director: William Gereghty
Apophis' Jaffa have been training human slaves to infiltrate the SGC.

310. Forever in a Day
Writer: Jonathan Glassner; Director: Peter DeLuise
During the final seconds of her life, Sha're reveals to Daniel the hiding place of her child.

311. Past and Present
Writer: Tor Alexander Valenza; Director: William Gereghty
Unfortunately for Daniel, who rather fancies her, the pretty young scientist with the blonde ringlets found on a planet of amnesiacs is actually the Destroyer of Worlds last seen in 'Prisoners'.

312. Jolinar's Memories

Writers: Sonny Wareham and Daniel Stashower; Director: Peter DeLuise

SG-1 is dispatched to Netu to rescue Jacob Carter from Sokar, counting on Sam's grasp of Jolinar's memories to get them out again.

313. The Devil You Know

Writer: Robert C. Cooper; Director: Peter DeLuise

The presence of Apophis, not so dead after all, complicates the escape from Netu.

314. Foothold

Writer: Heather E. Ash; Director: Andy Mikita

The SGC is overrun by aliens with the ability to mimic the appearance of SGC personnel, and Sam goes to Harry Maybourne for help.

315. Pretense

Writer: Katharyn Powers; Director: David Warry-Smith

The Tollans mediate a dispute between Skaara and the Goa'uld Klorel over possession of Skaara's body. Sam's cat makes a return appearance.

316. Urgo

Writer: Tor Alexander Valenza; Director: Peter DeLuise

Bad enough when the members of SG-1 are tagged like wild caribou by an inquisitive alien; things get worse when the implanted surveillance device develops a mind of its own and encourages the irresponsible consumption of pie.

317. A Hundred Days

Writer: V. C. James; Teleplay: Brad Wright; Director: David Warry-Smith

Stranded for months on an idyllic world with a woman who loves him, Jack eventually finds a measure of happiness, but he returns to Earth post-haste when the rest of SG-1 eventually reach him.

318. Shades of Gray

Writer: Jonathan Glassner; Director: Martin Wood

Shutting down the Antarctic gate didn't stop the theft of alien technology. Jack breaks emotional ties with the rest of his team and goes undercover to flush out the culprits.

319. New Ground

Writer: Heather E. Ash; Director: Chris McMullin

SG-1's very arrival through the Stargate threatens religious orthodoxy for a planet at war, and our heroes find themselves stuck in little metal cages being shocked with pointy sticks.

320. Maternal Instinct

Writer: Robert C. Cooper; Director: Peter F. Woeste

Daniel either does or doesn't receive enlightenment on the half-mythical world of Kheb, but he does find Sha're's child being raised by an Ascended being, Oma Desala.

321. Crystal Skull

Story: Michael Greenburg and Jarrad Paul; Teleplay: Brad Wright; Director: Brad Turner

After touching a crystal skull in an alien pyramid, Daniel is left wandering the corridors of the SGC like a spirit. SG-1 springs Daniel's grandfather, Nick, from a mental ward to get Daniel back.

322. Nemesis

Writer: Robert C. Cooper; Director: Martin Wood

Thor seeks Jack's help in destroying the Replicators – oversized, Erector-Set alien bugs – which have infested his ship and the Asgard galaxy.

Season Four: 2000–2001

401. Small Victories

Writer: Robert C. Cooper; Director: Martin Wood

Jack and Teal'c destroy Replicators on board a Russian submarine, Sam saves the Asgard homeworld, and Daniel frets.

402. The Other Side

Writer: Brad Wright; Director: Peter DeLuise

Posing as victims rather than the aggressors, fanatical eugenicists offer technology in exchange for raw materials. Daniel has misgivings; Jack and General Hammond have a mandate to procure new weapons.

403. Upgrades

Writer: David Rich; Director: Martin Wood

Anise outfits SG-1 with armbands (inscribed, fittingly enough, with advice from Spiderman's Uncle Ben) which turn the team into amiable but irresponsible superheroes.

404. Crossroads

Writer: Katharyn Powers; Director: Peter DeLuise

Teal'c's old flame comes to the SGC, claiming to have converted her almost mature symbiote from evil. She's wrong.

405. Divide and Conquer

Writer: Tor Alexander Valenza; Director: Martin Wood

Jack's and Sam's prevarications about their mutual feelings cause Anise's latest invention to finger them as brainwashed assassins.

406. Window of Opportunity
Writers: Joseph Mallozzi and Paul Mullie; Director: Peter DeLuise
Jack and Teal'c relive the same day repeatedly for three months, learning the language of the Ancients and how to juggle along the way.

407. Watergate
Writer: Robert C. Cooper; Director: Martin Wood
The Russians have opened a wormhole to a planet of sentient water, but must call on SG-1 to shut the gate down again.

408. The First Ones
Writer: Peter DeLuise; Director: Peter DeLuise
An adolescent Unas captures Daniel for dinner, but spares him after Daniel demonstrates self-awareness and the ability to acquire language.

409. Scorched Earth
Writers: Joseph Mallozzi and Paul Mullie; Director: Martin Wood
When two fragile civilisations lay claim to the same planet, Jack and Daniel go to irreconcilable extremes: Jack by arming a naqada bomb, Daniel by boarding the vessel Jack intends to blow up.

410. Beneath the Surface
Writer: Heather Ash; Director: Peter DeLuise
Stripped of their memories, SG-1 is sent to work in an underground power plant. Manual labour appears to suit them.

411. Point of No Return
Writer: Joseph Mallozzi and Paul Mullie; Director: William Gereghty
Martin Lloyd is sure he's from another planet, meant to return through the Stargate to do great deeds. SG-1 learns that he's got the 'other planet' part right.

412. Tangent
Writer: Michael Cassutt; Director: Peter DeLuise
A test flight of a retro-fitted Death Glider sends Jack and Teal'c hurtling out of the Solar System.

413. The Curse
Writers: Joseph Mallozzi and Paul Mullie; Director: Andy Mikita
Jack and Teal'c go fishing. Daniel attends his mentor's funeral and loses another old girlfriend to the Goa'uld.

414. The Serpent's Venom
Writer: Peter DeLuise; Director: Martin Wood
Teal'c is betrayed into the hands of Heru'ur's witchfinder general while the rest of SG-1 attempt to start an intra-System-Lord war by reprogramming an orbiting mine. Sam asks Daniel to accept the importance of zero on faith.

415. Chain Reaction

Writer: Joseph Mallozzi and Paul Mullie; Director: Martin Wood

Jack teams up with Maybourne to set things straight after General Hammond is forced into retirement. Hammond's replacement almost blows up the planet.

416. 2010

Writer: Brad Wright; Director: Andy Mikita

In the episode's title year, the former members of SG-1 discover Earth's decade-long alliance with the seemingly benevolent Aschen was, in fact, a very bad idea.

417. Absolute Power

Writer: Robert C. Cooper; Director: Peter DeLuise

When pressed to reveal the knowledge of the Goa'uld, Shifu, the koan-spouting Harsesis child, instead gives Daniel a teaching dream in which Daniel blows up Red Square and takes over the world.

418. The Light

Writer: James Phillips; Director: Peter F. Woeste

On a Goa'uld pleasure planet SG-1 becomes addicted to a visual narcotic, withdrawal from which causes a suicidal depression. Jack lies very badly about Daniel's interest in a curling championship.

419. Prodigy

Story: Brad Wright, Joseph Mallozzi and Paul Mullie; Teleplay: Joseph Mallozzi and Paul Mullie; Director: Peter DeLuise

Sam takes a personal interest in the career of a brilliant cadet while Jack and Teal'c oversee a scientific outpost haunted by killer lightning bugs.

420. Entity

Writer: Peter DeLuise; Director: Allan Lee

SG-1's computer is invaded by an entity, which then proceeds to take over Sam's mind.

421. Double Jeopardy

Writer: Robert C. Cooper; Director: Michael Shanks

SG-1's android doubles arrive on a world that is suffering the consequences of the real SG-1's previous visit.

422. Exodus

Writers: Joseph Mallozzi and Paul Mullie; Director: David Warry-Smith

Never one to think small, Sam destroys Apophis' fleet by blowing up a star after the Tok'ra decamp to a new base.

Season Five: 2001–2002

501. Enemies
Story: Brad Wright, Robert C. Cooper, Joseph Mallozzi and Paul Mullie;
Teleplay: Robert C. Cooper; Director: Martin Wood
The star Sam blew up in 'Exodus' flings both Apophis and SG-1 across the universe to the Replicator's galaxy. Further complicating matters, Teal'c has been brainwashed into believing he is once more First Prime of Apophis.

502. Threshold
Writer: Brad Wright; Director: Peter DeLuise
Teal'c endures a Jaffa deprogramming ordeal, reliving his service under Apophis.

503. Ascension
Writer: Robert C. Cooper; Director: Martin Wood
Exiled on a planet where his well-meant interference once destroyed a civilisation, an Ascended being, Orlin, falls in love with Sam and follows her home, where he builds a Stargate in her basement with mail-order parts to keep history from repeating itself.

504. The Fifth Man
Writers: Joseph Mallozzi and Paul Mullie; Director: Peter DeLuise
An alien who is being hunted by the Goa'uld uses his natural camouflage to make SG-1 believe he's the fifth member of their team.

505. Red Sky
Writer: Ron Wilkerson; Director: Martin Wood
Sam continues to be hard on stars, accidentally triggering a fatal chain reaction in the sun of a planet inhabited by pious worshippers of the Asgard.

506. Rite of Passage
Writer: Heather Ash; Director: Peter DeLuise
Before wiping out the inhabitants of Cassandra's planet (in 'Singularity'), Nirrti had been conducting a generations-long experiment in human evolution. When Cassie falls ill, Nirrti returns to continue her work.

507. Beast of Burden
Writer: Peter DeLuise; Director: Martin Wood
Daniel convinces a highly reluctant Jack to help rescue an Unas, Chaka, from slavery. Once freed, Chaka remains on the slavers' planet to free the rest of his kind.

508. The Tomb
Writers: Joseph Mallozzi and Paul Mullie; Director: Peter DeLuise
SG-1 and a Russian team wander around Marduk's ziggurat looking for a fabled Goa'uld weapon and trying to avoid a Goa'uld-infested, multi-legged carnivore.

509. Between Two Fires

Writer: Ron Wilkerson; Director: William Gereghty

When Goa'uld acquisition of new shield technology leaves Tollana without adequate defences, the Tollan government makes an ultimately unsuccessful secret deal with Tanith to provide bombs in exchange for their planet's continued survival.

510. 2001

Writer: Brad Wright; Director: Peter DeLuise

Despite the blood-spattered warning Jack sent back to himself in '2010', Earth nearly enacts a fatal treaty with the Aschen anyway.

511. Desperate Measures

Writers: Joseph Mallozzi and Paul Mullie; Director: William Gereghty

A dying industrialist is healed by implanting himself with a Goa'uld; Sam is kidnapped so his doctors can figure out how to get the Goa'uld out again.

512. Wormhole X-Treme

Story: Brad Wright, Joseph Mallozzi and Paul Mullie; Director: Peter DeLuise; Teleplay: Joseph Mallozzi and Paul Mullie

Unable to bear the mundane truth about his life, Martin Lloyd suppresses (most of) his memories, and successfully pitches what he does remember about the Stargate programme as a cable TV show.

513. Proving Ground

Writer: Ron Wilkerson; Director: Andy Mikita

SG-1 runs a training simulation for young recruits.

514. 48 Hours

Writer: Robert Cooper; Director: Peter F. Woeste

Teal'c's rescue from a gate accident is complicated by resistance from the NID and the Russians. Jack and Maybourne wring answers from the NID, and Colonel Chekhov caves in when Daniel says 'please'. First appearance of Rodney McKay.

515. Summit

516. Last Stand

Writers: 'Summit', Joseph Mallozzi and Paul Mullie; Director: Martin Wood
Writer: 'Last Stand', Robert C. Cooper; Director: Martin Wood

In this two-parter, Daniel infiltrates a summit of System Lords to release a Tok'ra-developed poison; meanwhile, the Tok'ra base itself falls under attack by Anubis.

517. Fail Safe

Writers: Joseph Mallozzi and Paul Mullie; Director: Andy Mikita

The Goa'uld pack an asteroid full of naqada and send it hurtling towards Earth. Sam saves the day by flying the asteroid through the planet.

518. The Warrior

Story: Christopher Judge; Teleplay: Peter DeLuise; Director: Peter DeLuise

Teal'c is thrilled by the rise of a charismatic new leader of the free Jaffa, and smiles more than he has in the last five years. Bad luck that K'tano is actually a Goa'uld in disguise.

519. Menace

Writer: James Tichenor; Director: Martin Wood

The creator of the Replicators is an android programmed with a child's mercurial temperament. Daniel tries to befriend her, but, with the base under attack, Jack decides she's too dangerous to live.

520. The Sentinel

Writer: Ron Wilkerson; Director: Peter DeLuise

SG-1 tries to repair the damage done to a planet's defences by a rogue NID team. A member of the NID team sacrifices himself to save the planet.

521. Meridian

Writer: Robert C. Cooper; Director: William Waring

Daniel receives a fatal dose of radiation but no thanks for preventing an explosion caused by Kelownan scientists who are 'tickling the tail of the dragon' in their own version of the Manhattan Project. Jack stops Jacob's subsequent attempt to heal Daniel, allowing him to ascend with Oma Desala instead.

522. Revelations

Writer: Joseph Mallozzi and Paul Mullie; Director: William Waring

Anubis finally makes his on-screen appearance, Heimdall discusses the delicate issue of Asgardian reproduction, and Daniel whistles like the wind through the corridors of the SGC.

Season Six: 2002–2003

Redemption

601. Part 1

602. Part 2

Writer: Robert C. Cooper; Director: Martin Wood

When Anubis launches an attack against Earth's Stargate, Rya'c and Jonas Quinn (who both have something to prove) help save the day.

603. Descent

Writers: Joseph Mallozzi and Paul Mullie; Director: Peter DeLuise

SG-1, Jacob and Major Davis save Thor's downloaded consciousness from the computer of Anubis' ship after the ship plunges into the Pacific Ocean.

604. Frozen

Writer: Robert C. Cooper; Director: Martin Wood

A woman found in the Antarctic ice near the site of the second Stargate infects her rescuers with a lethal virus. She dies before she can heal Jack, who, in extremis, accepts a Tok'ra symbiote.

605. Nightwalkers

Writers: Joseph Mallozzi and Paul Mullie; Director: Peter DeLuise

The Goa'uld in Adrian Conrad (of 'Desperate Measures') has been cloned by his own biotech company, and the immature symbiotes implanted in unsuspecting townsfolk.

606. Abyss

Writer: Brad Wright; Director: Martin Wood

Daniel begs Jack to ascend in order to escape Baal's soul-destroying cycle of death and revival in the sarcophagus. Jack demands another option.

607. Shadow Play

Writers: Joseph Mallozzi and Paul Mullie; Director: Peter DeLuise

The international resistance movement which Jonas' old professor believes will save the Kelownan planet from its deadly arms race is only a delusion born of mental illness.

608. The Other Guys

Writer: Damian Kindler; Director: Martin Wood

Civilian scientists come to the rescue when SG-1's rendezvous with a Tok'ra operative goes awry.

609. Allegiance

Writer: Peter DeLuise; Director: Peter DeLuise

An invisible Goa'uld assassin strains already difficult relations between refugee Tok'ra and rebel Jaffa at the Alpha site.

610. Cure

Writer: Damian Kindler; Director: Andy Mikita

After finding the Tok'ra queen in a *canopic* jar, the Pangarans have been processing her offspring to produce the miracle drug Tretonin.

611. Prometheus

Writers: Joseph Mallozzi and Paul Mullie; Director: Peter F. Woeste

Colonel Simmons and his pet Goa'uld, Adrian Conrad, hijack the X-303.

612. Unnatural Selection

Excerpt: Jeffrey F. King; Story: Robert C. Cooper and Brad Wright; Teleplay: Brad Wright; Director: Andy Mikita

On the Asgard homeworld, the Replicators have evolved into beings with humanoid forms and – with a single exception dismissed by his fellows as a mistake – singularly unpleasant personalities.

613. Sight Unseen

Writer: Sam Wilkerson; Director: Peter F. Woeste

Sam and Jonas discover a device that makes visible the giant bug creatures who live in a coexistent dimension.

614. Smoke and Mirrors

Story: Katharyn Powers; Teleplay: Joseph Mallozzi and Paul Mullie; Director: Peter DeLuise

Rogue elements within the NID frame Jack for the murder of Senator Kinsey.

615. Paradise Lost

Writer: Robert C. Cooper; Director: William Gereghty

Maybourne's plans for an off-world retirement in paradise go seriously awry. Not only does Jack follow him, but consuming the local flora causes paranoid delusions.

616. Metamorphosis

Story: Jacqueline Samuda and James Tichenor; Teleplay: James Tichenor; Director: Peter DeLuise

Nirrti has been continuing her grotesque experiments in human genetics on plague victims.

617. Disclosure

Writers: Joseph Mallozzi and Paul Mullie; Director: William Gereghty

The Stargate is revealed to ambassadors for the G-5 nations. Thor shows up personally to lobby for General Hammond's continued command of the SGC.

618. Forsaken

Writer: Damian Kindler; Director: Andy Mikita

SG-1 comes across a downed prison transport where the prisoners have overcome the guards.

619. The Changeling

Writer: Christopher Judge; Director: Martin Wood

While lying near death on a battlefield and sharing his symbiote with Bra'tac, Teal'c dreams that he's a fireman prepared to donate a kidney to his father-in-law. Daniel shows up in Teal'c's dream as a psychiatrist asking Teal'c to face the consequences of his decision.

620. Memento

Writer: Damian Kindler; Director: Peter DeLuise

SG-1 finds a lost Stargate on a planet which has tried to eradicate all memory of its people's past enslavement to the Goa'uld.

621. Prophecy

Writer: Joseph Mallozzi and Paul Mullie; Director: William Waring

Jonas starts having precognitive visions while the SGC is helping a mining colony escape the tyranny of a minor Goa'uld.

622. Full Circle

Writer: Robert C. Cooper; Director: Martin Wood

Despite his promises, Daniel can't save Abydos from Anubis. He doesn't find the Lost City either. Oma Desala ascends the entire population of the planet.

Season Seven: 2003–2004

701. Fallen

Writer: Robert C. Cooper; Director: Martin Wood

Oma Desala dumps Daniel, a naked amnesiac, near an encampment of nomads on a planet that is not home to the Lost City.

702. Homecoming

Writer: Joseph Mallozzi and Paul Mullie; Director: Martin Wood

Anubis attacks Jonas' homeworld. Teal'c enlists Baal's assistance in driving him off.

703. Fragile Balance

Story: Peter DeLuise and Michael Greenburg; Teleplay: Damian Kindler; Director: Peter DeLuise

The rogue Asgard scientist, Loki, creates a Jack O'Neill clone in order to hide his kidnapping of the real Jack. Since the cloned Jack is only 15, the subterfuge doesn't go unnoticed.

704. Orpheus

Writer: Peter DeLuise; Director: Peter DeLuise

Without the benefits of his symbiote, Teal'c has been feeling like he's not the Jaffa he once was. The mission to rescue Rya'c and Bra'tac restores his mojo.

705. Revisions

Writers: Joseph Mallozzi and Paul Mullie; Director: Martin Wood

The inhabitants of an environmental dome are rapidly running out of power and space, but an organic uplink to their community's mainframe keeps anyone from noticing.

706. Lifeboat

Writer: Brad Wright; Director: Peter DeLuise

The consciousnesses of doomed shipwreck victims are implanted in Daniel's mind.

707. Enemy Mine
Writer: Peter DeLuise; Director: Peter DeLuise
Daniel and Chaka negotiate peace between a population of Unas and the Pentagon's naqada mining interests.

708. Space Race
Writer: Damian Kindler; Director: Andy Mikita
Sam gets to have fun helping Warrick (last seen in 'Forsaken') compete in an interplanetary race.

709. Avenger 2.0
Writers: Joseph Mallozzi and Paul Mullie; Director: Martin Wood
Baal modifies Dr Felger's computer virus and shuts down the entire gate system.

710. Birthright
Writer: Christopher Judge; Director: Peter F. Woeste
SG-1 convinces the Hak'tyl, a band of Jaffa women who have fled the service of Moloch, to use Tretonin instead of stealing symbiotes from other Jaffa.

711. Evolution
Part 1
Story: Damian Kindler and Michael Shanks; Teleplay: Damian Kindler; Director: Peter DeLuise

712. Part 2
Story: Peter DeLuise and Damian Kindler; Teleplay: Peter DeLuise; Director: Peter DeLuise
Jack rescues Daniel from Honduran bandits who have been torturing him for information about a long-lost revivification device; the rest of SG-1 and Jacob manage to put a temporary crimp in Anubis' super-soldier programme.

713. Grace
Writer: Damian Kindler; Director: Peter F. Woeste
Marooned and concussed, trying to free the Prometheus and its crew, Sam has an ongoing conversation with aspects of herself who manifest as family and team members.

714. Fallout
Story: Corin Nemec; Teleplay: Joseph Mallozzi and Paul Mullie; Director: Martin Wood
Jonas' homeworld faces imminent destruction from a naqadria chain reaction, and his lab partner is a Goa'uld in service to Baal.

715. Chimera
Story: Robert C. Cooper; Teleplay: Damian Kindler; Director: William Waring
Sam meets a guy who's pretty nice despite his stalker-ish tendencies, and who, more importantly, isn't dead by the end of the episode; Sarah/Osiris

is manipulating Daniel's dreams in search of the Lost City of the Ancients.

716. Death Knell

Writer: Peter DeLuise; Director: Peter DeLuise

Seriously wounded, Sam flees an Anubis drone after an attack on the new Alpha site. The alliance among the Tok'ra, rebel Jaffa and Tau'ri finally breaks down.

Heroes

717. Part 1

718. Part 2

Writer: Robert C. Cooper; Director: Andy Mikita

A documentary filmmaker films the personnel of the SGC; Janet dies tending to a wounded soldier under fire.

719. Resurrection

Writer: Michael Shanks; Director: Amanda Tapping

A rogue NID sleeper cell tries to create its own Harsesis by engineering a human–Goa'uld hybrid.

720. Inauguration Day

Writers: Joseph Mallozzi and Paul Mullie; Director: Peter F. Woeste

Vice-President Kinsey tries to persuade the new president to change Stargate Command's administration.

The Lost City

721. Part 1

722. Part 2

Writers: Robert C. Cooper and Brad Wright; Director: Martin Wood

SG-1 still hasn't found the Lost City, but, with the knowledge of the Ancients once more downloaded into his head, Jack leads them to a weapon in Antarctica which destroys Anubis' fleet. Near death, Jack is placed in suspended animation.

Season Eight: 2004–2005

The New Order

801. Part 1

Writers: Joseph Mallozzi and Paul Mullie; Director: Andy Mikita

802. Part 2

Writer: Robert C. Cooper; Director: Andy Mikita

The new head of the SGC, Dr Weir, hosts negotiations with the Goa'uld System Lords; meanwhile, the new Asgardian homeworld is saved from the Replicators with Jack's help, but Fifth gets away with a Replicator version of

Sam. Jack is promoted to brigadier general and takes over Weir's position while she takes command of the Antarctic outpost and, later, the Atlantis Expedition (see the *Stargate: Atlantis* episode guide for more information on the spin-off series).

803. Lockdown

Writers: Joseph Mallozzi and Paul Mullie; Director: William Waring

Disembodied, semi-ascended Anubis is at the SGC and moving from host to host, finally escaping in the body of a Russian pilot.

804. Zero Hour

Writer: Robert C. Cooper; Director: Peter F. Woeste

Jack deals with a missing SG-1, squabbling delegates, threats from Baal and alien kudzu in advance of the president's visit.

805. Icon

Writer: Damian Kindler; Director: Peter F. Woeste

SG-1's arrival on a planet sparks civil and international war, trapping Daniel on the troubled world.

806. Avatar

Writer: Damian Kindler; Director: Martin Wood

Teal'c's warrior ego and fundamental pessimism are exploited by a battle simulation based on the Gamekeeper's technology, and he's trapped in the game until Daniel joins him.

807. Affinity

Writer: Peter DeLuise; Director: Peter DeLuise

Teal'c finally gets his own apartment, but ex-NID agents, now calling themselves the Trust, frame him for murder. Sam accepts Pete's marriage proposal.

808. Covenant

Story: Ron Wilkerson; Teleplay: Ron Wilkerson and Robert C. Cooper; Director: Martin Wood

An aerospace firm's CEO who intends to go public with the truth about Earth's contact with aliens is thwarted by the Trust and then co-opted by Sam.

809. Sacrifices

Writer: Christopher Judge; Director: Andy Mikita

Teal'c is vehemently opposed both to Rya'c's wedding and to staging open revolt against Moloch.

810. Endgame

Writers: Joseph Mallozzi and Paul Mullie; Director: Peter DeLuise

Walter goes for coffee, and the Trust steals the Stargate itself.

811. Gemini

Writer: Peter DeLuise; Director: William Waring

The Sam homonculus created by Fifth betrays both her creator and the original Sam Carter.

812. Prometheus Unbound
Writer: Damian Kindler; Director: Andy Mikita
The Prometheus is hijacked again, this time by a plucky (Daniel's term is 'fruitcake') ex-Goa'uld host, Vala Maldoran.

813. It's Good to be King
Story: Michael Greenburg, Peter DeLuise, Joseph Mallozzi and Paul Mullie; Teleplay: Joseph Mallozzi and Paul Mullie; Director: William Gereghty
A time-travelling Ancient left behind both his ship and a written future history on the planet where Harry Maybourne now rules as king.

814. Full Alert
Writers: Joseph Mallozzi and Paul Mullie; Director: Andy Mikita
Members of the Trust are taken over by Goa'uld, who manoeuvre the US and Russia to the brink of nuclear war.

815. Citizen Joe
Story: Robert C. Cooper; Teleplay: Damian Kindler; Director: Andy Mikita
Jack and a barber from Indiana have been sharing each other's memories for the past seven years.

Reckoning
816. Part 1
817. Part 2
Writer: Damian Kindler; Excerpt of Part 2 written by Robert C. Cooper; Director: Peter DeLuise
Anubis and the Replicators both plan to recreate all life in the Milky Way in their own respective images. Daniel dies again.

818. Threads
Writer: Robert C. Cooper; Excerpts by Damian Kindler; Director: Andy Mikita
After a long shift at the Diner of the Almost-Ascended, Oma finally takes on Anubis and saves the galaxy. Daniel briefly accepts ascension, but only so he can reject it again, and Selmak dies, taking Jacob with him. Sam breaks off her engagement with Pete.

Moebius
819. Part 1
Story: Jacob Mallozzi, Paul Mullie, Robert C. Cooper and Brad Wright; Teleplay: Jacob Mallozzi and Paul Mullie; Director: Peter DeLuise
820. Part 2
Teleplay: Robert C. Cooper; Director: Peter DeLuise

An improvident plan to travel into the past to steal a ZPM from Ra changes history, and geekier versions of Daniel and Sam who were never part of the now non-existent Stargate programme travel back in time to fix the future.

STARGÅTE: ATLANTIS
EPISODE GUIDE

LISA KINCAID

Season One: 2004–2005

101. Rising, Part 1
Writers: Brad Wright and Robert C. Cooper; Director: Martin Wood
A joint military and scientific expedition leaves Earth through the Stargate, on a one-way trip to the Pegasus Galaxy in search of the lost city of Atlantis.

102. Rising, Part 2
Writers: Brad Wright and Robert C. Cooper; Director: Martin Wood
The expedition faces failure when a lack of power nearly causes Atlantis to flood, and Sheppard must lead a team to rescue his people who were taken by a new enemy called the Wraith.

103. Hide and Seek
Story: Brad Wright and Robert C. Cooper; Teleplay: Robert C. Cooper; Director: David Warry-Smith
A shadowy alien – released from the Ancient lab where it was a specimen of study – stalks the corridors of Atlantis. McKay discovers the advantages and dangers of Ancient technology when he puts on a personal energy shield, and finds that he can't take it off.

104. Thirty-Eight Minutes
Writer: Brad Wright; Director: Mario Azzopardi
Major Sheppard is having a very bad day: first his team gets into a firefight with the Wraith, then he's bitten by an alien bug that refuses to let him go, and the damaged Puddle Jumper becomes lodged in the Stargate, preventing the team from reaching Atlantis and medical aid.

105. Suspicion
Story: Kerry Glover; Teleplay: Joseph Mallozzi and Paul Mullie; Director: Mario Azzopardi
Sheppard's team suffers a string of surprise attacks from the Wraith, and Weir believes that it's more than just a run of bad luck. The Earth personnel suspect a mole among the Athosians.

106. Childhood's End

Writer: Martin Gero; Director: David Winning

The failure of their Puddle Jumper leads Sheppard's team to a much-needed ZPM, and a society of children who believe that they are preventing Wraith attacks by committing ritual suicide at the age of 24.

107. Poisoning the Well

Story: Mary Kaiser; Teleplay: Damian Kindler; Director: Brad Turner

The Atlanteans offer scientific help to a world that is developing a drug to make its people unpalatable to the Wraith, but the drug results in high mortality for all those who take the inoculation.

108. Underground

Writer: Peter DeLuise; Director: Brad Turner

Sheppard's team attempts to negotiate for food supplies with one of Teyla's old trading partners. The Genii turn out to be more than simple farmers, however, and Sheppard must form an uneasy alliance in the hopes of working together to defeat the Wraith.

109. Home

Writers: Joseph Mallozzi and Paul Mullie; Director: Holly Dale

An alien planet with an unusual atmosphere provides the opportunity to open the gate to Earth, but the trip may be one-way. The expedition's senior members make the trip, only to find that they aren't home at all.

110. The Storm

Story: Jill Blotevogel; Teleplay: Martin Gero; Director: Martin Wood

Atlantis is evacuated when an enormous hurricane approaches, and the Genii take advantage of the weakened defences to stage an invasion.

111. The Eye

Writer: Martin Gero; Director: Martin Wood

With McKay and Weir held hostage and the storm threatening to destroy them all, Sheppard must reclaim the city on his own.

112. The Defiant One

Writer: Peter DeLuise; Director: Peter DeLuise

Sheppard's team investigates the wreckage of a Wraith supply ship that was downed 10,000 years ago by one of the Ancients' defence satellites. Unexpectedly, one of the ship's crew is still alive ... and very hungry.

113. Hot Zone

Writer: Martin Gero; Director: Mario Azzopardi

When a science team discovers a bio-lab and are unwittingly infected with a deadly virus, Atlantis initiates its own quarantine protocols and locks down the city. The scientists and medical team must create their own cure, while one of their own, running scared, attempts to breach the quarantine.

114. Sanctuary

Writer: Alan Brennert; Director: James Head

Sheppard's team visits a well-protected world that could be a safe home for refugees from Wraith feeding grounds. Sheppard brings the local 'priestess', Chaya, back to Atlantis in an attempt to persuade her to help, but suspicious McKay is proved correct when Chaya is revealed to be an Ascended Ancient, exiled to her former homeworld.

115. Before I Sleep

Writer: Carl Binder; Director: Andy Mikita; Excerpts: Brad Wright and Robert C. Cooper

Explorations of Atlantis lead to the discovery of a stasis chamber, which is occupied by a much older version of Dr Weir. This Weir – from an alternate timeline in which Earth's Atlantis Expedition was doomed to failure – recounts her journey back in time to the fall of Atlantis and the Ancients' retreat to the Milky Way Galaxy.

116. The Brotherhood

Writer: Martin Gero; Director: Martin Wood

Sheppard's team goes treasure hunting on the trail of a hidden ZPM, but they're hindered by allies with mysterious motives, and the interference of the Genii, who want the ZPM for themselves. Back on Atlantis, pilots are scrambled to defend the city against a lone Wraith dart, but the craft mysteriously self-destructs.

117. Letters from Pegasus

Writer: Carl Binder; Director: Mario Azzopardi; Excerpts: Jill Blotevogel, Robert C. Cooper, Peter DeLuise, Martin Gero, Kerry Glover, Mary Kaiser, Damian Kindler, Joseph Mallozzi, Paul Mullie and Brad Wright

The Wraith armada is drawing closer, and Sheppard's and Teyla's recon mission turns into a rescue when they're trapped on a planet during a culling. With little hope of saving Atlantis, the expedition team plans to send a transmission back to Earth warning of the Wraith threat and allowing the expedition members to send a last message to their loved ones.

118. The Gift

Story: Robert C. Cooper and Martin Gero; Teleplay: Robert C. Cooper; Director: Peter DeLuise

Teyla discovers that her gift for sensing the presence of the Wraith has a dark origin: as a result of Wraith experimentation with humans long ago, Teyla possesses Wraith DNA. She also discovers that she can tap into the

Wraith's telepathic network, but the talent leaves her vulnerable to the Wraith.

119. The Siege, Part 1

Writer: Martin Gero; Director: Martin Wood

With the Wraith fleet only days away from Atlantis, McKay leads a team attempting to repair an Ancient defence satellite, while Zelenka and Weir explore plan how they will destroy Atlantis to keep it out of Wraith hands.

120. The Siege, Part 2

Writers: Joseph Mallozzi and Paul Mullie; Director: Martin Wood

Reinforcements from Earth finally arrive through the Stargate, bringing news that Earth's second warship, *Daedalus*, is on the way, but help may come too late as the Wraith begin their siege of the city.

STARGÅTE GLOSSARY TERMS

LISA KINCAID

2IC – *Second in command*; in a military structure, the second-highest ranking person in a unit, who would assume command if the commanding officer were absent, incapacitated, or in bed with an alien princess.

Abydos – The first planet explored by a modern Stargate team. This world, which is in many ways similar to ancient Egypt, was the destination for the first expedition team in the motion picture.

Al'kesh – A mid-sized Goa'uld vessel, often used for reconnaissance and attacks from within a planetary atmosphere.

Ally – Alien governments and organisations who agree to help SGC personnel and then, occasionally, turn out to be not so helpful. See TOK'RA.

Alpha site – The designated evacuation or rendezvous site for SGC personnel, also used for the research and development of new alien-based technologies.

Ancestors – In the Pegasus Galaxy, the Athosians and others typically use this term to reference the Ancients.

Ancients – An advanced race of humanoids who died out or ascended thousands of years ago. Originally called the Altarans, they came to our galaxy a long time ago from far, far away, and were the builders of the Stargates, Atlantis, and many other wonderful and perplexing inventions such as time machines and enormous mega-weapons. The Ancients also once inhabited the Pegasus Galaxy but fled when they lost their war with the Wraith, returning to Earth and nearby systems. There, they were afflicted with a plague which wiped out most of their population; the last of them discovered the key to Ascension and left for a higher plane of existence.

Antarctic Treaty – The multinational treaty designating Antarctica as a non-militarised area used for peaceful purposes only. It also requires freedom of scientific investigation and cooperation and makes the Ancient outpost on Antarctica a global property. This resulted in the Atlantis Expedition becoming a multinational scientific expedition, rather than a US military operation.

Antarctica – The location of an Ancient outpost that was originally thought to be the Lost City of Atlantis, but turned out to be more like the Lost Storage Closet of the Ancients. Information found at the Antarctic outpost led to the discovery of the actual location of Atlantis. Antarctica has also been home to Earth's second Stargate, an Ancient on ice and a couple of million penguins.

Apostrophe – An article of punctuation which may be used to turn any everyday word or random collection of letters into an alien name or exclamation. For example, a few well-placed apostrophes can turn a plain old *potato* into a *po'tat'o*, which could be used as a name for anything from weapons to ships to Jaffa rituals involving meditation and nubile virgins.

Area 51 – The US military's top-secret research facility in the Nevada desert, where most of the artefacts and technologies recovered by SGC teams are stored and studied.

Area 52 – The official Pentagon designation for the SGC complex at Cheyenne Mountain.

Armbands – A set of alien devices discovered by the Tok'ra which are capable of greatly – but temporarily – boosting the wearer's speed and strength. The members of SG-1 were used as test subjects in trials of the armbands' use, and if the effects had been longer-lasting they may have even got around to picking out tights, capes and superhero names. Daniel Jackson was considering 'Doctor Heiroglyphico'.

Ascension – The process of letting go of one's physical form and ascending to a higher plane of existence. The Ascended are capable of remaining invisible but effecting the physical world, from moving objects to creating weather. They can also appear in various forms, looking like their old humanoid selves or floating glowy squids, and are also able to choose to descend, leaving the higher plane to return to a physical form.

Asgard – The little grey men of alien abduction lore, the Asgard are also the faces behind old Norse mythology, and have served a protective role in the development of human worlds.

Ashrak – A Goa'uld assassin and infiltrator, usually charged by System Lords to destroy their enemies.

ATA (*Ancient Technology Activation*) **Gene** – A specific gene possessed by some humans that allows them to use Ancient technology, much of which can only be operated by people with Ancient genes. It is also possible to create an artificial ATA gene effect using experimental gene therapy; however, the therapy is effective in only 48% of recipients.

Athosian – The first humans that the Atlantis Expedition comes into contact with in the Pegasus Galaxy. They enjoy a stout tea for breakfast and tend to become Wraith food for lunch. Some Athosians, like Teyla Emmagan, are capable of sensing the presence of the Wraith.

Atlantis – The Lost City of Earth lore, which as it turns out is actually an Ancient spaceship. Atlantis is approximately the size of Manhattan, with several piers extending off a main hub, and was probably the Ancient equivalent of a capital city. It comes fully loaded with shields, weapons systems, cryogenic chambers, lab experiments and dangerous viruses, as well as Puddle Jumpers and other useful accessories, and retails at the unbeatable price of free to any intergalactic explorers brave enough to go to the trouble of finding it.

Atlantis Expedition – A multinational scientific expedition on a joint mission with the US military, tasked with travelling to the Pegasus Galaxy in search of the Lost City of Atlantis. Once there, the expedition's focus became finding a ZPM to power the city's shields, forming trade relations with neighbouring worlds, fighting the Wraith, and discovering the Atlantean version of a jacuzzi.

Atlantis shield – An energy shield which, when activated, covers the entire city of Atlantis and is capable of easily protecting the city from attack and natural disaster.

AU – *Alternate Universe*. Some theories of quantum mechanics postulate that a new parallel universe is formed with each moment or decision; for instance, in one universe you may have had a bagel for breakfast, but an alternate universe version of you chose a croissant, thus leading to global thermonuclear war. It is possible for these alternate universes to be accessed using certain items of alien technology. *AU* is also a term used in fan fiction for stories which feature canon characters outside canon situations; for instance, a universe where O'Neill is a firefighter and Jackson is a psychologist, and neither know anything about the Stargate. See also QUANTUM MIRROR.

Blending – The Tok'ra term for introducing a Tok'ra symbiote into the body of a human host. It took the Tok'ra public relations office only two months to come up with that spin.

Blood of Sokar – A form of hallucinogenic truth serum devised by the System Lord Sokar, which aids in the interrogation of prisoners.

Body-swapping machine – A machine created by the inventor Ma'chello. When two people grip the handles at the same time, their consciousnesses trade bodies, and wacky high jinks ensue.

Canon – The set of facts presented within a television series that are generally considered to be inarguable; usually this means events, situations or characterisations which have actually been seen on-screen. Even authorised forms of media tie-ins are not typically considered 'canon' because they exist outside the main text of the series.

Canopic **jars** – Miniature stasis chambers, which are naqada-powered and may be used to store a Goa'uld symbiote in suspended animation for an indefinite period of time. Their appearance is similar to that of the *canopic* jars used in ancient Egypt to house the internal organs of a mummified corpse.

Cartouche – The cartouche room on Abydos was a map of the known Stargate system, providing SGC personnel with their first hint that the Stargate could take them to worlds other than Abydos. This cartouche was probably commissioned by Ra, and listed only those worlds known to the Goa'uld.

Chaapa'ai – The word used on Abydos, Chulak and many other Goa'uld-occupied worlds for the Stargate.

Chain of command – The line of authority which links all military personnel to superiors and subordinates. The chain of command allows a unit to continue even after the loss of a commanding officer; in the absence of superiors, the most senior officer automatically assumes command.

Chevron – The parts of the Stargate which light up and 'lock' as each symbol of a Gate address is successfully dialled.

Cheyenne Mountain Complex – Formerly a training site for nuclear missile launches, Colorado's Cheyenne Mountain is currently home to NORAD (North American Aerospace Defense Command) and Stargate Command, which stretches 28 levels deep into the mountain itself.

Cloaking device – The Goa'uld, Asgard and Ancients have all possessed some form of cloaking technology which allows them to make their ships literally invisible to the naked eye, and often undetectable by sensors and other technology.

The Committee – A cabal of high-powered businessmen who conspired to illegally appropriate alien technologies to enhance their own commercial product lines and to further their political agendas.

Cover stone – Found on top of the buried Stargate when it was originally unearthed in Egypt. The writing on the cover stone revealed the basic story of the Stargate and the Egyptian uprising which had led to its burial, and also provided the seven-symbol Gate address to Abydos.

Culling – The Wraith use a form of transporter beam in order to collect or 'cull' individuals from human settlements; these humans are consumed or stored for later use, and survivors are left to repopulate for the next culling.

***Daedalus*, The** – Earth's second space battlecruiser, sister ship to the prototype, *Prometheus*. It possesses sublight and hyperdrive engines, Asgard-designed shields and weapons, transport rings and docking for a complement of F-302 fighters.

***Daniel Jackson*, The** – A vessel roughly the size of a Goa'uld mothership, built by the Asgard, commanded by Thor, and named for Earth's own Daniel Jackson.

Dart – Small Wraith fighter craft, with weapons systems and culling transporters. They are not long-range vessels, but are built narrow enough to travel through Stargates.

Death – A semi-permanent state in the Stargate universe. Daniel Jackson, for instance, has not quite got the hang of it. See also SARCOPHAGUS and ASCENSION.

Death Glider – Small, short-range Goa'uld fighter craft, equipped with heavy weapons. Death Gliders are too wide to travel through the Stargate, and are usually deployed from motherships.

Detachment device – A piece of Tollan technology, which allows separation of Goa'uld symbiote and human host, allowing the host to think, act and speak independently without interference from the symbiote.

Dialling computer – Lacking a dialling device, the SGC devised their own computer systems which interface with the Stargate and allow them to dial out without a DHD.

Disruptor – A weapon which is capable of destroying Replicators by interfering with their systems on a molecular level. The weapon was initially created by Jack O'Neill utilising knowledge downloaded from an Ancient Knowledge Repository.

DHD – *Dial Home Device*. The console attached to most Stargates which allows the user to dial Gate addresses, much like the keypad on a telephone.

Drones – Ancient weapons that look a lot like flying calamari. Drones are capable of locking on to a target and following it, and can cause devastating damage; a Wraith Dart or other small craft can be completely destroyed by a single drone.

Event horizon – The surface of the 'puddle' formed by an open wormhole. Stepping into the event horizon takes you into the wormhole itself.

Eye of Ra – A large crystal which, when used with five other 'Eyes', can be used to construct a super-weapon. Anubis acquired all these Eyes and used them to assemble a super-weapon on his mothership, but the ship and weapon were later destroyed.

F-302 – Earth's second-generation space fighter (originally called the X-302), constructed with a blend of Earth technology and reverse-engineered Goa'uld Death Gliders. The F-302 is too wide to be flown through the Stargate, but can be dismantled, transported through the Gate, and then reconstructed on the other side. Its naqadria engine isn't capable of long-range travel, but short jumps into hyperspace are possible.

Failsafe – When Atlantis was abandoned by the Ancients, it was hidden beneath the ocean and protected by its energy shield; the failsafe, programmed by an Ancient, Janus, instructed the city to release from the ocean floor and rise to the surface if power levels ever became critically low enough that flooding seemed imminent. This failsafe saved the Atlantis Expedition from certain doom when they entered the city.

Fandom – Fans of a particular series. 'Fandom' refers to all fans in general, but more specifically to those who actively participate in the fan culture, particularly online or by attending conventions.

Fan fiction – Literature written by fans exploring an already established universe from television, film, games or other media sources. Fan fiction is one of the mediums fans use to make their viewing experience more interactive by authoring their own interpretations of events and situations based upon the original work.

Fanon – An idea which is so pervasive and well used in fandom that it is often mistaken for canon.

Fifth Column – The rebel Jaffa serving as covert agents for the rebellion within the ranks of Goa'uld armies.

First Prime – The commander of a Jaffa army, and a System Lord's right-hand man. All orders given to a Jaffa army by their Goa'uld master are typically relayed to the First Prime, who is effectively the general in charge of the entire force.

Foothold – An alien infiltration or invasion; when aliens manage to seize control of the SGC, it is called a 'foothold situation'.

Four Races – The alliance of Asgard, Ancients, Nox and Furlings which originally were the most advanced races in the Milky Way.

FRED - *Field Remote Expeditionary Device*. The FRED is a small motorised vehicle which is typically used as an equipment cart for trips through the Stargate. It can carry heavy loads, and may be controlled by remote or manually with a joystick.

Furlings – One of the Four Races. Though SGC personnel have explored worlds previously inhabited by the Furlings, they have yet to find any living trace of the Furlings themselves. See also FOUR RACES.

Gate address – The six-symbol address which, when used with the seventh point of origin symbol, can be used to dial another Stargate. Addresses longer than six symbols can be used to connect to Gates which are much farther away, in other galaxies.

Gateship – The overly obvious and ultimately unused first suggestion for naming the Puddle Jumpers. Though John Sheppard vetoed the idea of calling the vessels 'Gateships', the moniker has been seen in use in alternate realities.

GDO - *Garage Door Opener*. A small remote device carried by SG teams to allow them to safely return to Earth. While off-world, teams can dial Earth's Stargate and then enter their personal Iris Deactivation Code (IDC); this confirms their identity to the SGC's computers and signals SGC personnel to open the iris. Without a GDO and IDC, Earth personnel cannot return to Earth, for fear of being splattered against the closed iris.

Gen – Short for *general*, fan fiction which does not contain any particular romantic or sexual relationship or pairing.

Genetic memory – The inborn trait which grants each Goa'uld the memories and knowledge of all those who came before it in its family tree.

Genii – A race of humans in the Pegasus Galaxy who maintain a very rural facade to hide their industrial development. Though they have occasionally worked in tandem with the Atlantis Expedition to destroy the Wraith, the goal of the Genii is to keep their own people alive, and this often puts them at odds with the Atlanteans.

Glyph – The individual symbols which compose Stargate addresses. Most are constellations, and some signify particular planets as points of origin.

Goa'uld – A small snake-like creature with a four-pronged mouth and fins, which originally evolved in the waters of P3X-888. These creatures became capable of entering the bodies of other animals and controlling them. They are scavengers of knowledge and technology, and appropriated many of the devices they found around the galaxy to their own use, including the Stargates; this advancement allowed them to enslave primitive human cultures and begin building empires. Thanks to genetic memory, most Goa'uld possess megalomaniacal personalities, a flair for the dramatic, and truly horrific fashion sense.

Goa'uld-buster – A Mark-12A warhead; a nuclear device enhanced with naqada to create a larger explosion.

Gods – What the Goa'uld pretend to be, and what everyone thinks SG-1 are when they show up.

Hak'tyl – A Jaffa resistance movement using as its base of operations a planet of the same name. Led by a Jaffa, Ishta, and initially separate from the larger Jaffa liberation front and Fifth Column movement, the Hak'tyl worked independently to rescue Jaffa children from the Goa'uld Moloch, who ordered that all newborn girls be destroyed.

Harsesis – Human offspring born of two Goa'uld-infested humans. The Harsesis is born with the genetic memory of its Goa'uld parents, and therefore possesses all the knowledge of the Goa'uld.

Ha'tak – A Goa'uld mothership or 'pyramid ship'. These warships typically carry large numbers of troops and squadrons of Death Gliders, but are also capable of atmospheric manoeuvring and landing. They are equipped with heavy weapons which can be used to fire on other ships or bombard a planetary surface, and also possess shields and ring transporters.

Healing device – A Goa'uld device which can heal both internal and external injuries in humans and Jaffa. Use of the healing device requires naqada in the user's bloodstream, so only Goa'uld hosts and former hosts are capable of operating the device.

Heliopolis – The abandoned meeting place of the Four Races where they stored and exchanged information about their cultures and knowledge. It was first discovered by Earnest Littlefield, who accidentally became stranded on Heliopolis while performing experiments on Earth's Stargate in 1945. Littlefield was rescued 50 years later by SG-1, but the Heliopolis Stargate fell into the ocean, making the building inaccessible by Stargate.

Het – Short for *heterosexual*, fan fiction which contains romantic or sexual content between characters of opposite genders.

Hive ship – The Wraith version of a mothership. Hive ships are home to many Wraith, most of whom spend a great deal of time in hibernation, waiting for their human crop to breed so that they can feed again. Hive ships typically travel in convoy with smaller cruisers and Darts, and can carry large numbers of cocooned humans as food supplies.

Homeworld Security – A secret division of the United States government that oversees Stargate Command and all related programmes, such as the *Prometheus*, *Daedalus*, and F-302 research and construction, and the Atlantis Expedition.

Homing device – Mechanism installed in Death Gliders in Apophis' fleet which causes stolen Gliders to attempt to return to Apophis' mothership.

Humanform Replicator – Replicators that have duplicated the appearance – and sometimes the flaws – of human beings. They possess super-strength, can forcefully invade human minds, and are able to manipulate other Replicators. Reese was their progenitor, followed by others such as First, Fifth and a Replicator version of Sam Carter.

Hypoglycaemic reaction – A reaction in the human body caused by low blood sugar level, often brought on by not eating enough food. In Rodney McKay, it can cause spells of manly, hunger-induced passing out.

IDC – *Iris Deactivation Code*. Each member of the SGC's off-world teams has an individual code, which they can send through the Stargate using a Garage Door Opener (GDO). The IDC is a password recognised by the SGC computers, which authenticates the identity of the individual dialling Earth's Stargate. If an IDC is not transmitted, the iris will usually not be opened to accept incoming travellers.

Implantation – The initial act of deliberately introducing a Goa'uld symbiote to a host body, whether the symbiote is taking control of the host or is simply being stored in a Jaffa's incubation pouch.

Intar – A Goa'uld training weapon with non-fatal energy pulses, they can take the form of any human or Goa'uld weapon and are distinguishable by visible red crystal.

Iris – A shield made of trinium-reinforced titanium, which rests just slightly in front of the event horizon on Earth's Stargate. It allows a wormhole to form successfully, but will not allow unauthorised travellers to re-integrate on the Earth side. Any matter sent through the Stargate to Earth without a valid Iris Deactivation Code (IDC) will be splattered against the inside of the iris. Atlantis has a built-in Ancient version of an iris, which is composed of an energy field.

Jaffa – A race of humans who were genetically modified by the Goa'uld. They live longer than humans, heal faster and are overall healthier, but they are also used as incubators for larval Goa'uld symbiotes. The symbiote matures in the Jaffa's abdominal pouch and replaces the Jaffa's immune system, so, without artificial intervention (such as use of the drug *tretonin*), a Jaffa cannot survive without a symbiote; once the symbiote matures, the Jaffa must be implanted with another larva or be taken as a host by his own. The Jaffa have traditionally been used by the Goa'uld as slaves and have composed the main force of the System Lords' armies, but the beginnings of rebellion and the formation of the Jaffa Free Nation have made great advancements towards securing freedom for all Jaffa.

Jaffa Free Nation – The organisation which sprang from the initial Jaffa resistance, which attempts to unite all Jaffa under common leadership and with common goals.

Kelno'reem – A state of deep meditation, which is the Jaffa substitution for sleep. This period allows the Jaffa's *prim'ta* (symbiote) to heal any injuries and regenerate the Jaffa physically. Jaffa who carry a symbiote and are not able to kelno'reem with regularity will suffer failing health.

Kelowna – The planet whose inhabitants first introduced SG-1 to *naqadria*, a more unstable liquid form of naqada. Also the home of Jonas Quinn, who later became a member of SG-1.

Kheb – A world avoided by the Goa'uld but sacred to the Jaffa, who look upon it as the home of their souls in the afterlife. Oma Desala and the Harsesis Shifu sheltered on Kheb for a time, before being discovered there by SG-1.

Knowledge Repository – An Ancient device designed to store all the knowledge of their people. It has a tendency to grab unsuspecting travellers by the head and download all its information into their brains; in humans, this can be fatal, as the overflow of information eventually destroys the mind.

Koans – How deep is the koan, if you cannot decipher its meaning?

Kree – An all-purpose Goa'uld word usually directed at Jaffa warriors, as in 'Jaffa! Kree!' It can have a variety of meanings, such as 'Hey you', 'Stop', 'Go', and 'Kill that guy again'.

Kull Warriors – Humanoid super-soldiers created by the System Lord Anubis in response to the growing Jaffa rebellion. Anubis engineered a more mindless soldier, created and grown in a lab and implanted with a brainwashed Goa'uld symbiote. Their armour protects them from both bullets and energy weapons and they are immensely strong, but are not built to last.

Lifesigns detector – A hand-held Ancient device, which may only be operated by persons possessing the ATA gene. It detects and displays the position of various sorts of lifesigns, and is capable of differentiating between human and Wraith lifesigns.

Linvris – A league of lesser Goa'uld who plotted together to challenge the dominance of the System Lords. They were exterminated by a biological weapon planted by the inventor Ma'chello.

Long-range communication device – A large golden beach ball which, when interfaced with the Stargate, allows the Goa'uld to transmit audio and video communications instantly across great distances.

The Lost City – An Ancient city to which the SGC found references in Ancient texts; though they first assumed this to be a city that was lost, they eventually figured out that it meant the city was deliberately hidden. The Lost City was purported to possess powerful weapons and technologies, which the SGC hoped to utilise in their fight against the Goa'uld; however, the Lost City turned out to be Atlantis, home of sometimes dangerous technologies and 10,000-year-old dead plants.

Lo'taur – A human slave who serves as a sort of personal assistant to a Goa'uld. Most lo'taurs seem to be working towards a goal of eventually being implanted with a Goa'uld symiote themselves.

MALP – *Mobile Analytic Laboratory Probe.* A remote-controlled robotic vehicle which is sent through the Stargate on reconnaissance prior to any human traveller stepping through the event horizon. The MALP is equipped with scientific sensors and video and audio equipment, which allows the SGC to scout new planets and ensure that they have such desirable qualities as breathable air and attractive natives.

Memory device – A device used by the Goa'uld and Tok'ra which allows the wearer to vividly access memories. It can also be used with a holographic projector, which allows others to see the wearer's memories played out; it can be used as an interrogation device.

Mimic devices – Manufactured by an alien race which once attempted to invade the SGC, these devices are worn on the chest and allow the wearer to take on the appearance of another person. Each device is keyed to a specific individual, and requires that the person be scanned first in a larger machine.

MRE – *Meals Ready to Eat*. A standard meal ration used by the US military. Designed to be easily carried into the field, they are vacuum-packed and freeze-dried, and usually contain such elements as a main course (which usually tastes like chicken, even if it's meant to be macaroni and cheese), crackers, dessert, coffee, and a tiny bottle of hot sauce to make it all marginally edible.

Nanites – Tiny robots which can be introduced into the human bloodstream to do anything from storing knowledge to controlling ageing.

Naqada – The element that is not naturally occurring in Earth's Solar System, but is the basis of most Ancient (and, by extension, Goa'uld) technology, including the Stargates.

Naqada generator – Like a portable nuclear reactor, but powered by naqada.

Naqadria – An unstable liquid form of naqada, capable of incredible power generation.

NASA – *National Aeronautics and Space Administration*. The United States agency responsible for research in the field of space flight. Nobody bothered to tell them about the Stargate. Boy, are they going to feel like chumps when they find out.

NID – A US intelligence agency so secret that nobody (including the show's writers) knows what its acronym stands for.

Nish'ta – A substance used by the Goa'uld to make humans pliable for easy brainwashing.

Non-fraternisation – The policy set forth in Air Force Instruction 36–2909, Professional and Unprofessional Relationships, which boils down to 'no fishing off the company pier'.

Nox – One of the Four Races, very technologically advanced and not very helpful in the fight against the Goa'uld. They possess incredible healing abilities and lots of nifty cloaking technologies.

Off-world Activation – An off-world Stargate attempting to dial in to Earth. Unscheduled off-world activations tend to put the entire base on high alert.

Others, The – The ruling body of Ascended beings, who enforce Ascended rules of non-interference and general suckiness.

O'Neill, The – An Asgard ship designed entirely to fight the Replicators. It was destroyed before its construction could be completed.

P-90 – The favoured weapon of SG teams. It carries a 50-round top-loading magazine with teflon-coated ordnance and fires at a rate of 900 rounds per minute, but it doesn't do much good for SG teams who can't aim.

Page-turning device – A small hand-held device, which is used in conjunction with Goa'uld data storage tablets, allowing a reader to turn the 'pages' of data.

Pegasus Galaxy – A dwarf galaxy not too far from the Milky Way – relatively speaking – which is home to the Lost City of Atlantis.

Pel'tak – The bridge or command deck of a Goa'uld ship.

Personal shield – Both the Goa'uld and the Ancients created variations of personal energy shields, which protect the wearer from all sorts of personal trauma.

Prim'ta – The larval Goa'uld symbiote that is placed inside a Jaffa pouch for incubation.

Prometheus, **The** – Earth's first heavy space battlecruiser, complete with Asgard shields, beam technology and hyperdrive, Goa'uld transport rings and heavy weapons.

Protected Planets Treaty – A treaty between the Goa'uld and Asgard that places certain worlds – Earth included – under Asgard protection.

Protein marker – A biological remnant of Goa'uld presence that is left behind after the symbiote has died and been absorbed by the host body.

Puddle Jumper – A small Ancient ship designed to travel through the Stargate.

Quantum mirror – A device of unknown origin that allows the user to look into and access alternate universes.

Quarantine protocol – One of Atlantis' automatic defences, which automatically locks the city into quarantine when a biological threat is detected.

Red Phone – No different from any other phone, but it does have the Oval Office on speed-dial.

Remote Probe – A flying Goa'uld device used for reconnaissance, much like a MALP.

Replicators – A mechanical race capable of replicating themselves and taking on all sorts of forms, from little bugs to humans.

Ribbon device – A piece of gaudy Goa'uld costume jewellery which fits over the hand and allows the wearer to torture, kill and generally kick the asses of others.

Ring Transporter – A system of transportation involving a set of heavy naqada rings, used to 'beam' people or objects usually from a ship to a planet.

Rite of M'al Sharran – A Jaffa ritual in which a Jaffa's life passes before his eyes like a clip show.

Roshna – A drug used by the Goa'uld to enslave those who can't be used as hosts, so that they're dependent on the drug and can't be bothered with uprisings.

RPG – *Role-Playing Game*. A game in which players assume the role of a character of their own devising, who exists within and interacts with a larger fictional universe.

Sarcophagus – A Goa'uld device that can heal all manner of wounds, extend the user's life, and even resurrect the recently deceased, but can also cause addiction and change the user's personality for the worse.

Sarcophagus withdrawal – The withdrawal effects suffered by a person who's been exposed to a sarcophagus.

SF – *Security Forces*. The Air Force personnel who provide base security at the SGC.

SG teams – The teams assembled by the SGC to travel through the Stargate. Each team typically consists of four individuals, including military and scientific personnel, and is assigned a numbered designation. Some have a particular area of specialisation, such as first contact, engineering or diplomacy.

SGC – *Stargate Command*. The military organisation responsible for the use and security of the Stargate, overseeing all Stargate operations and missions.

SG-X – A human infiltration team assembled by Apophis and trained in SGC tactics.

Shol'va – The Goa'uld term for *traitor*, typically aimed at Jaffa who've renounced their false gods and single-handedly started a rebellion.

Simpsons, The – The cartoon family whose adventures dominate Jack O'Neill's regular entertainment viewing habits.

Slash – Fan fiction focusing on same-sex romantic or sexual relationships. The name comes from the slash between character names, as in 'Sheppard/McKay'.

Staff weapon – The cumbersome and extremely phallic energy weapon favoured by the Jaffa.

Stargate – The big ring made of naqada which people use to travel from one planet to another without the benefit of a spaceship; a sort of futuristic public transit. It 'flushes sideways'.

Stunner – A Wraith weapon that paralyses the target, so the Wraith can feed upon them.

Symbiote – See GOA'ULD.

System Lords – A sort of Goa'uld high council composed of the most powerful individuals.

Tablet device – A Goa'uld data storage unit that is read like a book. The alien version of a palm-top computer.

Takunitagaminituron – A Goa'uld automatic remote weapon, also called a 'tak' for short.

Tau'ri – The name the rest of the galaxy uses when referring to Earth or its people.

Telchak device – An Ancient device which could heal or regenerate living tissue. It was much too powerful to use on humans, but a Goa'uld named Telchak adapted the technology to create the Goa'uld sarcophagus.

Telepathy – One of the forms of communication utilised by the Wraith, who are able to tap into a sort of common neural network or hive mind.

Tel'tac – Goa'uld cargo ship; the minivan of the alien fleet.

TER – *Transphase Eradication Rod*. A device that can be used to detect the presence of an alien race called Reetu, who are capable of making themselves more or less invisible. Also works on other phase-shifting technology, such as that developed by the Goa'uld, Nirrti.

Terraforming – Transforming the landscape on another planet to make it more Earth-like. Often used as a general term for changing a planet's atmosphere to something breathable for humanoids.

Time machines – Devices that allow the user to travel not just from one physical location to another, but to different points in time. The Ancients were known to develop varieties of time travel devices, some of which worked better than others.

The Trust – A covert organisation composed mostly of ex-NID agents and with operatives placed in the SGC and Area 51. Their goal was to wipe out the entire Goa'uld race with biological weapons, but they didn't pull it off very well, and ended up being taken as Goa'uld hosts instead.

Tok'ra – A group of rebel Goa'uld who use covert tactics in an attempt to destroy the System Lords. They are distinguished from the Goa'uld by their professed belief that it is wrong to take a host by force, advocating a more properly symbiotic rather than parasitic relationship with the host with whom the symbiote ostensibly shares the body equally.

Tok'ra tunnel – Technology that allows the Tok'ra to quickly create underground tunnels from a single crystal, facilitating very fast set-up and dismantling of hidden bases.

Tollans – An advanced race who turn out to be a bunch of wusses. They are known mostly for refusing to share technology with Earth. Although their fate is unknown, they were most likely destroyed by the Goa'uld.

Torture stick – An alien cattle prod, but mostly used on people.

Trees – The most common life form in the galaxy, found on nearly every planet. They have a tendency to make any landscape look a lot like the area in and around Vancouver, British Columbia.

Tretonin – A drug which allows a Jaffa to survive without a larval symbiote.

Trinium – A valuable metal ore found on many planets outside Earth's Solar System. Once refined, it is a hundred times stronger and lighter than steel.

Turkey sandwich – The meal of choice for the discerning intergalactic traveller, at least in the Pegasus Galaxy.

UAV – *Unmanned Aerial Vehicle*. A small remote-controlled plane which carries surveillance and analysis equipment, allowing large and fast planetary surveys through the Stargate.

Unas – An intelligent reptilian race which served as the first hosts for the Goa'uld.

Wormholes – The connection that is formed between two Stargates, creating a conduit that sends matter from one end of the wormhole to the other.

Wormhole X-Treme! – A fictional television series, which is uncannily similar to SG-1; the creator of the series unknowingly drew his inspiration from the exploits of the SGC.

Wormhole vortex – The 'splash' (or 'flushing sideways') that accompanies the opening of a wormhole. Any matter within the vortex radius is vaporised by the extreme energy. Also sometimes referred to in fanon as the 'kawoosh'.

Wraith – A species of vaguely humanoid, vampire-like aliens who feed on humans by sucking out their life energy. Hobbies include hibernating, culling and attending Marilyn Manson concerts.

Wraith bug – A variety of giant alien insect which feeds on victims by draining their life energy, much like a Wraith; the two may be evolutionary cousins.

X-301 – See F-302.

X-302 – A second-generation Earth fighter, built with reverse-engineered Goa'uld technology but this time constructed entirely with Earth technology.

Zatarc – An individual who has been unknowingly brainwashed by the Goa'uld and programmed to become an assassin.

Zatarc detector – A form of lie detector invented by the Tok'ra to detect zatarcs. Its technology depends largely upon a sort of swishy circle display that changes colours. It is highly scientific and deeply inaccurate.

Zat'ni'katel – A hand-held Goa'uld energy weapon, also called a 'zat gun'. A single shot stuns, the second kills, and the third completely vaporises the target.

ZPM – *Zero Point Module*. A powerful Ancient power source used as a battery for all sorts of Ancient technology.

SELECTED INTERNET SOURCES

Sci Fi.com: Sci Fi Channel Official *Stargate SG-1* Site http://www.scifi.com/
stargate/

Sci Fi.com: Sci Fi Channel Official *Stargate: Atlantis* Site. http://
www.scifi.com/atlantis/

Sky One (United Kingdom) Official *Stargate SG-1* page. http://
www.skyone.co.uk/programme/pgeprogramme.aspx?pid=6

Stargate News Australia: Offers the usual mixture of images, convention
reports, blogs, news and awards for *SG-1* and *Atlantis*, geared towards
the Australian market. http://www.gasbo.net/stargate/news.htm

Sci Fi.com *Science Fiction Weekly* (Newsletter). http://www.scifi.com/sfw/

The *Stargate* section of Richard Dean Anderson's site. Remarkably well-
organised and full of useful information, including episode guides,
production notes, etc. http://rdanderson.com/

GateWorld: Your Complete Guide to Stargate This is the 'go-to' site for fans
wanting spoilers, interviews, pictures, articles and more. http://
www.gateworld.net/

Stargate SG-1 Role-Playing Game, Alderac Entertainment Group. A basic
description of the show and the game. http://www.stargatesg1rpg.com/
about.html

epguides.com and tv.com: Stargate SG-1 and Stargate: Atlantis Offers links to
TV.com's pages for the show's stars and episodes, including neat features
such as 'episode allusions', trivia, reviews, quotations and so on. The main
SG-1 and *Atlantis* pages feature original air dates for all episodes.
http://www.epguides.com/StargateSG1/http://www.epguides.com/
StargateAtlantis/

Arduinna's Stargate Handbook This has been referred to as the fan's bible
for series-related information, including episode guides, story-arc
descriptions and profiles on all the major characters, races and planets
featured on both *SG-1* and *Atlantis*. http://www.stargatehandbook.
org/

Gateguide: Stargate Website Directory for SG-1, Atlantis, The Movie Offers a
comprehensive links page for everything from convention reports to fan

sites (fiction, art, vids), charities, costuming and production crew, episode guides, transcripts and more. http://gateguide.net/

Stargate SG-1 Solutions Offers interviews, spoilers, convention reports, a forum, episode guide, transcripts, wiki. http://www.stargate-sg1-solutions.com/

Save Daniel Jackson Fan-run campaign site, now with additional features such as articles. An interesting look at fandom activism. http://www.savedanieljackson.com/history/home/home.shtml

Toward a Definition of Science Fiction – David Lavery. A handy table of definitions culled from science fiction writers and scholars. http://mtsu32.mtsu.edu:11090/305/Accessories/305OnlineSFDefinitions.html

DePauw University's *Science Fiction Studies* site. Searchable archive of the journal's tables of contents and links to article abstracts, plus a good links page for scholarly associations, journals and collections related to science fiction and fantasy studies. http://www.depauw.edu/sfs/

Ansible: SF News and Gossip David Langford's 'infamous British SF/fan newsletter, published since 1979'. http://www.dcs.gla.ac.uk/Ansible/

Internet Movie Database Offers comprehensive listings of production credits including: writers, directors, cast, guest stars, crew, air dates. A 'go-to' site for television and film details. Searchable. http://www.imdb.com

SELECTED BIBLIOGRAPHY

Ackermann, R. J., *Heterogeneities. Race, Gender, Class, Nation, and State* (Amherst MA, 1996)

Alice, Lynne, 'What is Postfeminism? Or, having it both ways', L. Alice (ed.) *Feminism, Postmodernism, Postfeminism: Conference Proceedings* (New Zealand, 1995)

Ang, Ien, *Living Room Wars: Rethinking Media Audiences for a Postmodern World* (New York, 1996)

Bakhtin, Mikhail M., *The Dialogic Imagination* (Texas, 1981)

Barr, Maureen, *Envisioning the Future: Science Fiction and the Next Millennium* (Middleton CT, 2003)

Bhabha, Homi K., *The Location of Culture* (London, New York, 1994)

Bondebjerg, Ib (ed.), *Moving Images, Culture and the Mind* (Luton, Bedfordshire, UK, 2000)

Brooks, Ann, *Postfeminisms: Feminism, Cultural Theory and Cultural Forms* (New York, 1997)

Budd, Mike, Steve Craig and Clay Steinman (eds), *Consuming Environments: Television and Commercial Culture* (New Brunswick NJ, 1999)

Burton, Graeme, *Talking Television: An Introduction to the Study of Television* (New York, 2000)

Butler, Judith, *Gender Trouble* (London, New York, 1990)

Cheung, Floyd, 'Imagining danger, imagining nation: Postcolonial discourse in *Rising Sun* and *Stargate*', *Jouvert: A Journal of Postcolonial Studies* 2, 2. Online, http://social.chass.ncsu.edu/jouvert/v2i2/ con22.htm

Clark, Stephen R. L., *How to Live Forever: Science Fiction and Philosophy* (London, New York, 1995)

Clover, Carol J., *Men, Women and Chainsaws: Gender in the Modern Horror Film* (Princeton NJ, 1992)

Cohan, Steven and Ina Rae Hark (eds), *Screening the Male: Exploring Masculinities in Hollywood Cinema* (New York, 1993)

Creeber, Glen (ed.), *The Television Genre Book* London, 2001)

Devereaux, Leslie and Roger Hillman (eds), *Fields of Vision: Essays in Film Studies, Visual Anthropology, and Photography* (Berkeley CA, 1995)

Douglas, Susan J., *Where the Girls Are: Growing Up Female with the Mass Media* (New York, 1995)

Duby, G. and M. Perrot (eds), *A History Of Women In The West* (5 vols) (Cambridge MA, London, 1992–1994)

Elrod, P.N. (ed.), *Stepping Through the Stargate: Science, Archaeology, and the Military in Stargate SG-1* (Dallas, 2004)

Erikson, Erik H., *Identity and the Life Cycle* (New York, 1959)

Flaherty, David H. and Frank E. Manning (eds), *The Beaver Bites Back: American Popular Culture in Canada* (Montreal, Kingston, 1993)

Fine, Gary Alan, *Shared Fantasy: Role-playing Games as Social Worlds* (Chicago, 1983)

Fiske, John, *Television Culture* (New York, 1987)

Fulton, Roger, *The Encyclopedia of TV Science Fiction*, 3rd edn (London, 1997)

Gallardo, Ximena C. and C. Jason Smith, *Alien Woman: The Making of Lt. Ellen Ripley* (New York, 2004)

Gamman, Lorraine and Margaret Marshment (eds), *The Female Gaze: Women as Viewers of Popular Culture* (Seattle, 1989)

Gasher, Mike, *Hollywood North: The Feature Film Industry in British Columbia* (Vancouver, 2002)

Gibson, Thomasina, *Stargate SG-1: The Illustrated Companion* (4 vols) (London, 2002–2005)

Helford, Elyce Ray (ed.), *Fantasy Girls: Gender in the New Universe of Science Fiction and Fantasy Television* (New York, 2000)

Hollinger, Veronica and Joan Gordon (eds), *Edging into the Future* (Philadelphia, 2002)

Hüppauf, Bernd, 'Modernism and the photographic representation of war and destruction', Leslie Devereaux and Roger Hillman (eds), *Fields of Vision: Essays in Film Studies, Visual Anthropology, and Photography* (Berkeley CA, 1995), pp.94–124

Inness, Sherrie A., *Tough Girls: Women Warriors and Wonder Women in Popular Culture* (Philadelphia, 1999)

—, (ed.), *Action Chicks: New Images of Tough Women in Popular Culture* (New York, 2004)

Irigaray, Luce, *Speculum of the Other Woman* (New York, 1985)

Jenkins, Henry, Tara McPherson and Jane Shattuc (eds), *Hop on Pop: The Politics and Pleasures of Popular Culture* (Durham NC, 2002)

Jenkins, Henry, *Textual Poachers: Television Fans and Participatory Culture* (New York, 1992)

Johnson-Smith, Jan, *American Science Fiction TV: Star Trek, Stargate and Beyond* (New York, 2005)

Laqueur, Thomas, *Making Sex* (Cambridge MA, 1990)

Laws, Robin, *Robin's Laws to Good Gamemastering* (Austin TX, 2002)

Lerner, Gerda, *The Creation Of Patriarchy* (Oxford, 1986)

—, *The Creation of Feminist Consciousness* (Oxford, 1993)

Magdar, Ted, *Canada's Hollywood: The Canadian State and Feature Films* (Toronto, 1993)

Malmgren, Carl D., 'Self and Other in SF: Alien encounters', *Science-Fiction Studies*, 20, 1 (March 1993), pp.15–33

Maltby, Richard, *Harmless Entertainment: Hollywood and the Ideology of Consensus* (Metuchen NJ, 1983)

McCaughey, Martha and Neal King (eds), *Reel Knockouts: Violent Women in the Movies* (Austin TX, 2001)

McGregor, Gaile, *The Noble Savage in the New World Garden: Notes toward a Syntactics of Place* (Bowling Green OH, 1988)

—, *The Wacousta Syndrome: Explorations in the Canadian Langscape* [sic] (Toronto, 1985)

Miller, Jeffrey S., *Something Completely Different: British Television and American Culture* (Minneapolis, 2000)

Miller, Mary Jane, *Turn Up the Contrast: CBC Television Drama Since 1952* (Vancouver, 1987)

Mulvey, Laura, 'Visual pleasure and narrative cinema', Leo Braudy and Marshall Cohen (eds), *Film Theory and Criticism* (New York, 1999)

Nazzaro, Joe, *Writing Science Fiction and Fantasy Television* (London, 2002)

Olson, Carl. *The Book of the Goddess* (Prospect Heights IL, 2002)

Olson, Scott Robert, 'Hollywood planet: Global media and the competitive advantage of narrative transparency', Robert C. Allen and Annette Hill (eds), *The Television Studies Reader* (London, New York, 2004)

Pevere, Geoff and Greig Dymond, *Mondo Canuck: A Canadian Pop Culture Odyssey* (Scarborough ON, 1996)

Scodari, Christine, 'Resistance re-examined: gender, fan practices, and science fiction television', *Popular Communications*, 1, 2 (2003), pp.111–130

Slusser, George E. and Eric S. Rabkin (eds), *Aliens: The Anthropology of Science Fiction* (Carbondale IL, 1987)

Solmsen, Friedrich, *Isis among the Greeks and Romans* (Cambridge, 1979)

Stafford, Greg and Robin D. Laws, *HeroQuest: Roleplaying in Glorantha*, (Concord CA, 2003)

Storm, Jo, *Approaching the Possible: the World of Stargate SG-1* (Toronto, 2005)

Suvin, Darko, *Metamorphoses of Science Fiction: On the Poetics and History of a Literary Genre* (New Haven CT, London, 1979)

Tasker, Yvonne, *Working Girls: Gender and Sexuality in Popular Cinema* (New York, 1998)

Todorov, Tzvetan, *The Conquest of America: The Question of the Other* (New York, 1992)

Topping, Keith, *Beyond the Gate: The Unofficial and Unauthorized Guide to Stargate SG-1* (Surrey, 2002)

Weldes, Jutta, *To Seek Out New Worlds: Exploring Links between Science Fiction and World Politics* (New York, 2003)

Westfahl, Gary (ed.), *Science Fiction, Canonization, Marginalization and the Academy* (Westport CT, 2002)

Wright, Brad et. al. *Stargate SG-1: the Essential Scripts*, Sharon Gosling (ed.) (London, 2004)

INDEX